THE ATHARVAVEDA

THE ATHARVAVEDA

M. BLOOMFIELD

GYAN

Published by

Gyan Publishing House
5, Ansari Road
Daryaganj, New Delhi-110002
Phone: 011-47034999, 9811692060
E-mail: books@gyanbooks.com

Distribution Network
gyanbooks.com
India, USA, Canada, UK, Australia

ISBN: 978-93-7169-180-2 (PB)

First Published, 1899

2nd Impression 2025

Printed at: Gyan Press, Delhi.

THE ATHARVAVEDA

Author: M. BLOOMFIELD

GRUNDRISS DER INDO-ARISCHEN PHILOLOGIE UND ALTERTUMSKUNDE
(ENCYCLOPEDIA OF INDO-ARYAN RESEARCH)
BEGRÜNDET VON G. BÜHLER, FORTGESETZT VON F. KIELHORN.
II. BAND, 1. HEFT, B.

THE ATHARVAVEDA

BY

M. BLOOMFIELD.

STRASSBURG
VERLAG VON KARL J. TRÜBNER
1899.

GRUNDRISS DER INDO-ARISCHEN PHILOLOGIE UND ALTERTUMSKUNDE
(ENCYCLOPEDIA OF INDO-ARYAN RESEARCH)
BEGRÜNDET VON G. BÜHLER, FORTGESETZT VON F. KIELHORN.
II. BAND, 1. HEFT B.

THE ATHARVA-VEDA AND THE GOPATHA-BRĀHMAṆA

BY
MAURICE BLOOMFIELD.

PART I. THE ATHARVA-VEDA IN GENERAL.

A. CHARACTER AND CHRONOLOGY OF THE ATHARVA-VEDA.

§ 1. External comparison with the other Vedas. — The Atharva-Veda is a collection of 730 hymns containing some 6000 stanzas, divided into 20 books. About one sixth of the mass, including two entire books (15 and 16), is written in prose, similar in style and language to the Brāhmaṇas[1]; the rest is poetry in the usual Vedic metres. The latter, however, are handled with great freedom, often betraying either ignorance or disregard of the Vedic metrical canons as applied to the poetry of the Rig-Veda[2]. Genuine tradition as to the authorship of the hymns there is none; the hymns themselves are silent; the reports of the Sarvānukramaṇikā[3] of the AV. are in this respect absolutely fatuous. Unlike the Rik, Sāman, and Yajus — the Vedas respectively of hymn of praise, chanted song, and sacrificial verses and formulas — the names of the AV. do not in the first place reflect the nature of the contents, or the manner of employment of its hymns. The name Brahma-Veda is very late, and does not in the main designate 'Veda of charms and incantations', but rather 'Veda of the bráhma' (holy word, or religion): the name was arrived at in a round-about fashion[4]. Other descriptive names, such as *bheṣajāni*, *yātu*, etc., are only partial descriptions, and, though familiar enough, were never used extensively. Instead, the association of this Veda is with mythic fire-priests of prehistoric antiquity, Atharvan and Aṅgiras (later also Bhṛgu), resulting in the names Atharvāṅgirasaḥ, Bhṛgvaṅgirasaḥ and finally Atharvaveda[5]. It has been assumed that this association is entirely secondary, due to the natural desire to adorn these otherwise almost nameless compositions with an antiquity and dignity which do not belong to them[6]. But the names *atharvan* and *aṅgiras* are well ingrained in the poems themselves, in a sense very much the same as that of the oldest title of the AV. (*atharvāṅgirasaḥ*)[7]. Hence it may be well to remember that the Atharvanic rites as well as the Hindu ceremonies connected with home-life (*gṛhya*) centre about the fire, in distinction from the greater Vedic ceremonies (*śrauta*) which are in the main concerned with oblations of soma. It is therefore possible to believe that the Vedic Hindus, when they said of these charms that they were *atharvāṇaḥ* and *aṅgirasaḥ*, meant 'fire-charms', i. e., charms pronounced when some oblation, not soma, was poured or thrown into the fire[8].

§ 2. Relative chronology of the popular and hieratic literatures. — Anyhow this difference of nomenclature between the three Vedas on the one side and the Atharvan on the other is an important and profound one in the history of Vedic literature. Leaving aside the beginnings of speculative theosophic literature which are represented freely in both types (RV. and AV.), we are lead to two main divisions of Vedic literature, the three Vedas with their soma-sacrifices, and the AV. with the house-ceremonies (*gṛhya*), i. e., respectively, the hieratic and the popular religion. The statement put in this form is of importance for the relative chronology of the Atharvan writings: it becomes evident at once, and from the ethnological point of view *a fortiore*, that there can have been no period of Vedic history in which house-customs and mantras of essentially Atharvanic character were wanting, while at the same time the more elaborate hieratic mantras and soma-sacrifices were present. In fact, in some form or other both are prehistoric. The hieratic religion joins the Avestan *haoma*-worship; the Atharvanic charms and practices are very likely rooted in an even earlier, perhaps Indo-European, antiquity[9]. At least, he who does not regard the analoga between Atharvanic charms and practices and those of the Teutonic and other I. E. peoples as entirely accidental (anthropological) must hesitate to ascribe all the mantras of the AV. and Gṛhyasūtras to a late Vedic period[10]. In the case of some, e. g. the wedding-charms and the funeral hymns, this is manifestly impossible; it is not less so in the case of at least some hymns embodied in the AV. Saṃhitās alone, as, e. g. 4. 12. This point of view gains much firmness from a complete survey of the vast armory of charms, blessings, and curses contained in the AV., such as may be gained by reading over the analysis of the vulgate as given in this book (Part III). What is the nature of the impulse which created *ex nihilo*, at a late period so strong and popular a need, and with it such elaborate means of satisfaction; what were the conditions which exempted the earlier and therefore more primitive Vedic time from these needs and their gratification? It has been assumed that the more intimate blending of the Vedic people with the barbarous aborigines of India may have contributed much to the vulgarization of the beliefs and literature of the Vedic Hindus. This is certainly true to some extent, but it does not account for a literature of such extent and character as the Atharvan. This is, after all, only to a limited extent suggestive of aboriginal barbarism: demonolatry with all other things that are hideous and uncanny make up only a part of fhe AV. and the related Gṛhya-literature; nor is it possible to demonstrate that even all that is borrowed from outside sources. Contrariwise, Atharvanic charms are often pervaded by a more genuine 'Aryan' spirit than the more artistic prayers to the gods of the Rigvedic pantheon (e. g. 3. 12; 3, 30; 4. 8; 7. 36 and 37). That the differences in language, style, and metre between AV. and RV. are by no means always to be interpreted as chronological but rather as dialectic; and that the songs of the lower grades of the people were sure to be composed in a language slightly different from that of the higher priestly families will be shown below (§ 38 and 42).

§ 3. Chronology of the Atharvan redaction. — Yet there can be no doubt that the existing collections of the Atharvan are the final product of a redactional activity much later than that of the RV., and that many hymns and prose pieces in the AV. date from a very late period of Vedic productivity. The Atharvan hymns as well as the Gṛhya-rites present themselves in a form thoroughly Rishified and Brahmanized; even the mantras and rites of the most primitive ethnological flavor have been caught in the drag-net of the priestly class and made part of the universal Vedic religion.

Thus the AV. with its popular beliefs poses outwardly in the same attitude of dignity as the RV. with the soma-rites, i. e. Brahmanical priests handle charm and hocus-pocus as religion, not as superstition. As a natural consequence the Vedic pantheon is brought down and made to participate in the common people's customs and superstitions. But one feels the difference; they are employed mechanically, they have become sterile, and only rarely develop their character beyond the point at which the RV. leaves them. Agni, Indra, the Maruts, Bṛhaspati, etc., are mentioned most always in series which show that the Vedic gods have become indifferently of equal value. Being of old slayers of demons, they are needed, of course, against the darkling brood of demons, goblins, wizards, and witches which rise above the horizon from the lowest depths of the folks consciousness: demon-slayers they are in the AV., and little else. Even ethical Varuṇa with his spies, by virtue of his unrivaled facilities for ferreting out hostile, i. e., *eo ipso* sinful, schemes of enemies and sorcerers, figures familiarly. Such criticisms as are called out by this inherently difficult and paradoxical condition of things in the midst of a people capable of higher thought, belong to a rather late time. While all this has been going on speculative theosophic thought which seems never to have been wanting in India, has also moved from such beginnings as are found in the RV. to a greater degree of subtlety and mysticism: the sublimated pantheism of the Upaniṣads has been reached nearly, if not quite. Everything is grist to the mill of the Atharvan: not only are entire theosophic hymns fitted out as weapons against the hated enemy and wizard, but individual speculative formulas and theosophic entities have joined the claptrap that is supposed to be effective against 'him that hates us and whom we hate'. This explains the extraordinary fact that a hymn like 8. 6, resting upon the lowest bathos of folk-lore, can exist peaceably by the side of such fine-spun theosophic lucubrations as the two hymns to Skambha 'Support' (10. 7 and 8) which present the knowledge of brahma and ātman as the highest goal; or that *asat* 'non-being', the perplexing cosmogonic conception, may be turned against performers of spells (4. 19. 6)[11]. From such phenomena as these, rather than the word-forms, or demonological contents of the hymns, the evidence of a later time must be extracted: the concurrent use of popular, hieratic, and philosophical themes for practical purposes, often manifestly secondary, betokens a highly reflective, manipulating period of Brahmanical activity.

§ 4. Relation of the AV. to the Brāhmaṇas, and the Dharma-texts. — Indeed the word Brahmanical which has just now been used is to be taken, it seems, in its narrower sense, namely, the period of the composition of the Brāhmaṇa-texts. The observant reader of a commentary on the AV., such as has been published by the author in SBE., vol. XLII, will find abundant evidence that the spirit of the Brāhmaṇa-texts — I refrain from saying Brāhmaṇa period because there never was a period devoted exclusively to the composition of Brāhmaṇas — asserts itself mightily in the collection of the AV. as a whole. Above all, these hymns run the whole gamut of the pretensions and demands of the Brāhmaṇa priesthood in the style of the Brāhmaṇa-texts themselves. The Brahmans in the AV., as in the Brāhmaṇa-texts, call themselves *deva*, 'gods'[12]; their claims reach the highest pitch. A comparison of WEBER's 'Collectanea on the Castes'[13] with the chapter in this book on the 'Prayers and imprecations in the interest of Brahmans' (§ 56) fixes pretty definitely the lower limit in the relative chronology of the Atharvan diaskeuasis: it belongs to an advanced period of Brahmanical literary activity; there is nothing in the way of assuming that the composition of such texts as AB. and ŚB. preceded the redactions of the Atharvan Saṃhitās. The sparse geographical data of the AV., especially the mention of the rivers Yamunā and Varaṇāvatī and the regions of the Aṅgas and Magadhas[14], point to an acquaintance with India far enough to the east and south-east to accommodate the scene of action of the Brāhmaṇa-texts. Among zoographic facts pointing in the same direction the most conspicuous is the Atharvan's familiarity with the tiger, the inhabitant of the swampy forests of Bengal, perhaps more narrowly the region about Benares[15]. The inevitable and doubtless prehistoric (Indo-Iranian) distinction, on the one hand, between priests, chieftains, and free commoners, all three *ārya*, and the aboriginal servitor-class (*dasyu, śūdra*) has advanced in the AV., so that the line is drawn sharply not only between the two (*ārya* and *śūdra*) but also between the first three, *brāhmaṇa*, *kṣatriya* and *vaiśya*[16]. The knowledge of anatomy, human and animal, has advanced nearly if not quite so far as in the Brahmanical accounts of the *aśvamedha* and *puruṣamedha*[17]. The hymn 11. 7 which deifies the leavings of the porridge (*ucchiṣṭa*) is not only full of hair-splitting scholastic theosophy, but also contains a long catalogue of the *śrauta*-sacrifices and the technical forms of recitation of hymns and liturgic chant. The combination of the two gods Tvaṣṭar and Savitar and their assimilation to Prajāpati reflects the spirit of the Brāhmaṇas (see 2. 26. 1; 3. 8. 2; 7. 17. 4). In another direction the AV. reaches an advanced period of literary activity, namely in the marked development of expiatory hymns (*prāyaścitta*); the entire tract of hymns, AV. 6. 110—121, deals with sin (*pāpa, enas, kilbiṣa*, etc.) very much in the same spirit as the Vidhāna-texts and the Dharma-texts. Thus the chapter of this book on 'Expiation of sin and defilement' (§ 58) touches at many points the paragraph entitled 'Religious delinquencies' in Jolly's 'Recht und Sitte' p. 115 ff.; as also the *prāyaścitta*-chapters, Svidh. 1. 5 ff. Especially noteworthy are 6. 117—119 which apparently aim to salve the conscience for unpaid debts (*ṛṇa*), in part gambling-debts; and 6. 112 and 113 which deal with the class of sins 'wiped off' by the gods from themselves upon the 'scape-god' Trita, sins like the marriage of a younger brother before the older, abortion, and murder of Brahmans[18]. This class of hymns together with the closely related so-called *kūṣmāṇḍa*[19], TA. 2. 3—6, mark, as has hardly been noticed, the longest line of contact between mantra and dharma, and the matter is of some importance in determining the relative chronology of the Atharvan redaction as very late. Of course dates, real dates, in Vedic literature prior to Buddha and the Epic are still 'pins set up only to be bowled down again'. So true is this that fortunately no knowing attempts have been made as yet to fix either the date of the composition of the individual hymns or the redaction. This much is clear that the chronology of each hymn, and each antiquarian and institutional theme, must be viewed from an ever changing critical position, and with a particularly constant regard of the related facts of the whole Vedic tradition: to mass the testimony of the AV. at any one point, to speak, except for occasional convenience, of the period of the AV., seems an even more pernicious error than the bundling together of the facts of the so-called 'Rigvedic' period into one package, separate from all the rest of the early Brahmanic antiquity.

Madhusūdanasarasvatī, Prasthānabheda, IS. I, 16 (Deussen, Allgemeine Geschichte der Philosophie, vol. I, part 1, p. 50); Sāyaṇa, Introduction to his commentary on the AV.; Alberuni, India (Sachau's translation), p. 129 ff.; Colebrooke, Essays[2], vol. I, p. 13, 80 ff.; Bohlen, Das alte Indien, vol. I, p. 128; Lassen, Indische Alterthumskunde, vol. I, p. 523; Roth, Zur Litteratur und Geschichte des Weda, p. 5, 13, 37 ff.; Abhandlung über den Atharva-Veda (Tübingen 1856); Der Atharva-Veda in Kaschmir (Tübingen 1875); Max Müller, HASL. p. 446 ff.; Chips from a German Workshop, vol. I, p. 9 ff.; WEBER, IS. I, 289, 294 ff.; XIII, 331 ff.; Indische Literaturgeschichte[2], p. 11, 161 ff.; WHITNEY, JAOS. IV, 254; OLS. I, p. 18 ff.; Sanskrit Grammar, p. XVI; LUDWIG, Der Rig-Veda, vol. III, p. 28, 341 ff.; L. v. SCHROEDER, Indien's Literatur und Cultur, p. 170 ff.; KAEGI, The Rig-Veda (ARROWSMITH's translation), p. 4, 97; R. T. H. GRIFFITH, Hymns of the Atharva-veda (translation), in the preface; HARDY, Die Vedisch-brahmanische Periode, p. 190 ff.; OLDENBERG, Die Religion des Veda, p. 17 ff.; HOPKINS, Religions of India, p. 151 ff.; BLOOMFIELD, Hymns of the Atharvaveda, SBE. XLII, Introduction; ANONYMUS, The Atharva-Veda described, London and Madras 1897 (missionary tract).

[1] Book 16 contains, however, some passages which are written in cadenced prose from which it is possible to extract at least single metrical pâdas. This is true of much other prose material in the AV. (as also in the YV.), so that it is not unfrequently difficult to decide whether a given hymn or stanza is prose or poetry: prose and loose verse are mixed up in the AV. to an extent not quite reached in any other class of Vedic writings. Cp. WHITNEY, Index Verborum, p. 5. — [2] See below, § 38. — [3] Below, § 19. — [4] Below, § 9 and 33, and more fully, SBE. XLII, p. LVIII, and LXV ff. — [5] See § 8 and 9. — [6] WEBER, IS. I, 295; Omina und Portenta, p. 347; WL.[2], p. 164; WHITNEY, OLS. I, 18. — [7] SBE. XLII, p. XXI and XXXI ff. — [8] The connection of *atharvan* with fire is Indo-Iranian (Avestan *athravan*); cp. SPIEGEL, Eranische Alterthumskunde, III, p. 559; Die arische Periode, p. 232; HAUG, Essays on the Parsis, p. 280, 294; GEIGER, Civilization of the Eastern Iranians, vol. II, p. 48 ff.; and many other writers. HAUG's attempt to show that the Avesta is acquainted with some Atharvan collection under the name *apãm aiviṣtiṣ* has only historical interest: see, Brahma und die Brahmanen, p. 43 ff.; Essays, p. 182. — [9] Cp. KNAUER, Festgruss an ROTH, p. 64 ff.; WINTERNITZ, The Mantrapâṭha of the Âpastambins, p. XLIV. — [10] ADALBERT KUHN, KZ. XIII, p. 49—74; 113—157; SBE. XLII, p. 313, 386, 454. Cp. STENZLER, Über die Sitte, Appendix to his translation of AG.; HILLEBRANDT, Ritual-Litteratur, p. 2. — [11] See § 59. — [12] See 5. 11. 11; 6. 13. 1; 114. 1; 11. 1. 23; 12. 3. 38; 4. 23; 19. 62. 1. Cp. ZIMMER, p. 205 ff.; SBE. XLII, Index, under, 'Brahman-priests'. — [13] IS. X, 1—160. — [14] ZIMMER, p. 5, 20, 31; the interpretation of *varaṇâvatî* is, however, quite doubtful: SBE. XLII, p. 376. — [15] ZIMMER, p. 79. — [16] See, 5. 17. 9; 6. 13. 1; 7. 103. 1; 12. 5. 46; 15. 8. 1 ff.; 19. 32. 8; 62. 1. — [17] See, 9. 6 and 7; 10. 2, etc. — [18] See BLOOMFIELD, Contributions. Seventh Series. AJPh. XVII, 430 ff.; JOLLY, p. 116. — [19] See § 58, note 3.

B. HISTORICAL CHARACTER OF THE ATHARVAN, AND ITS RELATION TO THE HOUSE-BOOKS.

§ 5. **The mutual relations of the AV. and the Gṛhya-sûtras, and their historical value.** — Ancient India, as is well known, has no history in the ordinary sense, no secular history. In lieu thereof the history of its religion and the history of its institutions are unrivaled among the peoples of olden times in their continuity and completeness. Especially the obscurer and more sluggish currents of ordinary daily life, a knowledge of which is so important for the true estimate of a people, are laid bare to the eye of the historian by an altogether unusual kind of tradition. We are not left to reconstruct a picture of the private life of the Vedic Hindu from scattered, incidental statements of their ancient literature alone. Valuable as such statements are, more trustworthy perhaps, as far as they go, than intentional descriptions, they are yet certain to be fragmentary, and to yield but a hazy outline of the subject. In addition to such incidental statements Vedic literature has preserved native systematic treatises on home-life which have searched out and stated systematically a well-defined body of facts connected with the every-day existence of the individual and the family. These are the Gṛhya-sûtras, or house-books, composed as formal treatises at a comparatively late Vedic period[1], but reporting practices and prayers of great antiquity[2]. This class of texts owe their existence to the religious view which the Hindus were led to take of the entire course of their lives. In its even daily course, as well as in its crucial moments, the life of the Hindu is surrounded by a plethora of religious forms;

it is, as it were, sacramental throughout. The beliefs of the folk did not forever flow in a separate undercurrent beneath the open-air religion, scorned by the latter as superstition, but they were at an early time imbedded within the religion. The Gṛhya-sūtras, as in a measure also the Śrauta-sūtras[3], resulted from a codification of popular beliefs undertaken by the Brahmans at a time when these beliefs had been completely harmonized with the Brahmanical order of things, as well as with the divine law and the personal needs and demands of the gods.

It is not to be doubted that the simple practices which are at the bottom of the systematic house-books were at all times accompanied by prayers to such gods, genii, and demons as peopled the fancy of the simple folk[4]. To be sure the Gṛhya-sūtras in their finished form are later redactorial products of schools of Vedic learning, and as such participate to a large extent in the entire stock of hymns, stanzas, and liturgic prayers of their particular school without careful regard to the original purpose for which these hymns, stanzas, etc., were composed[5]. In other words, as the practice of home-rites passed more and more into the hands of the Brahmans, the latter did not stint them their spiritual learning; they decked out the practices with mantras often ludicrously misapplied to the situation. We may also suppose that many ancient prayers were remodelled by the Brahmans to accord better with their own religious ideas and literary habits. Yet it is impossible to believe that marriage-ceremony, burial-rite, medical charm, exorcism and the like can ever have been carried on without prayer, and it will be ultimately a distinct task of Vedic study to find out what are the original gṛhya-mantras and gṛhya-formulas in distinction from the later importations. Such a body of prayers would be even more fit to be trusted as a report of early customs than the Sūtras themselves, they would cancel for themselves all suspicion that we are dealing with individual trumped up fancies. The prayers of the Gṛhya-sūtras are either woven into the account of the practices themselves, or they are preserved as separate collections (*mantra-brāhmaṇa*, *mantra-pāṭha*): the Saṃhitās of the AV. are, as it were, Mantra-pāṭhas on a large scale, broader in scope and freer from school-influence than those of the house-books proper. We may expect to find in their hymns a picture of the private antiquities of ancient India, painted on a large canvass with no particular choice of favored subjects placed in the fore-ground; a picture such as cannot be furnished by the Gṛhya-sūtras, because they limit themselves eclectically to good or pious subjects in the main. The light and the shadows, the good and the evil in the life of this ancient people must appear in due proportion.

§ 6. Scope of the AV. as a record of ancient life. — This expectation the hymns of the AV. fulfil quite amply. Supported by its own ritual book, the Sūtra of Kauśika, which reports the practices connected with these hymns in a way that is on the whole trustworthy, the AV. furnishes an almost complete picture of the ordinary life of the Vedic Hindu. The AV. deals with the themes of the house-books proper and is, of course, supplemented by these interesting and important treatises. The life of the average Arya from the cradle to the funeral-pyre is depicted by the AV. with greater freedom and completeness than in the house-books; the difference, as I have said before, is that the AV. is not at all squeamish in the choice of its themes, and exhibits the ordinary Hindu not only in his aspect of devout and virtuous adherent of the Brahmanic gods, and performer of pious practices, but also as the natural semi-civilized man: rapacious, demon and fear-ridden, hateful, lustful, addicted to sorcery. The variety of practices and beliefs connected with house and home, field and cattle, love and marriage, trade and village-politics, is also far greater in the AV. than in the house-books. But it contains in addition much that is wanting or barely touched upon in the Gṛhya-sūtras. The analysis of the AV. which forms the third part of this work exhibits this difference even in the headings of its separate paragraphs. Thus the medical charms (§ 50) present a complete picture of primitive Hindu medicine, a theme that is hardly indicated in any other department of Vedic literature. The house-books have nothing that corresponds to the theme, 'Prayers and imprecations in the interest of Brahmans' (§ 56); very little that corresponds to the 'Royal rites' (§ 55): these two chapters hold the earliest fairly systematic account of the two superior castes, the Brahmans and the Kṣatriyas. The 'Women's rites' (§ 53), the 'Charms to secure harmony, influence in the village-assembly' (§ 54), and many other less prominent themes, though not entirely absent in the house-books, are also characteristically Atharvan. It may be said fairly that the house-books are excerpts from the broad sphere of life with all its realities, excerpts which were begun in a certain mood that governed the choice of subjects, and that this choice became traditional in all non-Atharvanic Vedic schools. Thus all Gṛhya-sūtras present in the main the same selections, their many differences notwithstanding[6]: the circle or endless chain of human existence: birth, confirmation, Brahman disciplehood, arrival at man's estate, marriage, householdership and again birth, etc., with many intermediate rites. Other matters are treated only incidentally and in a subsidiary way. Not only are the Gṛhya-sūtras restricted to the more pious and orderly aspects of daily life, but they deal also in the main with those practices which are of a regular, permanent, or periodic character — *nityakarmāṇi* as the theologians call them — whereas the AV. is engaged largely with occasional and optional practices (*naimittika, kāmya*). To this the AV. owes its flavor of romance and unexpectedness. As the reader works his way hymn by hymn through the Atharvan collections, arranged with a degree of gaucherie hardly to be excelled[7], he is surprised and bewildered by the number and variety of subjects, by the insistent way in which the obscurer relations and emotions of human life are brought to the surface and exploited. And there is left finally the definite impression that the precious literary diligence of the Hindus has in this instance preserved a document of priceless value for the institutional history of early India as well as the ethnological history of the human race, that in this respect the AV. is a document as precious as is the RV. on the side of mythology and formal priestly religion.

[1] See OLDENBERG, SBE. XXX, p. XVII ff. — [2] Note in this connection, e. g., the way in which the proper noun *atithigva*, 'presenting a cow to guests', in the RV., has embalmed an essential feature of the *arghya*, the rites at the reception of an honored guest; see Contributions. Seventh Series. AJPh. XVII, 424. — [3] HILLEBRANDT, Ritual-Litteratur, p. 1 ff. — [4] Quite the opposite view is advocated by OLDENBERG, l. c., p. X: it has been criticized by WINTERNITZ, The Mantrapāṭha of the Āpastambins, p. XLIV. — [5] Cp. E. W. FAY, Johns Hopkins University Circulars, May, 1890, vol. IX, nr. 81, p. 74; SBE. XLII, p. XLIII ff. — [6] For a comprehensive view of the themes of the Gṛhya-sūtras see OLDENBERG's synopsis, SBE. XXX, p. 300—307; for a description in detail, HILLEBRANDT, l. c., p. 41 ff. — [7] See § 36 ff.

C. THE NAMES OF THE ATHARVA-VEDA AND THEIR MEANINGS[1].

§ 7. The compound Atharvāṅgirasaḥ and the meaning of its two members, Atharvan and Aṅgiras. — The oldest name of the fourth Veda is the dvandva-plural *atharvāṅgirasaḥ* (AV. 10. 7. 20), the name found at the head of the manuscripts of the Śaunakīya-Saṃhitā. More or less secondary and irregular forms and derivatives, such as occur in the expressions *atharvāṅgirasi śrutam*, Mahābh. 3. 305. 20 = 17066[2]; *kuśalam atharvāṅgirase*, Yājñ. 1. 312; *kṛtyām atharvāṅgirasīm*, Mahābh. 8. 40. 33 = 1848; *atharvāṅgirasīḥ śrutīḥ*, Manu 11. 33; *atharvāṅgirasaṃ tarpayāmi*, Baudh. Dh. 2. 5. 9. 14, are of later growth. The name *atharvan* and its derivatives are employed growingly throughout the literature, whereas the name *aṅgiras* by itself occurs but in a single Vedic passage, TS. 7. 5. 11. 2 = Kāṭhaka Aśvamedhagrantha (*aṅgirobhyaḥ svāhā*), as the designation of the fourth Veda[3]. Quite frequently, however, the members of the compound *atharvāṅgirasaḥ* are separated so that each is mentioned by itself, but always in more or less close vicinity to one another, showing that the Atharvans and Aṅgirases had a separate existence, and that the AV. consists of these two component parts. In fact, in a considerable range of the literature especially of older times the term *atharvan* refers to the auspicious practices of the Veda, the *bheṣajāni* (AV. 11. 6. 14), those parts of the Veda which are recognized by the Atharvan ritual and the orthodox Brahmanical writings as *śānta*, 'holy', and *pauṣṭika*, 'auspicious'; the term *aṅgiras* refers to the hostile sorcery practices of the Veda, the *yātu* (ŚB. 10. 5. 2. 20), or *abhicāra*, which is terrible (*ghora*).

This view of the double character of the AV. is expressed most plainly and familiarly in the Gopathabrāhmaṇa. Thus 1. 2. 21 and 1. 5. 10, *ṛci yajuṣi sāmni śānte 'tha ghore*; in the last-named case GB. substitutes these five Vedas for the *trayī* in the corresponding passage, ŚB. 12. 3. 3. 2, upon which GB. is based. These two Atharvanic Vedas assume such reality in the mind of the author of GB. as to be furnished each with an independent *vyāhṛti*, to match *bhūr*, *bhuvaḥ*, *svaḥ* of the *trayī*, namely, *oṃ* for the Atharvan = *śānta*; *janat* for the Aṅgiras = *ghora*: GB. 1. 2. 24 and 1. 3. 3. In 1. 3. 3 the *vyāhṛtis* of the *trayī* are sandwiched in between *oṃ* and *janat* for protection (*gup*: see GB. 1. 1. 13). Cp. also 1. 1. 5, 8 and 1. 3. 4. In the ritual practices, Vait. 5. 10; GB. 1. 2. 18 the same distinction is maintained in behalf of two classes of plants, one of which is described as *śānta*, or *ātharvaṇa*; the other, used in hostile sorcery, as *āṅgirasa*. The latter word has assumed in the Kauśika the meaning of *ābhicārika* or *ghora*, and the fifth Kalpa of the AV. goes by the names Āṅgirasa-kalpa, Abhicāra-kalpa, and Vidhāna-kalpa. The words *āṅgirasa* = *ābhicārika*, and *pratyāṅgirasa* as referring to 'counter-witchcraft' (*pratyabhicaraṇa*) are also used in Vidhāna-texts outside of the AV., in fact as designations of such texts, e. g. Rig-vidhāna 4. 6. 4[4]; with this pejorative use of the word we may perhaps also connect the fact that the Purāṇas count the Āṅgirasa-Veda as one of the four Vedas of the Parsis (Maga), the other three, Vada, Viśvavada, and Vidut, also conveying thinly veiled contempt for the religious books of a foreign religion[5]. What is even more significant, the distinction between Ātharvaṇa-Veda and Āṅgirasa-Veda is also recognized by the non-Atharvanic Brāhmaṇas and Sūtras, and also associated by them in explicit terms respectively with *śānta* and *ghora*. At ŚB. 13. 4. 3. 3 ff.; AŚ. 10. 7. 1 ff.; ŚŚ. 16. 2. 9 ff.; on the occasion of the *pāriplava*, at the horse-sacrifice, sections from these two Vedas are recited: AŚ. and ŚŚ. specify that a *bheṣajam* (*śāntam*) be recited from the Ātharvaṇa-Veda, a *ghoram* (*ābhicārikam*) from the Āṅgirasa-Veda. Cp. also PB. 12. 9. 10; 16. 10. 10, and the names of apocryphal sages and divinities like Bhiṣaj Ātharvaṇa, in contrast with Ghora Āṅgirasa, as also Śaṃyu Ātharvaṇa and Śānti, the wife of Atharvan[6]. Possibly the assumed inferiority of the Aṅgiras in the Brāhmaṇa-legends of the contests between the Ādityas and Aṅgiras also points to the uncanny, devilish character of the latter, and may be derived from the same sphere of conceptions: the Aṅgiras regularly appear as vanquished victims, similar to the Asuras in their struggles with the Devas[7].

The AV. Saṃhitā marks the same distinction very clearly. At 11. 6. 14 four Vedic mantra-categories are indicated by the expressions *ṛcaḥ, sāmāni, bheṣajā*, and *yajūṁṣi*; here the choice of the word *bheṣajā* is eclectic and one-sided. Its precise complement is ŚB. 10. 5. 2. 20, where *yātu* and the *yātuvidaḥ* are placed by the side of the three Vedas and their representative priests. That *bheṣaja* and *yātu* are complements of one another appears from AV. 6. 13. 3, *namas te* (sc. *mṛtyoḥ*) *yātudhānebhyo, namas te bheṣajebhyaḥ*. The *bheṣajā* of AV. 11. 6. 14 and the *yātu* of the ŚB. passage make up together what is embraced in the name *atharvāṅgirasaḥ* (AV. 10. 7. 20). The Saṃhitā also associates markedly the term *āṅgirasa* with aggressive sorcery and the practice of spells (*kṛtyā*). Thus 8. 5. 9, *kṛtyā āṅgirasīḥ*; 10. 1. 6, *pratīcīna āṅgirasaḥ ... pratīcīḥ kṛtyā ākṛtyā 'mūn kṛtyākṛto jahi*; cp. also 12. 5. 52, and 6. 45. 3 = RV. 10. 164. 4. And the distinction between Atharvanic and Aṅgirasic plants appears also in 11. 4. 16 (cp. 8. 7. 17), probably in the same sense as in the Atharvan ritual, i. e. in the sense, respectively, of 'holy' and 'witchcraft' plants. Finally the late Pariśiṣṭa hymns, AV. 19. 22 and 23, repeated in the Uttamapaṭala, Ath. Pariś. 46. 9 and 10, deal with and state subdivisions of *āṅgirasa* and *ātharvaṇa* texts, each separately; cp. GB. 1. 1. 5, 8, and 1. 3. 4.

§ 8. Cause of the distinction between Atharvan and Aṅgiras. — As regards the chronology and cause of this differentiation of *atharvan* and *aṅgiras* the texts offer but scant information. The association of both names (and later of the name *bhṛgu* also) with the texts and practices of the fourth Veda may be sought in their character of mythic fire-priests, or fire-churners: the homely practices of the AV. may have been in charge of human fire-priests in distinction from soma-priests[8]. As regards the terrible aspect of the Aṅgiras as compared with the Atharvans, we may point to RV. 10. 108. 10, where Saramā threatens the Paṇis with the *aṅgirasaḥ ... ghorāḥ*. More important is the Aṅgirasic character of Bṛhaspati, the divine Purohita: in Kauś. 135. 9 Bṛhaspati Āṅgirasa appears as the representative, or the divinity of sorcery; in the Mahābh. he is frequently called *aṅgirasāṃ śreṣṭhaḥ*. In his function of body-priest of the gods he exercises against hostile powers those fierce qualities which are later regarded as Aṅgirasic in the broader sense, cp. RV. 10. 164. 4 = AV. 6. 45. 3, where Bṛhaspati figures as Pratīcīna ('Back-hurler') Āṅgirasa. Still less obvious are the reasons why the word *atharvan* should be particularly associated with *śānta* and *bheṣaja*; perhaps this was accomplished by simply contrasting it with *aṅgiras*, after the latter had assumed its sinister sense[9]. In any case at an early time the terms *atharvāṇaḥ* in the sense of 'holy charms', and *aṅgirasaḥ* in the sense of 'witchcraft charms', joined the more distinctively hieratic terms *ṛcaḥ, yajūṁṣi*, and *sāmāni*, as characteristic types of Brahmanical literary performances. But this distinction was at a later period again abandoned; in the end the name *atharvan* and its derivatives (*atharvāṇaḥ, ātharvaṇāni, ātharvaṇāḥ, ātharvaṇika, atharvaṇa, atharvāṇa*, and, finally, *atharva-veda*)[10] prevail as designations of the charms and practices of the fourth Veda, without reference to their strongly diversified character.

§ 9. The terms Bhṛgvaṅgirasaḥ, Brahmaveda, and the designations of Atharvan priests. — Two other designations of the AV. differ from the preceding in that they are the product of a later Atharvanic literary age; neither of them are found in the Saṃhitā, both are almost wholly restricted to the ritual texts of the Atharvan itself. They are the names *bhṛgvaṅgirasaḥ* and *brahma-veda*. The term *bhṛgvaṅgirasaḥ*, as far as is known, occurs only in Atharvan texts. Though *bhṛgu* in this compound takes the place of *atharvan*, the terms *bhṛgavaḥ* or *bhṛguveda* do not occur, except that the Cūlikā-Up. 11 designates the Atharvan collection of mantras as *bhṛguvistara* (schol., *bhārgava-*

granthāḥ). The term *bhṛgvaṅgiras*, almost always in the compound *bhṛgvaṅgirovid*, is the favorite designation of the AV. in the Atharvan ritual texts; it makes a show, in fact, of crowding out designations based upon the stem *atharvan*[11]. And there is an indefinable tendency to magnify the importance of the term *bhṛgu* at the expense of the others, as when the cosmogony GB. 1. 1. 3 creates Bhṛgu before Atharvan; or when GB. 1. 2. 22 says that the Atharvans and Aṅgiras are the eyes of Bhṛgu; or when the Cūlikā-Up. 10 says that the Bhṛgus are foremost among the Atharvans (*atharvāṇo bhṛgūttamāḥ*): if this is taken seriously at all it reflects rather the result than the cause of the substitution of the name *bhṛgu* for *atharvan*. There is indeed no valid reason why the term *bhṛgu* has succeeded in encroaching so far upon the term *atharvan*. The following may, however, be remarked. The three words *atharvan*, *aṅgiras*, and *bhṛgu* are in general equivalent, or closely related mythic names, concerned with the production, or the service of the fire. Occasionally in the mantras (RV. 10. 14. 6) they are found all together, or *bhṛgu* is found in company with *atharvan* (RV. 10. 92. 10), or with *aṅgiras* (RV. 8. 43. 13). This inter-relation continues in the Yajus and Brāhmaṇa-texts[12] in such a way that the juxtaposition of *bhṛgu* and *aṅgiras* becomes exceedingly frequent, broaching on the complete synonymy reached in ŚB. 4. 1. 5. 1, where the sage Cyavana is designated either as a Bhārgava, or as an Āṅgirasa. Perhaps the frequency of this collocation suggested to the Atharvavedins a mode of freshening up the more trite compound *atharvāṅgirasaḥ*; of any more conscious reason for the preference of the word *bhṛgu* the texts show no trace.

The term *brahma-veda* whose origin is discussed below (§ 33) likewise belongs to the sphere of the Atharvan ritual. Outside of the Atharvan there is but a single unquestionable occurrence, ŚG. 1. 16. 3. Even in the Atharvan Upaniṣads the term is wanting, curiously enough[13]. The earliest occurrences, aside from ŚG., are Vait. 1. 1; GB. 1. 1. 22; 2. 16, 19; 5. 15, 19; 2. 2. 6. The word is common in the Pariśiṣṭas[14]. The supposition that ŚB. 14. 8. 14. 1—4 = Bṛh. Up. 5. 13. 1—4 with its series, *uktham* (= *ṛk*), *yajuḥ*, *sāma*, *kṣatram*, alludes to the Atharvan as the Veda of the Kṣatriyas is at present no more likely than when it was advanced by the author, SBE. XLII, p. XXV ff. Cp. also WEBER, Verz. II, p. 1203. The RV. Prātiśākhya 16. 54 (55) mentions a Vedic book or collection by the name of *subheṣaja*, 'collection of remedial charms', probably only another way of saying *bheṣajāni*, i. e. the auspicious Atharvan charms; cp. the expression *saubheṣajaṃ chandaḥ*, GB. 1. 5. 23 (p. 85, bottom). Curious is ALBERUNI's statement (India, SACHAU's translation, vol. I, p. 129) that the AV. does not consist of the same compositions as the Rik and Yajus, but of a third kind called *bhara* 'song of praise' (RV.).

Designations of priests devoted to the AV. are wanting in the Saṃhitās, unless the terms *bhṛgu* and *āṅgirasa*, AV. 5. 19. 1, 2 are intended as such. The Atharvan ritual texts use *brahman* and *bhṛgvaṅgirovid*, in addition to derivatives from the stem *atharvan*. Very late is the use of the bahuvrīhis *pañcakalpa* and *pañcakalpin*, 'one who practices with the five Kalpas of the AV.': Mahābh. 12. 342. 99 = 13258; 13. 14. 309 = 901; Mahābhāṣya (IS. XIII. 455); and as titles of scribes of Atharvan ritual texts[15]. Whether the word *mātṛkalpika* in the Mahābhāṣya bears any relation to the AV. is still an unsettled point: see Kauś. Introd. p. LVIII.

1 The present chapter is an abstract of the essay on this subject, SBE. XLII, p. XVII—XXVIII, with certain not unimportant corroborative additional details that have come to hand since the date of that publication. Cp. HILLEBRANDT, Ritual-Litteratur, p. 169. — 2 Bombay ed., *atharvāṅgirasi śrutam*; Calcutta, however,

atharvaśirasi śrutam. — 3 Later this designation crops out in grammatical writings, in the superscription of Ath. Prātiś., and in the Mahābhāṣya to Pāṇini 5. 2. 37 (cp. IS. XIII. 433). — 4 BLOOMFIELD, JAOS. XI. 387 ff.; SBE. XLII, p. XVIII ff. — 5 Cp. WILSON in REINAUD's Mémoire sur l'Inde, p. 394; WEBER, IS. I, 292, note; WL.² 164, note. — 6 SBE. XLII, p. XXI. — 7 Cp. WEBER, IS. I. 291 ff.; and below, § 52, note 3. — 8 Cp. KNAUER, Festgruss an Roth, p. 64 ff. — 9 A dash of popular etymology may have helped the process: *a-tharvan* 'not injuring'; cp. *thurv* in the sense of 'injure', Dhātupāṭha 15. 62, and perhaps MS. 2. 10. 1; also the roots *tūrv* and *dhūrv* with similar meanings. — 10 SBE. XLII, p. XXV. — 11 See Kauś. 63. 3; 94. 3, 4 (cp. 137. 25; 139. 6); Vait. 1. 5; GB. 1. 1. 28, 39; 2. 9, 18 (end); 3. 1, 2, 4. The term is familiar in the Pariśiṣṭas and in the AV. Anukramaṇī; cp. WEBER, Omina und Portenta, p. 346 ff.; WEBER, Verz. II. 89 ff.; SBE. XLII, p. XXVI ff. — 12 See the passages cited SBE. XLII, p. XXVII, note. — 13 See ib. p. XXVIII, note. — 14 See WEBER, Verz. II, 88 ff. — 15 SBE. XLII, p. XXVIII; WEBER, Verz. II. 96 (cp. also 919 and 921).

D. THE SCHOOLS OF THE ATHARVA-VEDA.

§ 10. **Character and sources of the reports on the schools of the AV.** — Hindu tradition has fixed upon the number nine as expressing the extent to which the Atharvanic collections of hymns, or their employment in the hands of the Atharvanic practitioners was diversified by differences of treatment in Atharvanic schools (*śākhā*, *caraṇa*, *bheda*). Numerical statements of this sort are apt to be apocryphal; and the differences which represent to the Hindu mind sufficient reason for positing an independent *śākhā* vary greatly in scope and importance. They may be due to genuine differences in the extent and arrangement of the hymn-collections themselves; to differences of ritualistic employment of one and the same hymn-collection (*sūtra-śākhā*); to the existence of independent Upaniṣads among the votaries of the same *śruti*-products in all other respects; or to other more trivial points, at times of great obscurity[1]. These differences great and small are lumped together in the traditional Atharvanic count of nine śākhās, without perspective or sense of proportion; their analysis, moreover, is rendered somewhat uncertain owing to the modulations which the names of the śākhās have been subjected to in the course of time, inside and outside of the Atharvan, and even more by the portentous amount of blundering report on the part of the scribes unacquainted with these names.

The reports on the Atharvan śākhās are from the following sources: 1. The two Caraṇavyūhas: one, counted as the fifth Pariśiṣṭa of the White Yajur-Veda, registers the schools of the AV. in chapter one; another, figuring as the 49th Pariśiṣṭa of the AV., treats the same subject in briefer form. — 2. Incidental mention in Pāṇini, the Mahābhāṣya, and other grammatical literature. — 3. The very late over-systematic reports of the Purāṇas, and other late literature, e. g. the Saṃskāragaṇapati of Rāmakṛṣṇa. — 4. Incidental mention throughout the literature of the Atharvan, to which may be added Sāyaṇa's list of the śākhās in the introduction to his commentary to the AV., p. 25[2]. — Sāyaṇa's statement coincides with that of the AV. Caraṇavyūha, and it would seem that these two authorities present a correct list of the śākhās as known in their day: the different versions of other texts are due to blunders, and more or less conscious malformations and additions on the part of writers farther removed from the sphere of the Atharvan. Accordingly the traditional nine śākhās are as follows:

§ 11. **The nine śākhās of the AV.** — 1. The Paippalāda (also, Paippalādaka, Paippalādi, Pippalāda, Paippala, Paippalāyana, &c.), a patronymic derived from the name of a teacher Pippalādi. In the Atharvan literature itself these names do not appear prior to the Pariśiṣṭas and the Upaniṣads[3], being unknown even in Kauś., Vait., and GB. The name occurs as the designation of a group of mantras which figure as an appendix to the Nakṣatrakalpa, whenever that text figures as the first Pariśiṣṭa; these mantras are in fact derived from AVP[4]. Again, AV. 19. 56—58 in the Śaunakīya are designated as *paippalāda-mantrāḥ* at the end of Ath. Pariś. 8. This is significant in the light of the close relationship of book 19 of AV. with AVP. The so-called *pippalādi-śānti-gaṇa*, Ath. Pariś. 34. 20, begins with the pratīka, *śaṃ no devī* (vulgata 1. 6) which is in all probability the opening verse of the Kashmirian śākhā. Further Ath. Pariś. 2. 3, 6; 23. 10; 24. 14; 41. Caland, Ahnencult, p. 96, 107, 243 ff., has reconstructed a considerable part of a Paippalāda-śrāddhakalpa, and surmises that the school of the Paippalāda is older than the Śaunakīya. The tradition of the Atharvan Upaniṣads distributes them largely, and very secondarily, among the two more important schools, the Śaunaka and the Paippalāda; one of the older Upaniṣads, the Praśna, is regularly and probably with good reason assigned to the Paippalāda[5]. Cp. also the end of Garbha-Up. The Brahma-Up. opens with a conversation between Śaunaka and Pippalāda. The name occurs also frequently in the colophons of Atharvanic writings, and is contained in all systematic reports of the śākhās, Atharvanic and otherwise[6].

2. The Tauda or Taudāyana, written frequently, Stauda and Staudāyana. Appears in the literature itself only Ath. Pariś. 23. 3, *ā skandhād uraso vā 'pī 'ti staudāyanaiḥ smṛtā* (sc. *araṇiḥ*). The śākhā-reports have propagated this name with a brood of variants, often of the most ignorant character, contributing nothing to the real history of the name[7].

3. The Mauda or Maudāyana are mentioned several times in the Pariśiṣṭas. Especially, an interesting passage, 2. 4, declares that only Śaunaka and Paippalāda priests are fit to be Purohitas, whereas the kingdom whose spiritual care is in the hands of priests of the Jalada or Mauda schools rapidly goes to destruction[8]. Otherwise the names occur Ath. Pariś. 23. 3 (*mauda*), and 24. 10 (*maudāyana*), and in all systematic accounts of the śākhās with the usual corruptions[9].

4. The Śaunakīya or Śaunakin. The term Śaunakin occurs by the side of Devadarśin, Kauś. 85. 8. At Vait. 43. 25 a *śaunaka*-sacrifice is prescribed for such as desire to become adepts in sorcery (*śaunakayajño 'bhicārakāmasya*): the force and originality of this testimony is somewhat impaired by the occurrence of a similar statement KB. 4. 7 (cp. ŚŚ. 3. 10. 7), as we may not be sure that the RV. Brāhmaṇa has in mind an Atharvan doctor. In Ath. Paddh. at Kauś. 1. 6 the Vait. is cited as Śaunakīya-sūtra; the title of the published Prātiśākhya of the AV. (vulgata) is Śaunakīyā Caturādhyāyikā[10]: and the terms *śaunaka*, *śaunaki*, and *śaunakīya* are common in the AV. Pariśiṣṭas. The Atharvan Upaniṣads also regard Śaunaka as one of their great teachers (Muṇḍaka 1. 1. 3; Brahma 1); one of them appears under the name of Śaunaka-Upaniṣad (Shavank, in Anquetil's translation)[11], and the commentators on these texts are apt to ascribe them for the most part either to the school of Śaunaka or to that of Paippalāda. Finally all the systematic reports of the śākhās present the name, though often corrupted almost beyond recognition[12].

5. The Jājala. The form of this name, which is obscured by the usual blunders in the systematic reports, may be considered as established on the strength of the unequivocal statement Ath. Pariś. 23. 2, *bāhumātrā devadarśair jājalair ūrumātrikā* (sc. *araṇiḥ*); cp. Sāyaṇa, Introduction, p. 25. The *ācārya* eponymous of the school seems to have been Jajali, as reported by the Mahābhāṣya[13].

6. The Jalada, mentioned in the polemic statement, Ath. Pariś. 2. 4,

reported above under Mauda. In addition *jaladāyana,* Ath. Pariś. 23. 2, *jaladāyanair vitastir vā* (sc. *araṇiḥ*) *ṣoḍaśe 'ti tu bhārgavaḥ.*

7. The Brahmavada. Not found in Atharvan literature outside of the Caraṇavyūha; the outside reports of the śākhās all present the name, mostly with variants more or less corrupt.

8. The Devadarśa or Devadarśin. They occur Kauś. 85. 7, in opposition to the Śaunakin; in the grammatical gaṇa *śaunaka* in the form *devadarśaninaḥ*; and in Ath. Pariś. 23. 2, see above under 5. The śākhā-lists in spite of great corruption intend the same name.

9. The Cāraṇavaidya. Mentioned by Keśava at Kauś. 6. 37, and Ath. Pariś. 23. 2: *cāraṇavaidyair jaṅghe ca maudenā 'ṣṭāṅgulāni ca* (length of the *araṇi*). The śākhā-lists all have the name.

§ 12. Estimate of the historical value of the śākhās, and their relation to the teachers of the Sūtras. — Aside from a difference of opinion on the part of the Śaunakin and Devadarśin in a trivial matter of measurements at Kauś. 85.7,8; and the polemic confrontation of the Śaunakin and Paippalāda with the Mauda and Jalada (above under 3), the only direct statement as to the belongings of these śākhās is, that Kauśika's Sūtra was used by four of them, the Śaunakīya, Jājala, Jalada, and Brahmavada[14]. With the exception of the names Śaunaka (°kin) and Devadarśa (°śin) neither Kauś., Vait., nor GB. include these śākhā-names among those of the teachers to whom they have occasion to refer[15]. The Rishis and teachers of GB. are largely non-Atharvanic and wholly unusable for a reconstruction of Atharvan literary history, owing to the licentious way in which this late text has pilfered the entire Brahmanic literature[16]. Those of Kauś. and Vait., on the other hand, have the true ring: Kauśika, Yuvan Kauśika, Bhāgali, Māṭhara, Śaunaka (Kauś. and Vait.), Gārgya, Pārthaśravasa, Kāṅkāyana, Paribabhrava, Jāṭikāyana, Kaurupathi, Iśuphāli and Devadarśa (Kauś.). In addition Kauś. 140. 18 and Vait. 1. 3; 5. 13; 7. 16 mention *ācāryāḥ* in the plural; both texts refer also to nameless authorities (*eke, ity āhuḥ*)[17]. The absence of these names from the śākhā-list of itself stamps the latter as an exceedingly late evolution, quite as late or later than the theory of the five Atharvanic Kalpas. Just as it is impossible to explain the elevation of the insignificant Śāntikalpa to a place among the five Kalpas by the side of the real Sūtras of the AV., whereas the equally trivial Āsurīkalpa must content itself with a place among the Pariśiṣṭas[18], so it is impossible to say why the Cāraṇavaidya, Mauda, and Jalada figure as śākhās whereas the Bhārgava who are mentioned with them, Ath. Pariś. 23. 2, are excluded from this honor. Several of the śākhā-names are not patronymics; they seem to point to professional phases of Atharvanic life rather than to school-differences. Thus the Brahmavada seem to allude to the function of Atharvan theologians as Brahmans (fourth priests) at the Śrauta-ceremonies[19]; the Cāraṇavāidya to the profession of wandering medicine-men; and Jalada ('water-giver') to the exceedingly common sorceries with water[20]. Anyhow, the śākhā-list is a medley of things of very different importance, and the tradition that the Kauś. is the book of rites (*saṃhitā-vidhi*) of four of these śākhās indicates pretty clearly that these 'school'-differences did not extent in every case to the Saṃhitās themselves, nor even to different Sūtras of the same Saṃhitā.

§ 13. The two Saṃhitā-śākhās, the Śaunakīya and the Paippalāda. — At this date there have been found no texts representing either Saṃhitā-śākhās, or Sūtra-śākhās, in addition to the vulgate Saṃhitā and the Kashmirian Saṃhitā. That the vulgate, together with Kauś., Vait., and GB., belongs to the school of Śaunaka may be regarded as certain. The AV. Prātiśākhya bears the title Śaunakīyā Caturādhyāyikā: it is the phonetic manual of the vulgate, and no other text[21]. The Ath. Paddh., at Kauś. 1. 6, designates Vait. as the Śaunakīya-sūtra; the dependence of Vait. upon Kauś. is certain: the Kauś. is therefore also a Sūtra of the Śaunakin[22]. The tradition alluded to above, that Kauś. is *catasṛṣu śākhāsu śaunakādiṣu saṃhitāvidhiḥ* points to the same conclusion independently, as does also Kauś. 85. 7, 8 where the Sūtra sides with the Śaunakin against the Devadarśin. Again the Kauś. cites the initial hymn of the vulgate (*ye triṣaptāḥ*) as *pūrvaṃ* (or, *triṣaptīyaṃ*) *sūktam*, and in general cites its hymns by pratīka, reproducing occasional orthographical or textual blunders: the school-correspondence of the two texts is quite complete[23]. On the other hand Kauś. as well as Vait. quote hymns from the Kashmirian version in full (*sakalapāṭha*)[24]; they cannot therefore belong to the Paippalāda. Being themselves Śaunakīya, the vulgata is by this perfect correspondence also stamped as Śaunakīya, as there is no evidence that this term was the designation of a special Sūtra-śākhā.

Hardly less conclusive is the evidence that the Kashmirian Saṃhitā belongs to the school of the Paippalāda, in accordance with the statements in the colophons of the Tübingen MS. of that Veda[25]. The text is there described as *ātharvaṇikā-paippalāda-śākhā*. The evidence of the Pariśiṣṭas on this point is given above under Paippalāda (p. 12): especially significant is the *pippalādi śāntigaṇa*, Ath. Pariś. 34. 20 (Kauś. 9. 7, note), doubtless so called because it begins with the pratīka *śaṃ no devī*, the probable opening verse of AVP. The fact that the name *paippalāda* is found associated rather loosely with Atharvan productions in general[26] is paralleled frequently in the history of the Vedic śākhās and is not sufficient to cast doubt upon this conclusion. Neither Brāhmaṇa nor Sūtras seem to have been preserved in this school; at least neither Vedic nor Atharvan literature have the least thing to say about any such works. The discovery of this śākhā in a single birch bark MS. was due to the ingenuity and the efforts of ROTH: the reasons which led this scholar to surmise its existence, a history of its discovery, and a brief comparison of it with the vulgate was published by him in a Tübingen Programme in 1875, entitled 'Der Atharvaveda in Kaschmir'; cp. the same author in the Atti del IV. Congresso Internazionale degli orientalisti, vol. II, p. 89—96. A photographic reproduction of the Tübingen MS. is proposed by the present author[27]. The readings of the Paippalāda texts in those parts of the Veda which correspond with the Śaunakīya are to be presented in WHITNEY's posthumous translation and critical apparatus of the Śaunakīya[28]. Connected passages of AVP. are occasionally cited in full in Kauś. and Vait.; the Paippalāda form of AV. 11. 2 appears in a Ṛcaka of the Kāṭhaka school, described by VON SCHROEDER[29]. Sāyaṇa in his commentary to the Śaunakīya occasionally adopts readings from the Paippalāda[30].

§ 14. Brief account of the Paippalāda-śākhā. — The AVP. like the Śaunakīya is divided into 20 books, subdivided into anuvākas and sūktas; the latter, like the books themselves, are sometimes designated as kāṇḍas. The relation of AVP. to the vulgata (represented in the sequel by the numbers in brackets) is as follows: the opening stanza of AVP. was in all probability the stanza *śaṃ no devī* (1. 1. 6), as was surmised by ROTH, p. 16; the opening stanza of the Śaunakīya, *ye triṣaptāḥ*, heads the second anuvāka of the first book of AVP.[31]. The pratīkas of the remaining books are: 2. *arasaṃ prācyam* (4. 7. 1); 3. *ā tvā gan* (3. 4. 1); 4. *hiraṇyagarbhas* (4. 2. 7); 5. *piśaṅgabāhvai sindhujātāyai*; 6. *tad id āsa* (5. 2. 1); 7. *suparṇas tvā* (5. 14. 1); 8. *kathā diva asurāya* (5. 11. 1); 9. *ūrdhvā asya* (5. 27. 1); 10. *na tad vido yad*; 11. *vṛṣā te'ham*; 12. *imaṃ stomam arhate* (20. 13. 3); 13. *agnis takmānam*

(5. 22. 1); 14. *indrasya nu* (2. 5. 5); 15. *samyag digbhyaḥ*; 16. *antakāya* (8. 1. 1); 17. *satyaṃ bṛhad ṛtam* (12. 1. 1); 18. *satyenottabhitā* (14. 1. 1); 19. *doṣo gāya* (6. 1. 1); 20. *dhītī vā ye* (7. 1. 1).

Books 1—7 of the Śaunakīya reappear for the most part in AVP.; 8—14 almost completely. Of 15 there is only the beginning; 16 and 17 appear for the most part. On the other hand the funeral-hymns, book 18, are wanting entirely. Of the two supplementary books, 19 and 20, the latter including the *kuntāpa*-hymns is wanting in AVP., except those stanzas which are not *kuntāpa* and are not borrowed from the RV.[32]; book 19 with the exception of about 12 of its 72 hymns is scattered through the AVP., showing that this supplement to the Śaunakīya is largely derived from its sister-śākhā. The arrangement of the two Vedas is to a certain extent on parallel lines: books 1—5 of the Śaunakīya are contained in 1—9 of AVP.; books 8—11 in the large book 16; book 12 in 17; books 13, 14, 16, 17 in 18: the one notable divergence concerns 6 and 7 of the Śaunakīya: they appear in 19 and 20 of AVP. The variations between the two texts range all the way from inconsiderable variants to complete change of sense. Perfect textual correspondence between parallel stanzas and hymns of the two śākhās is comparatively rare. About one eighth or one ninth of AVP. is original, being found neither in the Śaunakīya nor in any other of the accessible collections of mantras[33].

[1] Cp. OLDENBERG, Die Hymnen des Rig-Veda, p. 430 ff. — [2] See, MAX MÜLLER, HASL. p. 371; WEBER, IS. I. 152, 296; III. 277—8; XIII. 434—5; Omina und Portenta, p. 412—3; WL.[2] p. 170; RĀJENDRALĀLAMITRA in the introduction to the Gopatha-Brāhmaṇa, p. 6; Śabdakalpadruma, s. v. *veda*; ROTH, Der AV. in Kaschmir, p. 24 ff.; SIMON, Beitraege zur Kenntniss der vedischen Schulen, p. 31; BLOOMFIELD, JAOS. XI. 377—8; Kauśika, Introduction, p. XXXI ff. — [3] See JACOB'S Concordance, under *pippalāda*, and *paippalāda*. — [4] See ROTH, AV. in Kaschmir, p. 12; the mantras are printed in, BLOOMFIELD, Seven Hymns of the AV., AJPh. VII, 486—7. — [5] See COLEBROOKE, Essays I[2], p. 93; DEUSSEN, Sechzig Upanishad's, pp. 531, 559. — [6] See Kauś., Introd., p. XXXIII. — [7] See, ibid. p. XXXIV. — [8] JAOS. XI. 378 note. — [9] Kauś., ibid. — [10] WHITNEY, JAOS. VII. 333 ff. — [11] DEUSSEN, Sechzig Upanishad's, p. 867 ff. — [12] Kauś., ibid. XXXV. — [13] IS. XIII. 435. — [14] Sāyaṇa, Introduction, p. 25, and Keśava and Atharvapaddhati in their respective introductions. — [15] JAOS. XI. 385; Gopathabrāhmaṇa, List of proper names, at the beginning of the edition. — [16] See below § 65, 66. — [17] See the indexes, especially Kauś. p. 373. — [18] JAOS. XI. 378 ff.; Kauś. Introd. p. XXXVI; MAGOUN, Āsurīkalpa, AJPh. X. 165 ff.; cp. below, § 16. — [19] See below, § 33. — [20] Cp. SBE. XLII, Index, under 'waters'; and the items, *apāṃ sūktāni, abhiṣekagana, jīvāḥ, mahāśānti, śaṃbhūmayobhū, salilāni,* etc. in Kauś., Index B, p. 383 ff. — [21] The Kauś. follows some of the orthoepic peculiarities of the vulgate as described by AV. Prātiś.; see Kauś., Introd., p. XXXVIII. — [22] The GB. is in turn dependent upon Vait. and exhibits no independent school-traits; see below § 64. — [23] Kauś. Introd. p. XXXVIII ff. — [24] Kauś. 72; 91; 107; 115; Vait. 10. 17; 14. 1; 24. 1: see ROTH, AV. in Kaschmir, p. 23; GARBE, Vaitāna-Sūtra (text), p. VII; JAOS. XI. 377. — [25] ROTH, ibid. p. 12; Kauś. Introd. p. XXXIII. — [26] So, e. g., the Praśna-Upaniṣad, because the teacher Pippalādi figures in it; see above, p. 12; Kauś. ibid.; WHITNEY, Index verborum, p. 2, note. — [27] JAOS. Vol. XX, p. 184 ff. — [28] See, JAOS. XV, p. CLXXIII. — [29] See note 24; v. SCHROEDER, Die Tübinger Kaṭha-Handschriften, p. 14 ff. (SWAW. 1898, vol. CXXXVII, part IV; cp. IS. XVIII. 417). Some stanzas of AVP. are quoted also in GB.: see ROTH, ibid. p. 23. — [30] WHITNEY, Festgruss an R. v. Roth, p. 92. — [31] Cp. Kauś. Introd. p. XXXVII. — [32] See WHITNEY, Index Verborum, p. 2; cp. below § 62. — [33] See, ROTH, ibid. p. 15—20.

E. BRIEF SKETCH OF ATHARVANIC LITERATURE.

§ 15. **The Saṃhitās, Sūtras, and Brāhmaṇa.** — The literature of the Atharvan comprises the two collections of hymns connected by tradition respectively with the schools of Śaunaka and Paippalāda[1]. The latter exists only in a single hitherto unpublished saṃhitā-manuscript without pada-pāṭha or commentary; the former in numerous mss. of both saṃhitā and pada-pāṭha, except that no pada-text of the so-called *kuntāpa*-hymns has as yet come to light[2]; it probably does not exist at all. It has been edited by ROTH and WHITNEY (Berlin 1855). The pada-pāṭha of the Śaunakīya is characterized in relation to other pada-texts by WEBER, IS. XIII. 6 ff. It is particularly blundering in the corrupt book 19, but also liable to serious error elsewhere; e.g., it divides *stuvannemi* into *stuvan nemi*, instead of *stuvann emi* (4. 28. 3[b]), or *yadyāmam* into *yad yāmam*, instead of *yady āmam* (6. 116. 1[a]). A fragmentary commentary on the Śaunakīya with an elaborate introduction, containing a valuable sketch of the more important accessory Atharvan texts, and an Atharvanic view of the character and importance of the AV., is as usual ascribed to Sāyaṇa; this commentary is now in the course of publication[3]. The most important accessory text of the AV. is the Sūtra of Kauśika[4]. It comprises, along with a good deal of peculiar matter, the themes ordinarily treated in the Gṛhya-sūtras, and, in addition, what may be called an Atharva-Sūtra proper, or a Vidhāna-Sūtra: cp. the frequent designation of the text as *saṃhitā-vidhi*[5]. The Kauś. belongs to the Śaunakīya-school, or to a school deviating from the Śaunakīya only in minor matters; there is however a later tradition that it was used as the Sūtra of four of the Atharvanic schools or śākhās, the Śaunakīya at the head[6]. In addition to the commentary of Dārila, the Paddhati of Keśava, and other minor Paddhatis, the Kauś. seems also to have been commented upon by Bhadra and Rudra[7]; judging from quotations of these writers (Kauś. p. 312, 338, and 352) their works are composed in ślokas of a late Smṛti-character. The Atharvan has also a Śrauta-sūtra, the authorless Vaitāna-Sūtra which also belongs to the school of Śaunaka; the published text contains eight adhyāyas[8]: an appendix called Yajñaprāyaścitta-sūtra, or Vaitāyana, consists of six adhyāyas which are as yet unedited[9]. SHANKAR PANDIT in the introduction to AV. 11. 2 mentions a commentary on Vait., called Ākṣepa by Somāditya. The relation of Vait. to Kauś. and the AV. Saṃhitā is quite peculiar as compared with the inter-relation of the corresponding texts in other schools. As a rule the Gṛhya-sūtras are dependent upon the Śrauta-sūtras; they refer to them familiarly, and do not describe a second time performances which have been treated in the Śrauta-sūtras. The two Atharvan Sūtras reverse this relation: there is no point in which Kauś. depends upon Vait.; on the other hand the dependence of Vait. upon Kauś. is apparent at almost every step. The Vait. treats the Kauś. as though it were a Saṃhitā; the ritual practices and independent mantras of Kauś. are taken for granted, and alluded to as understood by and known to the *śrauta*-priests practicing with Vait. From the point of view of the other Śrauta-sūtras the Vait. may be judged as follows: it is not the product of practices in *śrauta*-ceremonies which have slowly and gradually developed in a certain high priestly school, but a somewhat conscious product, made at a time when the Atharvavedins began to feel the need of a distinctive Śrauta-manual to support their claim that the AV. is a canonical Veda of independent and superior character. Vait. 1. 8 acknowledges its dependence upon the Yajur-Veda[10]. To the Śaunaka-school belongs also the single Brāhmaṇa of the AV., the Gopatha-brāhmaṇa which is in turn later than and dependent upon the Vaitāna: see § 64.

§ 16. The Kalpas and the Pariśiṣṭas. — With the above-mentioned Sūtras three other texts of slight intrinsic importance are associated: Hindu tradition persistently states that the ritual literature attached to the AV. consists of five Kalpas[11]. The (*pūrva-*)*mīmāṅsā*-teacher Upavarṣa[12] goes so far as to assert that these five are *śruti* (*vedatulya*), contrasting them with others that are *smṛtitulya*[13]. Priests practicing with these five kalpas are known as *pañcakalpa* or *pañcakalpin*[14]. The rather variable nomenclature of these texts is: 1. The Kauśika-sūtra, or Saṃhitā-vidhi, or Saṃhitā-kalpa. 2. The Vaitāna-sūtra, or Vitāna-kalpa[15]. 3. The Nakṣatrakalpa. 4. The Śānti-kalpa. 5. The Āṅgirasa-kalpa, or Abhicāra-kalpa, or Vidhāna-kalpa. The last three are Pariśiṣṭas, intrinsically not at all more interesting than many of the numerous Atharvan texts of that class: why they should have been deemed worthy of a place by the side of the real Sūtras does not appear. No mss. of the Āṅgirasa-kalpa have as yet come to hand, nor are there any announced in the ms. catalogues: our previous surmise that the text would bear upon the sixth book of Kauś. is rendered probable by Sāyaṇa's brief summary of its contents (introd. p. 28). The Nakṣatrakalpa is called a Pariśiṣṭa outright, and is frequently found at the head of the Pariśiṣṭa-mss.; this text, as well as the still more trivial Śāntikalpa are in the main of an astronomic-astrologic character[16]. The Pariśiṣṭas, according to Hatfield's count 72 in number[17], deal with a great variety of subjects; leaving aside the Nakṣatrakalpa (nr. 1) and its appendix, the so-called Paippalādā Mantrāḥ (nr. 1[2]), they begin with a considerable number of texts in the nature of *rājakarmāṇi* (royal rites), and end with a little less numerous a class of *adbhutāni* (omens and portents), thus continuing in these, as in other cases, the tradition of the Kauś. (14—17, and adhyāya XIII). A considerable number of these texts are devoted to grammatical, text-historical, or astronomical subjects, of a degree of interest that calls for a critical edition of the entire collection. Quite a number of them are even now edited or adequately discussed: the Paippalādā Mantrāḥ (1[2]) have been reproduced by Bloomfield[18]; the Indramahotsava (19) is very similar to the corresponding chapter, Kauś. 140; the Skandayāga or Dhūrtakalpa (20), a kind of a thieves' manual, has been edited and translated by Goodwin[19]; the Gaṇamālā (32) is worked up in connection with the corresponding groups in the Kauś.[20]; the Āsurīkalpa (35), a witch-craft practice undertaken with the *āsurī*-plant, has been edited and translated, with the aid of a native commentary, by Magoun[21]; the Śrāddhakalpa (44) has been edited and translated by Caland[22]; the Uttamapaṭala (46) is treated in part by Weber[23]; the Kautsavya-(or, Kautsavaya-)niruktanighaṇṭu (48) has been commented upon and compared with Yāska's Nighaṇṭu by Bloomfield[24]; the Caraṇavyūha (49) is discussed by Weber[25]; the Grahayuddha (51) has been edited by Weber[26]; the Adbhutaśānti (67) is for the most part reproduced and translated by Weber[27]; the Auśanasādbhutāni has been edited and translated by Hatfield[28]. Aside from Pariśiṣṭas and Paddhatis there exist also mss. of certain prayer and ritual books of a yet slighter importance and probably later date than the Pariśiṣṭas; e. g. an Atharvatarpaṇam; the Ātharvaṇapramitākṣarā of Vāsudeva; the Ṣoḍaśopacārapūjā; and *rahasya*-texts[29]. Hemādri in the Vratakhaṇḍa of the Caturvargacintāmaṇi presents an Atharvakavidhāna[30]. For an Atharvavedoktaṃ jyotiṣam written by a *pañcakalpin* see Weber, Verz. II, p. 96; for a similar text called Āraṇyaka jyotiṣam, Haug, IS. IX. 174.

§ 17. On the Smṛti of Paiṭhīnasi. — The question raised by the present author[31] as to whether Paiṭhīnasi, the reputed author of a work on *dharma*, belongs to the AV., has been answered in the affirmative by Pischel[32], Caland[33], Jolly[34], and Hillebrandt[35]. Pischel regards Paiṭhīnasi as the author of a Dharma-śāstra in mixed prose and ślokas; Caland and Jolly as the author of a Dharmasūtra. And Caland concludes that Paiṭhīnasi was at any rate an Atharvanic writer, because the Śrāddhakalpa of this author reconstructed from Hemādri's citations, is related to the Atharvan *śrāddha*-texts[36]. It would seem possible, however, that there existed more than one Paiṭhīnasi.

The Ātharvaṇīya-paddhati describes him as an author of a Paddhati; the citations in the Atharvanic commentaries[37] seem to point to a knowledge of special Atharvanic rites so particular as to make it seem quite likely that some Paiṭhīnasi was the author of a very late metrical text, dependent directly upon the Kauśika. Paiṭhīnasi in the Pariśiṣṭas is called Mausalīputra; he seems also not likely to have been the author of the *dharma*-text in question. At any rate it will be well to remember that if all references to Paiṭhīnasi are intended for the *dharma*-writer it will not be easy to assign to him too late a date.

§ 18. The Atharvan Upaniṣads. — With the AV. are associated traditionally the great mass of the Upaniṣads[38], in fact all except those that belong definitely to schools of the other three Vedas. Some of these, even, appear in Atharvanic recensions, e. g., the Kena (SV.), Bhṛguvallī, Ānanda-vallī (Taittirīya-Upaniṣads = TA. 8 and 9), and Bṛhannārāyaṇa (= Mahānārāyaṇa = TA. 10)[39]. What ought to be an authoritative statement of the number and names of the Atharvan Upaniṣads is the list of 27 presented by the 49th Pariśiṣṭa, the Caraṇavyūha[40]; they are: 1. Muṇḍaka. 2. Praśna. 3. Brahmavidyā. 4. Kṣurikā. 5. Cūlikā. 6. Atharvaśiras. 7. Atharvaśikhā. 8. Garbha. 9. Mahā. 10. Brahma. 11. Prāṇāgnihotra. 12. Māṇḍūkya. 13. Nādabindu. 14. Brahmabindu. 15. Amṛtabindu. 16. Dhyānabindu. 17. Tejobindu. 18. Yogaśikhā. 19. Yogatattva. 20. Nīlarudra. 21. Pañcatāpinī (°tāpanīya). 22. Ekadaṇḍisaṃnyāsa. 23. Aruṇi. 24. Haṁsa. 25. Paramahaṁsa. 26. Nārāyaṇa. 27. Vaitathya. The majority of the names in this list require no explanation: the Pañcatāpanīya is doubtless the Nṛsiṁhapūrvatāpanī; one ms. reads Dvitāpanīya, having in mind probably the additional Nṛsiṁhottaratāpanī. The term Ekadaṇḍisaṃnyāsa is otherwise unknown as a designation of an Upaniṣad: the stem *ekadaṇḍin* (cp. schol. to PB. 19. 4. 7) occurs in Brahma 3; Paramahaṁsa 3; and Gopīchandana 5; cp. the ms. listed as a Dharmaśāstra under the title Ekadaṇḍisaṃnyāsavidhiḥ, by Śaunaka, in Stein's Catalogue of Sanskrit MSS. at Jammu, p. 84. I do not venture to assume that the text is identical with the well-known Saṃnyāsa-Upaniṣad. The Vaitathya is the independent name of the second of the four parts of Gauḍapāda's Kārikā to the Māṇḍūkya, all of which are usually counted as independent Upaniṣads[41]. The presence in this list of the work of a personal author makes for the belief that it, like all other Upaniṣad lists, is late and eclectic, representing the learning of some particular scholar or coterie of scholars. It does not coincide with any other historical collection, as, e. g., the collection of the Muktikā-Upaniṣad; the Persian translation of the Oupnekhat in Anquetil-Duperron's Latin translation; Nārāyaṇa's collection; Colebrooke's collection; or the lists of the Chambers collection[42]. Jīvānanda's 'Atharvaṇopanishat' (Calcutta 1891), to be sure, contains 29 Upaniṣads, but they are copied, apparently, from the unfinished edition in five fasciculi, printed in the Bibliotheca Indica. They also are the result of an independent selection of the minor Upaniṣads, differing from that of the Pariśiṣṭa in the choice and order of the texts. There is in fact no complete collection of Upaniṣads, because the term Upaniṣad does not represent a closed canon but an indefinitely extensible type of literature 'which has not been formally concluded and which may yet be continued in the present or the future'. The number of Upaniṣad-names counted by Weber in 1876[43] was all in all 235, including apocrypha; even a Moslemic Allopaniṣad figures among them. The judgment of the intrinsic and historical value of the Atharvan Upaniṣads does not therefore depend upon any one collection; their value — in the first instance their historical value — depends upon the degree of regularity with which they occur in the collections. Even so it is obvious that literary products of the most diversified character (cp., e. g., the

Gāruḍa, a snake-charm) have found their way into the principal collections, all of which are probably relatively late, so that finally the chronology and the value of each Upaniṣad will have to be determined by its style, contents and other inner criteria[44].

Deussen, extending and developing a suggestion of Weber, divides the Atharvan-Upaniṣads into five clearly defined classes[45]: 1. Pure Vedānta-Upaniṣads, i. e., such as continue the Vedānta doctrines of the older texts without undue development of the notions of *yoga* (concentration, and abstraction from all mundane matters), *saṃnyāsa* (asceticism), or Śivaitic or Viṣṇuitic symbolism, beyond where these ideas had developed in the older Upaniṣads. 2. Yoga-Upaniṣads, i. e., such as presuppose the Vedānta ideas, and in addition advise concentration upon the morae of the sound *om*, especially its last half mora (*nāda*). 3. Saṃnyāsa-Upaniṣads, i. e., those which recommend and describe a life of asceticism as the practical result of the doctrines of the Upaniṣads. 4. Śiva-Upaniṣads, i. e., such as interpret the popular god Śiva or one of his *mūrtis* (Īśāna, Maheśvara, Mahādeva, etc.) as a personification of the Ātman. 5. Viṣṇu-Upaniṣads, i. e., those which similarly transform Viṣṇu or one of his *avatāras* (Nārāyaṇa, Nṛsiṁha, Rāma, Kṛṣṇa) into human manifestations of the Ātman. Of these classes the first (cp. AV. 10. 7 and 8; 11. 4 and 8), the third (cp. AV. 11. 5) and the fourth (cp. AV. 4. 28; 11. 2) might be expected to be in organic touch with the hymns of the AV. But this is not the case: the Atharvan Upaniṣads are connected with the AV. Saṃhitā by ties that are but little more close than those that connect them with the Vedic mantras in general. There is one notable exception, the Cūlikā, which presents (śloka 10 ff.) characteristically as '*mantropaniṣad*' an almost complete catalogue of the cosmogonic and theosophic hymns of the AV., naming them by well-selected catch-words, such as *brahmacārin* (11. 5), *skambha* (10. 7 and 8), *ucchiṣṭa* (11. 7), etc.[46] Otherwise the Atharvan hymns are cited only sporadically, not more frequently or familiarly than mantras of the other Vedas[47]. In addition the relation of these texts to the AV. is of the loosest sort: they are apt to add the name of the AV. to that of the *trayī* more regularly than the older Upaniṣads[48], and the names of their holy Rishis are to a considerable extent those of earlier as well as later Atharvanic tradition: Atharvan, Aṅgiras (from which Muṇḍaka 1. 1. 2 abstracts Aṅgir), Bhṛgu, Śaunaka, Pippalādi. The last two are the names of two Atharvan schools, being the only names of the traditional śākhās that are mentioned in the AV. Upaniṣads. With one or the other of these two school-names the commentators are apt to associate loosely and inconsistently the individual Upaniṣads as special school-products[49]: Colebrooke, e. g., reports that the first fifteen in his count belong to the Śaunaka-school; or the colophon of the Praśna states that itself belongs *pippalādātharvaṇe śākhāyām* (!)[50]. But, aside again from the Cūlikā which distinctly refers to the Śaunakīya, there is little or nothing in the texts themselves that binds them to one or the other Atharvan school, or for that matter, to the AV. itself, as a whole. This is rather striking at the first glance, because the theosophic hymns of the AV. seem to herald the Upaniṣad speculations more loudly than the theosophic mantras of the other Vedas, and because the later ritual literature of the AV., notably the GB., professes to be devoted to a knowledge of the brahma. The GB., moreover, notably in its first prapāṭhaka, resembles the Upaniṣads in diction and style; especially its speculations on the syllable *om* remind one of the *yoga*-class of Upaniṣads. Indeed one of the treatises of GB., the *om*-cosmogony[51] was regarded as an Upaniṣad by the Persian translators: the Pranou (Praṇava) in Anquetil's translation is almost identical with GB. 1. 1. 16—30, a fact which will be of especial interest to WEBER and DEUSSEN[52]. Another treatise, that on the *gāyatrī* (GB. 1. 1. 31—38)[53] describes itself at the end as an Upaniṣad: it also suggests, without being at all like it, the Shavank of ANQUETIL'S Oupnekhat[54]. But there was probably, nevertheless, a greater break in time between Mantra and Upaniṣad in the AV. than in the other Vedas: the older AV. Upaniṣads doubtless grew up in priestly communities that practiced with the AV.; the more secondary and recent ones are the products of later mystic, ascetic, and sectarian speculations which were compelled to associate themselves also with the AV., because less rigid school discrimination obtained at all times in the AV., and because the canons of the other Vedic schools were definitely closed. As it is texts like the Jābāla or the Nīlarudra (cp. VS. 16 and 13) are in some aspects paradoxical members of a collection that professes to be Atharvanic. The bibliography and contents of the Atharvan Upaniṣads may now be studied conveniently, aside from WEBER'S pioneer treatment, in connection with DEUSSEN'S excellent translations with introductions (Sechzig Upanishad's, p. 531 ff.).

§ 19. Grammatical and text-historical treatises. — Of grammatical and text-historical books the most important is the AV. Prātiśākhya, the so-called Śaunakīyā Caturādhyāyikā, in WHITNEY'S careful edition[55]. BÜHLER has reported on another AV. Prātiśākhya different from the preceding[56]. A grammatical text called Ātharvaṇasūtra by Pāṇinīya seems to have been known to Trikāṇḍamaṇḍana[57]. The so-called Nirukta-nighaṇṭu of Kautsavya or Kautsavaya (Ath. Pariś. 48) is a collection of glosses similar to Yāska's Nighaṇṭu, not a *nirukta*-text at all[58]. Note also the Varṇapaṭala, Ath. Pariś. 47. The Caraṇavyūha and the Uttamapaṭala, interesting for the history of Atharvan texts, have been mentioned above (p. 17). The unpublished Bṛhatsarvānukramaṇikā of the AV. is a very late and secondary text of that sort; its statements, especially those on the authorship of the hymns (mostly gods or semi-divine beings) are of minimal value[59]. The Pañcapaṭalikā is another text of the nature of an Anukramaṇī, mostly metrical[60]. The Caraṇavyūha mentions four related texts as '*lakṣaṇagranthāḥ*', namely, *caturādhyāyikā prātiśākhyam pañcamapaṭelikā* (!) *daṃtyoṣṭhavidhir bṛhatsarvānukramaṇī ca*[61]. A work on accentuation, the Svara-śāstra was known traditionally to one of the Pandits of SHANKAR PANDIT'S acquaintance[62].

WEBER, Verz. I. 82 ff.; II. 79 ff.; WL.², p. 161 ff.; BLOOMFIELD, JAOS. XI. 375 ff.; HILLEBRANDT, Ritual-Litteratur, p. 35 ff.

1 Some data on the Paippalāda (AVP.) are presented (on ROTH'S authority) above, p. 14 ff; for the Śaunakīya see the entire second part of this book. — 2 See ROTH, AV. in Kaschmir, p. 8; WHITNEY, Index Verborum, p. 4; the *kuntāpa*-hymns are analyzed below, § 63. — 3 See the introductory notes below p. 40. — 4 The Kauśika-Sūtra of the Atharva-Veda, with extracts from the commentaries of Dārila and Keśava. Edited by MAURICE BLOOMFIELD (Vol. XIV of JAOS.); cp. HILLEBRANDT, Ritual-Litteratur, p. 36. — 5 WINDISCH, Literarisches Centralblatt, Nov. 21, 1891, column 1663 ff. — 6 See above, p. 13; cp. PISCHEL, GGA., April 15, 1891, nr. 8, p. 283. — 7 JAOS. XI, p. 376; Kauś. Introd. p. XV and XVII. — 8 Edited and translated by RICHARD GARBE, respectively, London, 1878, and, Strassburg, 1878. The Vait. begins with the words, *atha vitānasya*. On a remote possibility of connecting the Vaitāna with the name Kaśyapa, see JAOS. XI. 377. — 9 See GARBE, Introd. to his edition, p. V; WEBER, Verz. II, p. 83; EGGELING, Cat. nr. 367; BLOOMFIELD, AJPh. XVIII, 352. — 10 JAOS. XI. 379 ff.; HILLEBRANDT, l. c. p. 36 (AJPh. ibid.). — 11 JAOS. ibid. 376 ff.; HILLEBRANDT, l. c. — 12 COLEBROOKE, Essays II², 319 ff. — 13 The latter class is represented probably by Pariśiṣṭa-texts like the Āsurī-kalpa, or the Dhūrta-kalpa (Skandayāga). — 14 See above, p. 10. — 15 Occasionally the name Śaunakīya-sūtra may be expected to turn up: cp. JAOS. ibid. p. 377, note 3. — 16 JAOS., ibid. p. 378; Kauś. Introd. p. XIX. Summaries of both texts are given by SĀYAṆA, Introduction, p. 27 ff.; WEBER, Nakṣatra II, p. 392 ff. The Nakṣ. is occasionally referred to by its initial words *kṛttikā rohiṇī*,

WEBER, Verz. II, p. 89, l. 7. — 17 JAOS. XIV, p. CLVI ff.; cp. WEBER, Verz. I, p. 89 ff.; II, p. 87 ff. — 18 AJPh. VII, p. 485 ff. — 19 JAOS. XV, p. V ff. — 20 See Index B, p. 383 ff. — 21 Baltimore Dissertation: AJPh. X. 165—197. — 22 Ahnenkult, p. 95, 240 ff. This Śrāddhakalpa belongs to the school of Śaunaka. Out of Hemādri's Caturvargacintāmaṇi CALAND, ibid. p. 243 ff., has reconstructed a Śrāddhakalpa belonging to the Paippalāda-school; he also presents fragments from the same source of *śrāddha*-ceremonies according to the *smṛti* of Paiṭhīnasi (p. 109 ff.); cp. the next paragraph. — 23 WEBER, IS. IV. 431 ff. — 24 JAOS. XV, p. XLVIII ff. Cp. also the curious *nighaṇṭu*-like passage, TB. 3. 10. 1. — 25 WL.², p. 170 (cp. IS. III. 247 ff.); WEBER, Verz. I. 92; II. 88. — 26 IS. X. 317 ff. — 27 Omina und Portenta, p. 320 ff. — 28 JAOS. XV. 207 ff. — 29 For a list of such texts see JAOS. XI, p. CLXXI, and cp. AUFRECHT's Catalogus Catalogorum. The Atharvatarpaṇam is, of course, likely to be the same as Ath. Pariś. 43. — 30 WEBER, Verz. I, p. 332. — 31 JAOS. XI. 376; Kauś. Introd. p. XXII ff. — 32 GGA., 1891, nr. 8, p. 283. — 33 Ahnenkult, p. 99, 109 ff. — 34 Recht und Sitte, p. 12 ff. — 35 Ritual-Litteratur, p. 36. — 36 CALAND, ibid. 95, 107 ff. — 37 Kauś. Introd. p. XVII ff. — 38 MHASL., p. 328 ff.; MAX MÜLLER, ZDMG. XIX. 137 ff.; WEBER, IS. I. 247 ff., 380 ff.; II. 1 ff., 170 ff.; III. 324 ff.; IX. 1 ff.; IStr. II. 135; III. 585 ff.; WL.² 170 ff. (especially p. 171, note 3); DEUSSEN, Sechzig Upanishad's, p. 531 ff. — 39 WL.², p. 172 ff. — 40 WEBER, Verz. II. 88; HATFIELD, JAOS. XIV, p. CLX. — 41 DEUSSEN, ibid. p. 575, 583 ff. — 42 Ibid. p. 532 ff.; WEBER, Verz. I. 95. — 43 WL.², p. 171, note 3. — 44 DEUSSEN, ibid. — 45 IS. 251; WL.², p. 173; DEUSSEN, p. 543. — 46 See below, § 59. — 47 E. g. AV. 3. 20. 1: Jābāla 4; AV. 4. 1. 1: Atharvaśiras 1; AV. 4. 4. 1: Saṃnyāsa 1; AV. 6. 96. 1: Prāṇāgnihotra 1; AV. 10. 2. 26—27: Atharvaśiras 6; AV. 10. 8. 27: Atharvaśiras 1; AV. 11. 4 to be compared with Praśna 2. 7 ff.; AV. 11. 4. 13: Muṇḍaka 2. 1. 7; AV. 11. 8: Saṃnyāsa 3, and Kaṇṭhaśruti 5; AV. 18: Saṃnyāsa 1. — 48 Cp. below, § 24. — 49 DEUSSEN, ibid. p. 531. — 50 Kauśika, Introduction, p. XXXIII. — 51 See below, § 68. — 52 IS. IX. 49 ff.; Sechzig Upanishad's, p. 858 ff. The Praṇavopaniṣad is catalogued by BURNELL, Sk. MSS. in the palace of Tanjore, 33ᵇ; STEIN, Catalogue of Sanskrit Manuscripts at Jammu, p. 31; Catalogue of the Oriental Manuscript Library in Madras, p. 52; cp. also TAYLOR, Catalogue of Oriental MSS. in Fort St. George, II, 472. — 53 See below, § 69. — 54 DEUSSEN, p. 867 ff. — 55 JAOS. VII. 333—615; X. 156—171; cp. IS. IV. 79 ff.; V. 451 ff.; IStr. II. 230 ff.; WL.², p. 168. — 56 SPAW. 1871, p. 77. — 57 BHANDARKAR, Report 1883—4, p. 30. — 58 BLOOMFIELD, JAOS. XV, p. XLVIII ff. — 59 WEBER, Verz. II. 79 ff.; and in the introductions of his translations of AV., books 3—5, IS. XVII. 177 ff.; XVIII. 1 ff.; SHANKAR PANDIT in his edition of the AV. vol. I, Critical note, p. 17 ff. — 60 See the passages extracted by SHANKAR PANDIT, ibid. p. 18—23; cp. JAOS. XI. 376. — 61 WEBER, Verz. II. 89. — 62 SHANKAR PANDIT, ibid. p. 15 (top.).

F. THE POSITION OF THE ATHARVA-VEDA IN HINDU LITERATURE IN GENERAL.[1]

§ 20. General estimate of the AV. — The Atharvan is a sacred text in more than one respect: aside from the materials which it shares with the other Vedas the majority of its hymns are benevolent or highly religious (theosophic); these cannot at any time have been received with any other sentiment than esteem. Even the sorceries of the AV. necessarily show a double face: they are useful to oneself, harmful to others. Thus there arises a conflict of emotions which lasts throughout the history of recorded Hindu thought and is summed up in the final orthodox and stereotyped view that the Atharvan is used 'to appease, to bless, and to curse'[2]. In the long run there arose withal a strong wave of popular aversion against the Veda whose most pointed teaching is after all sorcery. This appears from the discussions of the Hindus themselves as to the orthodoxy of that Veda[3]; from the conscious efforts of the later Atharvan writings to vindicate its character and value; from the allegorical representation of the Atharvan as 'a lean black man, sharp, irascible, and amorous'[4]; and from occasional statements of the Vedic and Classical texts.

§ 21. The Atharvan in the RV. — The RV. has no specific designation for Atharvan charms, although it contains a goodly number of such charms. No great importance is to be attached to this silence; the praises to the gods in connection with the great soma-sacrifices offer but scant occasion for the mention of sorcery, or the plainer practices of every-day life. Yet sorcery and house-practices there were in India at all times[5]. The failure of the RV. to mention such charms by a collective name like *atharvāṅgirasaḥ* must be gauged by the slenderness of its opportunities to mention the Veda as a generic name (cp. 8. 19. 5), or Vedic collections or redactions in particular (10.90.9)[6]. There is no proof that even the oldest 'Rigvedie period', or the most ancient Hindu tradition accessible historically, excluded writings which would be entitled to the name of Atharvan-charms by their subject-matter, form (metre), or style: even the absence of generic names, such as *bheṣajāni*, *atharvāṇaḥ*, *aṅgirasaḥ*, for such compositions may be due to accidental silence. The existing redactions of the AV., to be sure, betray themselves as later than the RV. redaction in many ways, especially by the character of the variants in those mantras which they share with the RV.[7]; certainly also a good many of existing Atharvan hymns are later than the bulk of the RV. Nevertheless, we cannot escape the conclusion that hymns of the Atharvanic type were composed simultaneously with, or even prior to those of the Rigvedic (*śrauta*) type[8].

§ 22. The Atharvan in the AV. itself. — The AV. alludes to its own class of compositions but rarely: 10. 7. 20 (*atharvāṅgirasaḥ*); 11. 6. 14 (*bheṣajā*); cp. also 19. 54. 5, and 19. 22. 1; 23. 1[9]. There is to be noted also a decided advance in the association of the names Atharvan, Aṅgiras and Bhṛgu with the practices and the conditions which these hymns are aimed at: e. g. 4. 37. 1 where the Atharvans appear as slayers of the Rakṣas; see also 4. 3. 7; 5. 19. 1; 10. 6. 20. Especially noteworthy is the evident association of the word *āṅgirasa* with sorcery and spells, and the somewhat less clear corresponding correlation of *ātharvaṇa* with auspicious charms (see above, p. 8). Otherwise the attitude of the AV. is much the same as that of the Yajus-texts: the three Vedas are often mentioned without the fourth by way of esoteric restriction to the sphere of the great Vedic (*śrauta*) ritual. Thus it augurs no contempt or neglect of the Atharvan, if in a charm constructed for the purpose of obtaining a knowledge of the Vedas (7. 54: Kauś. 42. 9), only *ṛk*, *sāman*, *yajuḥ*, *veda*, and oblation (*haviḥ*) are mentioned: the person who here desires Vedic learning is not in training for Atharvan priesthood, and therefore does not take care to include this special branch of learning. A similar passage in a RV. Sūtra (AG. 3. 3. 1—3) does not hesitate to include the AV. on the same occasion. Even the GB. which certainly cannot be accused of Atharvaphoby (see § 66) is caught napping once or twice, and omits the AV. from systematic statements of Vedic compositions: 1. 1. 23 and 24. In fact this very omission shows that the AV. Saṃhitā, unlike its ritualistic adjuncts (see § 30), is in no wise engaged either in self-glorification, or in polemics against the other Vedas: the Atharvan poets certainly are quite unconscious of any disadvantages inherent in their text, or of any contemptuous view of the AV. on the part of the adherents of the other Vedas.

§ 23. The Atharvan in the Śrauta-texts. — The position of the AV. in the *śrauta*-literature in general depends altogether on the practical character of these texts as exponents of the great Vedic sacrifices: these, by their very nature, exclude direct interest in the systematic charms of the *bheṣajāni* and *ābhicārikāṇi*. Such sorcery as is interwoven with the *śrauta*-performances obtains independent expression in metrical stanzas and prose formulas (*yajus*) which are thoroughly Atharvanic[10]. But in the *śruti* the sphere of the Atharvan is restricted to matters that are incidental and subsidiary, intended merely to pave the way for the main issue, the successful dispatch of the sacrifice to the gods, and the undisturbed gratification of the priests (*iṣṭi* and *pūrti*). Under these circumstances pronounced hostility against the AV., such as crops out at a later and more reflective age, would be a paradox, too silly even for the Yajus-texts and the Brāhmaṇas. Rigid consistency is, of course, not to be expected; witchcraft blows hot and cold from the same mouth: according as it is turned towards the inimical forces, human and demoniac, or is turned by others against oneself, it is regarded as useful or noxious. The AV. takes the same view by implication, as may be gathered from a comparison of 2.12 with 7. 70, or 2. 7 with 6. 13 and 37. It is a question throughout of my sorcery or thy sorcery. The poet of RV. 7. 104. 15, 16 exclaims 'May I die to-day if I am a sorcerer', and makes complaint against his enemy who calls him, though he is pure, a sorcerer, and against the real sorcerer who pretends that he is pure. Though *yātu* here, as at AV. 1. 7 and 8, is regarded as devilish, the writer of ŚB. 10. 5. 2. 20 is not prevented from placing the *yātuvidaḥ*, 'those that are skilled in sorcery', in solemn array with the representatives of the holiest forms of literature, the *bahvṛcaḥ* etc. On the other hand even *bheṣajam* 'cure, medicine', the altruistic province of the Atharvan, though well regarded in general, does not come off without a sneer[11]: we may trust that the canons of social standing and literary appreciation of a people that produced the better types of Vedic literature could not fail, in the proper mood, to estimate at its right value the wretched hocus-pocus of the *bheṣajāni*, though these were the best that the Vedic period had produced for the relief of bodily ailment. Yet the Veda without charms and sorcery would not be the Veda, and the *śrauta*-texts are not in the position to throw stones at the Atharvan. Anyhow a sober survey of the position of the AV. in the *śruti* shows that this Veda, while not within the proper sphere of the greater concerns of Vedic religion, is considered within its own sphere as a Veda in perfectly good standing; the question of its relative importance, its authority, and its canonicity is not discussed, nor even suggested.

Accordingly the mythic personages Atharvan, Aṅgiras, and Bhṛgu, and their descendants (Ātharvaṇa etc.), whose proper names in the course of time are restricted more and more to the sphere of the Atharvan, continue in the *śruti* to be designations of demigods and Rishis[12]. These names are held in honor no more and no less than other eponyms, it being reserved for the later Atharvan writings to extol them beyond measure, and to claim for them a special position as typical Vedic saints. And this is true although the *śruti* occasionally feels the connection between these names and the sphere of the Atharvan, as when KS. 16. 13 mentions a Rishi Bhiṣaj Ātharvaṇa, the KB. 30. 6 a Rishi Ghora Āṅgirasa[13]; or when PB. 12. 8. 6 states that Dadhyañc Āṅgirasa was the chaplain (*purodhānīya*) of the gods. Even more clearly does this appear from the way in which the hymns of the AV. are alluded to in the *śruti*. Ordinarily the texts are preoccupied with the sacrificial literature in the narrower sense, and hence devote themselves to the mention and laudation of the *trayī vidyā*. On the other hand, whenever the *śrauta*-texts mention, or draw upon other literary forms like *itihāsa*, *purāṇa*, *gāthā*, *sūtra*, *upaniṣad*, and many others, the Atharvan is regularly included, and that too, almost invariably in the following order: the three Vedas occupy the first three places; the AV. holds the fourth place, and next follow in variable arrangement the types *itihāsa* etc. Typical examples are: TS. 7. 5. 11. 2 = KS., Aśvamedhagrantha, 5. 2 (*aṅgiras* alone); ŚB. 10. 5. 2. 10;

11. 5. 6. 4—8; 13. 4. 3. 3ff.; TB. 3. 12. 8. 2; TA. 2. 9. 2; 10. 7. 8; 11. 2; AŚ. 10. 7. 1 ff.; ŚS. 16. 2. 2 ff.

§ 24. The Atharvan in the Upaniṣads. — The position of the AV. in the Upaniṣads is much the same as in the *śruti* in general. Aside from the Atharvan Upaniṣads, which refer more freely to the AV., it is introduced but rarely, and in the same way as in the Śrauta-texts, i. e., preceded by the *trayī*, and followed by a variable list of other types of composition: e. g. BṛhU. 2. 4. 10; 4. 1. 2; 5. 11; ChU. 3. 1—4; 7. 1. 2, 4; 2. 1; 7. 1; MU. 6. 32 and 33. Very much more numerous are the cases in which the *trayī* alone occurs[14], showing that the draughts upon the AV. and the subsequent literary compositions are, in general, made under the excitement of formulaic solemnity. Needless to say, the Upaniṣads with their eye aloft alike from hymn, sacrificial formula, and witchcraft-charm, have no occasion to condemn the AV., aside from that superior attitude of theirs which implies and diplomatically expresses condemnation of the entire Veda that is not *brahmavidyā*. Even the Atharvan Upaniṣads do not in general sound either the polemic or the apologetic note of the ritualistic writings of the AV. The late Praṇava (Pranou) assumes the superiority of the AV.[15], but the Praṇava is a part of the Gopatha-Brāhmaṇa (§ 68). Besides this there is only an interpolated passage in the Praśna that tries to secure at any cost the correlation of the Atharvan with the highest *brahma*[16]. The authority of Atharvan teachers, Sanatkumāra, Aṅgiras, Paippalāda, etc. is, of course, invoked, by way of imparting to those texts an esoteric school-character. But in general, all that may be said is, that these tracts mention the fourth Veda along with the other three more frequently than the Upaniṣads of other schools, that the AV. is quietly added to the *trayī*, whether other literary forms like the *itihāsapurāṇam*, etc., appear in the sequel or not. Thus the four Vedas alone: Nṛsiṁhapūrvatāpanī 1. 2 and 4; 2. 1; Atharvaśiras 1; Muktikā 12—14; Mahā 3; the four Vedas with other literary categories: Muṇḍaka 1. 1. 5; Nṛsiṁhapūrvatāpanī 5. 9. Even these Upaniṣads, however, occasionally lapse into the more frequent habit of the bulk of the Vedic literature, and fail to refer to the AV., whether consciously or unconsciously, it seems impossible to say: Muṇḍaka 2. 1. 6; Praśna 2. 6; Nṛsiṁhatāpanī 5. 2; Brahmavidyā 5ff. As a class the Atharvan Upaniṣads are engaged neither in defending the AV. from attack, nor in securing for it any special degree of prominence.

§ 25. The Atharvan in the Gṛhya-sūtras. — In the Gṛhyasūtras one would expect a greater degree of intimacy with the Atharvan, and hence a more frequent and less formulaic reference to its writings, since in more than one sense the Gṛhyasūtras are themselves Atharvanic. Many of their mantras are identical with, or variants of those contained in the AV. But even the Gṛhya-rites, popular, nay vulgar, as they must have been in their untrammeled beginnings were, so to speak, Rishified, and in time passed through a process of school-treatment which enstranged them from the Atharvan, and assimilated them, as far as possible, to the RV., SV., and YV., as the case may be. Thus the battle-charm AG. 3. 12, instead of drawing upon the very abundant mantras of this kind in the AV.[17], is decked out with the scattering material of this class in the RV. Nowhere is there a marked degree of literary relationship with the AV. Sometimes the Atharvan is mentioned in the manner which is normal in the *śruti*, i. e., preceded by the *trayī*, and followed by other varieties of composition: AG. 3. 3. 1—3; ŚG. 1. 24. 8; HG. 2. 19. 16. But in ŚG. 1. 16. 3 (*brahmaveda*); PG. 2. 10. 7 (*atharvaveda*); 2. 10. 21 (*atharvaṇām*); HG. 2. 3. 9; 18. 3; 20. 9 (*atharvaveda*) there is a distinct advance along the line of later development in the more distinct and familiar mention of the fourth Veda; this is not balanced altogether by the cases of restriction to the *trayī* (ŚG. 1. 22. 15; 24. 2; HG. 1. 5. 13; 2. 13. 1), or to two Vedas (AG. 1. 7. 6 = ŚG. 1. 13. 4 = PG. 1. 6. 3; GG. 1. 6. 19; 3. 2. 48), because these passages are to a considerable extent quotations, or modified mantras from the *śruti*. The true value of this testimony is chronological, not sentimental: the Gṛhyasūtras, as much as their subject-matter is akin to the AV., are not imbued with a sense of its especial value and importance, any more than the *śrauta*-texts. They handle their materials in a self-centred fashion; their reference to the AV. is formulaic in every single instance; and the greater frequency with which it is mentioned marks the later chronology of the composition of the Gṛhyasūtras into formal treatises[18]. This is illustrated significantly by the list of Rishis at the *tarpaṇa* in the Gṛhyasūtras of the RV.[19]: here Sumantu whom very late tradition designates as the source of Atharvan-lore[20], but who figures not at all in Atharvan texts, is given a prominent place. From such a late period of Atharvanic development do the Gṛhyasūtras derive their consciousness of the AV.

§ 26. The Atharvan in the law-literature (dharma). — There is yet another field of literature whose roots also reach down to the Veda, namely that of the law-books *(dharma)*: in the legal Sūtras, Śāstras, and Smṛtis, especially in their so-called *vyavahāra*-chapters, judgment must be finally passed on the unclean and sinister phases of Atharvanic activity. Here the golden rule must come up for consideration. The need of doing unto others what one would have others do unto oneself, and leaving the opposite undone, is sure to be felt and expressed. In the *dharma*-texts also the AV. retains in a measure its place by virtue of its profound hold upon popular beliefs, because indispensable sciences like medicine and astrology are Atharvanic by distinction, and because the Atharvan priest performs, especially for the king, inestimable services in the injury and overthrow of enemies. The king's chaplain (*purohita*) was in all probability as a rule an Atharvan priest (cp. Yājñav. 1. 312). But incantations, sorceries, love-charms and the like do work injury, and the *dharma*-texts pronounce with no uncertain voice the judgment that the Atharvan, useful or indispensable as it is under certain circumstances, is on the whole inferior in character and position, that its practices are impure, and must be either strictly regulated, or prohibited by the proper punishments.

The AV. is not mentioned by name very frequently in the Dharma-texts[21]. A number of times it presents itself in the normal and formal Vedic manner, i. e. preceded by the *traividya*, and followed by other literary types, especially the *itihāsapurāṇam*, e. g. ViDh. 30. 37; BDh. 2. 5. 9. 14; Yājñav. 1. 44; Auśanasa 3. 44; Karmapradīpa 2. 5. 10. A little less frequently it holds the position of the fourth Veda in cases where no subsidiary literature is mentioned: BDh. 3. 9. 4; 4. 5. 1; VāDh. 22. 9; Auśanasa 3. 86; Vṛddha-Hārīta 3. 45. The Atharvaśiras (Śiras), an Upaniṣad connected with the AV., is often mentioned, with respect of course, e. g. GDh. 19. 12; VāDh. 22. 9; BDh. 4. 1. 28; ViDh. 55. 9; Auśanasa 4. 5. More pointedly the sacred texts of the AV. are recommended as the true weapons with which the Brāhmaṇa may slay his enemies, Manu 11. 33 (*śrutīr atharvāṅgirasīḥ*); the king must choose as his Purohita one skilled in the Atharvan and Aṅgiras (*atharvāṅgirase*), Yājñav. 1. 312; the same behest is implied GDh. 11. 15, 17, where the king is enjoined to take heed of that which astrologers and interpreters of omens tell him, and to cause the Purohita to perform in his house-fire expiatory rites (*śānti*), rites for prosperity (*maṅgala*), and witchcraft-practices against enemies (*abhicāra*)[22]. Such a Purohita is *eo ipso* an Atharvan priest. At BDh. 2. 8. 15. 4; ViDh.

73. 11; 81. 4 the demons called *yātudhāna* are driven out by means of sesame, in perfect accord with AV. 1. 7. 2. In the Atri-Saṃhitā (Jīvānanda's collection, vol. 1, p. 45) Atharvan priests skilled in astrology are recommended for the performance of śrāddhas and sacrifices. Cp. also ViDh. 3. 75; 71. 66; Manu 7. 217; Yājñav. 1. 332.

Thus far the *dharma*-texts express regard for the AV. and conscious dependence upon its literature and its practices. But the dubious quality of the fourth Veda sounds from notes pitched in a different key. In the first place the omission of the AV. from Vedic lists which characterizes the *śrauta*-texts, is continued in the *dharma*-texts, here as there without pronounced disapproval. Thus notably in the prohibition of the other Vedas while the sound of the Sāmans is heard, only RV. and YV. are mentioned: GDh. 16. 21; VāDh. 13. 30; ViDh. 30. 26; Manu 4, 123, 124. Other cases in which the *traividya* is mentioned without reference to the AV. are BDh. 2. 8. 14. 4, 5; 4. 5. 29; Manu 1. 23; 3. 145; 11. 263—6; 12. 112; Yājñav. 2. 211. The inferiority of the AV. is stated outright at ĀpDh. 2. 11. 29. 10, 11, where it is said that the knowledge of women and Śūdras forms a supplement to the AV.[23]; yet more brusquely ViDh. 5. 191 counts him that recites a deadly incantation from the AV. as one of the seven kinds of assassins. More frequently performances which imply the use of the AV. are decried and punished, though the Veda is not mentioned by name. Magic rites with intent to harm enemies, and curses in general cause defilement: they are visited with severe penances, e. g. ĀpDh. 1. 9. 26. 7; BDh. 2. 1. 2. 16; GDh. 25. 7; ViDh. 37. 26; Manu 9, 290; Yājñav. 3. 289 (contrariwise Manu 11. 33). The practice of medicine is emphatically described as impure here as in the Brāhmaṇas[24], e. g. ĀpDh. 1. 6. 18. 20; ViDh. 51. 10; GDh. 17. 17; VāDh. 14. 2, 19; Manu 3. 152; Yājñav. 1. 162: the charge, of course, reflects upon the AV. Astrology and fortune-telling are impure professions, e. g. BDh. 2. 1. 2. 16; ViDh. 82. 7; VāDh. 10. 21; Manu 3. 162: that these occupations were Atharvanic seems to follow from AV. 6. 128; Kauś. 50. 15 (cp. Atri-saṃhitā, above). An especially pointed reflection against the AV. is implied in the prohibition of *mūlakriyā* or *mūlakarman*, 'practises with roots', ViDh. 25. 7; Manu 9. 290; 11. 64: the brunt of this charge is without doubt directed against the AV. (see, e. g. 1. 34; 6. 138), though practices of this kind are not wanting outside of that Veda (cp. RV. 10. 145, and the Gṛhyasūtras). Finally, GDh. 15. 16; ViDh. 82. 12; Manu 3. 151; 4. 205, he that sacrifices for the common herd (*grāma-yājaka*) is impure: we may presume that this kind of activity was largely, if not entirely in the hands of Atharvan priests; cp. SBE. XLII, p. xl, note.

§ 27. The Atharvan in the Mahābhārata. — The position of the AV. in the Mahābhārata is characterized by the single statement that its importance as a Veda, and its canonicity, are finally and completely established; that its practices are familiarly known and, in general, not subjected to any particular criticism. The great collection deals so largely with the interests of the Kṣatriyas as to preclude any conscious discrimination against the AV., since this Veda also is largely engaged in the interest of the kings (*rājakarmaṇi*)[25]. Frequently, to be sure, the prevailing Vedic habit of speaking of the threefold Veda is continued mechanically[26], but the high regard for the Atharvan and its unchallenged position in the canon are proved by the quasi-cosmogonic passages in which the four Vedas figure in close affinity with the personified creator. Thus, at 5. 108. 10 = 3770 Brahman is said to have first sung the four Vedas, and at 3. 203. 15 = 13560 Brahman has the epithet Caturveda; and similarly much else of this sort[27]. By itself the AV. is mentioned frequently either with direct praise, or in a position of indisputable usefulness. E. g. at 2. 11. 19 = 437 the *atharvāṅgirasaḥ* personified, are mentioned honorifically along with other Vedic Rishis; at 5. 18. 5 = 548 ff. Aṅgiras praises Indra with mantras of the AV., hence Indra declares that this Veda shall thenceforth have the name *atharvāṅgirasa*. At 12. 342. 99 = 13258 ff. Prajāpati declares that Atharvan sages fashioned him into an Atharvan priest devoted to the practice of the five kalpas (*pañcakalpam atharvāṇam*); at 3. 305. 20 = 17066 Kuntī knows Atharvan mantras (*atharvāṅgirasi*[28] *śrutam*) which compel the gods to appear; and so on[29]. It is, of course, not to be expected that the Atharvan and its practices, notwithstanding their establishment in the good graces of the Epic writers, shall come off entirely without criticism; there must have been persons aching under its supposed inflictions, and moods alive to a full sense of its vulgarity. In such cases the Epic reflects entirely the spirit of the *dharma*-texts. Thus physicians are declared to be impure, 12. 36. 28 = 1322; 13. 90. 13 = 4282; or, practices of bad women with charms and roots are condemned, 3. 39. 6 = 2237 ff. Magic or sorcery is in general regarded as good, but yet it is possible in the view of the Epic to bewitch right so as to make it wrong, to be a *dharmābhicārin* (12. 140. 42 = 5288), or to use foul *māyā* (7. 30. 15 = 1316 ff.): the Atharvan duplicity is ineradicable.

§ 28. The Atharvan in Sanskrit, Jaina, and Bauddha literature.— In Sanskrit literature in general the AV., though not mentioned very frequently, is just as firmly established as in the Mahābhārata. The Rāmāyaṇa refers to the AV. but once (2. 26. 21); but the Daśakumāracarita (twice, chap. 2, p. 94, and chap. 3, p. 108), the Kirātārjunīya 10. 10, and the proverbs here and there, exhibit it in undiminished usefulness and respect. Suśruta's Āyurveda is naturally acquainted with the oldest source of Hindu medicine: 1. 89. 19; 122. 10. The Purāṇas always speak of the fourfold Veda, and present the AV. in the exalted position given it in its own ritualistic literature (see the next chapter): *paurohityaṃ śāntipauṣṭikāni rājñām atharvavedena kārayed brahmatvaṃ ca* (Viṣṇu-Purāṇa, Prasthānabheda, p. 16, l. 10). The Matsya, as quoted by Sāyaṇa in the introduction to the AV., p. 6, orders that the Purohita shall compass the mantras and the Brāhmaṇa of the AV.; and the Mārkaṇḍeya claims that the king consecrated with its mantras enjoys the earth and the ocean (Sāyaṇa, ibid.)[30]. On the other hand the Jainist and Buddhist literatures naturally cap their small esteem of the Veda in general with occasional express condemnation of the practices of the AV. Thus the Sūtrakṛtāṅga-sūtra 2. 27 forbids the incantations of the Atharvan (*atharvaṇī*); or the Aṭṭhakavagga 14. 13 of the Sutta-nipāta forbids the practice of the Āthabbaṇa-Veda. To the condemnation of practices essentially Atharvanic is devoted the Mahā Sīlam in the second chapter of the Tevijja-sutta; similarly the Vinaya, Kullavagga 5. 32. 2[31].

§ 29. The Atharvan in grammatical, lexical, and text-historical works. — In grammatical, lexical, and text-historical treatises the Atharvan still occupies a somewhat uncertain position. Pāṇini 4. 3. 133; 6. 4. 174 has *ātharvaṇika* (cp. the *gaṇa* to 4. 2. 63), without defining its position[32]; the Mahābhāṣya not only mentions its Saṃhitā (Śaunakīya or Paippalāda) by the term *viṃśino 'ṅgirasaḥ*[33], but is peculiar in placing it, or rather its opening stanza, *śaṃ no devī*, at the head of the list of Vedic writings[34]: the scholiast explains this unusual position of the AV. on the ground that all sacrifices begin with the expulsion of demons (*rakṣas* and *piśāca*) from the sacrificial ground. Weber prefers to think that the Vedas of the *śrauta* (*traividya*) had at that time become obsolete and were only mentioned for form's sake. Perhaps the growing importance of the office of the Brahman, the fourth type of priest, at the Vedic sacrifice, and the growingly frequent tenure of this office by Atharvan priests, accounts for the unusual attitude of Patañjali[35]. Or we may bear in mind the special practical importance of this Atharvan stanza as a purificatory prayer in the morning, manifested by the fact that it is placed at the head of many Śaunakīya-MSS. where it does not originally belong[36]. The Ātharvaṇika are also cited respectfully in the Anupada (3. 12) and Nidāna Sūtras (2. 12) of the SV.[37] in connection with teachers of other Vedic schools; similarly Sāyaṇa to Mahānārāyaṇa Up. (IS. II. 100, note 2). The Caraṇavyūhas treat the AV. as the fourth Veda, on the same plain as the other Vedas[38]; the Bṛhaddevatā 5. 15 knows the *atharvāṅgirasāḥ mantrāḥ* in active practice. Of lexical texts the Amarakośa does not mention the AV.; in the Medinīkośa Atharvan figures as the name of the Veda[39]. But a writer as late as Hemacandra, 249, may still describe the AV. as an extract (*uddhṛti*) from the *traividya*[40].

1 This chapter is a revised abstract of the investigation on this subject printed by the author, SBE. XLII, p. XXVIII—LVI; the paragraph at the end, on the position of the AV. in the grammatical and kindred literature, is added to the original treatment of the subject. — 2 MADHUSŪDANASARASVATI (IS. I. 16); KEŚAVA to Kauś. 1. 1; DEVA to KŚ. 15. 7. 11, and elsewhere. — 3 ALBERUNI, India (SACHAU's translation), vol. I, p. 129, reports that the AV. is less in favor with the Hindus than the other Vedas. According to BURNELL, Vaṁśabrāhmaṇa of the SV., p. XXI, the most influential scholars of Southern India still deny the genuineness of the AV. — 4 RĀJENDRALĀLAMITRA, in the introduction to GB., p. 4. — 5 Cp., e. g. RV. 1. 191; 7. 50; 7. 104; 10. 128; and see AUFRECHT's edition of the RV., vol. II, p. 670 ff. — 6 See SBE. XLII, p. XXX, note 3. — 7 See above, § 3; below, § 42. — 8 KNAUER, Festgruss an ROTH, p. 64 ff., and in opposition to our view, OLDENBERG, DLZ. March 13, 1897 (p. 366 ff.). On the metrical and linguistic criteria for the relative dates of RV. and AV. poetry see below, § 38, 42. — 9 The word *brahma* which is catalogued with the *trayī*, 11. 8. 23; 15. 6. 3 (cp. also 15. 3. 7) does not refer to the AV., but is the broader and higher term for religion in general; cp. RV. 10. 71. 11, and see below, § 33. — 10 E. g., 'I dig (pits) that destroy the Rakṣas etc.': TS. 1. 3. 2. 1; MS. 1. 2. 10; VS. 5. 23; ŚB. 3. 5. 4. 8. — 11 E. g. TS. 6. 4. 9. 3; MS. 4. 6. 2; ŚB. 4. 1. 5. 14. — 12 SBE. XLII, p. XXXIV ff. — 13 Cp. above, p. 8. — 14 See JACOB's Concordance, s. vs. *ṛgveda*, *ṛṅmaya*, *ṛc*; *yajurveda*, *yajurmaya*, *yajus*; *sāmaveda*, *sāmamaya*, *sāman*. — 15 IS. I. 296; IX. 51. — 16 SBE. XLII, p. XLII, note 2. — 17 Ibid. p. 117 ff. — 18 OLDENBERG, SBE. XXX, p. 1 and XVII ff. — 19 AG. 3. 4. 4; ŚG. 4. 10. 3; Śāmbavya-Gṛhya, IS. XV. 153. Cp. IS. XIV. 441; WL.², p. 165. — 20 ROTH, AV. in Kaschmir, p. 28. — 21 For detailed statements see SBE. XLII, p. XLVI ff. — 22 This is the stereotyped summary of the functions of the AV., *śāntapuṣṭikābhicārika*; see p. 8. — 23 Cp. BÜHLER, SBE. II, p. XXIX. — 24 SBE. XLII, p. XXXIX ff. — 25 SBE. XLII, p. 111 ff.; Kauś., chapters 14 to 17. — 26 See A. HOLTZMANN, Das Mahābhārata, vol. IV, p. 5. — 27 SBE. XLII, p. LII. — 28 Calcutta ed., *atharvaśirasi*. — 29 Ibid. LIII. — 30 Ibid. LIV ff. — 31 Ibid. LVI. — 32 IS. V. 77. For Pāṇini's acquaintance with the so-called *hṛdya*, see below § 53. — 33 Cp. TS. 7. 5. 11. 2 = Kāṭhaka Aśvamedhagrantha, and the superscription of the Ath. Prātiśākhya. — 34 IS. XIII. 431 ff.; XIV. 441; WL.², p. 165, note 3. — 35 See next chapter, § 33. — 36 Kauś. Introd. p. XXXVII. — 37 IS. I. 43, 45; XIII. 144, 146; WL.², p. 90, 165. — 38 IS. III. 277 ff. — 39 Pet. Lex. s. v. *atharvan*, 2. — 40 IS. I. 297, bottom.

G. THE ATHARVA-VEDA IN THE VIEW OF ITS RITUALISTIC LITERATURE[1].

§ 30. The attitude of the ritual texts towards the Atharvan and its priests. — From the preceding chapter we may gather that the Saṃhitā of the AV. and the Atharvan Upaniṣads allude with predilection and in terms of praise to their own kind of compositions, to the mythical sages who are their reputed authors, and to Atharvanic priests. Of any systematic attempt to make battle against the ancient threefold Veda or its adherents there is no sign. Similarly the ritual texts of the AV. allude preferably, and yet incidentally, to their own Veda, and as occasion offers, bring to the front the priests schooled in it: e. g. Kauś. 63. 3; 139. 6; Vait. 1. 5; Ath. Pariś. 46. 2, etc. But over and above this the ritual texts raise certain special claims regarding the position of the AV. among the Vedas, and they demand with obvious polemic intention that certain offices shall be reserved for Atharvan priests. The position of these texts may be stated under three heads. First, they are not content with the rather vacillating attitude of the non-Atharvanic texts which restrict the honorific mention of the fourth Veda to more or less well-defined occasions, especially to moods when it appears desirable to call into requisition the entire range of Vedic literary compositions in addition to the *trayī vidyā* (e. g. *itihāsa*, *purāṇa*, etc.). Secondly, the office of the Brahman, the fourth priest at the *śrauta*-ceremonies, is said by them to belong to an Atharvavedin, and Vait. and GB. in fact exhibit the *bhṛgvaṅgirovid* in possession of that office. Thirdly, a similar claim is advanced in respect to the office of the Purohita; the king must choose an Atharvan priest conversant with the Atharvan writings as his chaplain or house-priest: *purohita, guru,* or *brahman,* as he is variously called. The latter claim is supported, as has been shown, to some extent by later Brahmanical treatises not derived from Atharvan schools[2].

§ 31. Exaltation of the Atharvan, and the office of the Brahman in the ritual texts. — As regards the first point, the GB. 1. 1. 4—10 describes the cosmogonic origin of the universe and the Vedas from the lone *brahma.* Vedic texts in general ignore the AV. in these creative fancies, but in the GB. the Atharvan and Aṅgiras texts are placed at the head: the other Vedic texts (1. 1. 6) as well as the subsidiary compositions (*sarpaveda* etc., 1. 1. 10) are relegated to the rear. GB. 1. 3. 4 lauds the AV. as the most important religious manifestation (*etad vai bhūyiṣṭhaṃ brahma yad bhṛgvaṅgirasaḥ*); GB. 1. 5. 25 ends with the assertion that the students of the *trayī* reach, to be sure, the highest heaven, but that the Atharvans and Aṅgiras go even beyond to the great worlds of Brahma (*ata uttare brahmalokā mahāntaḥ*). In fact the leading theme at the heart of the composers of the GB. is to carry to the front the AV. and its adherents[3], and only rarely, as if by mistake, does this text omit the AV. from its Vedic lists (above, § 22). And in the same way Vait. 6. 1 places the AV. at the head of the four Vedas, not to speak of the even more energetic exaltation of the Atharvan in the Pariśiṣṭas. As regards, secondly, the Brahman, the overseer of the *śrauta*-sacrifices, Vait. 1. 1; 11. 2 (GB. 1. 2. 16) state that he must be conversant with the Brahma-Veda, or Atharvāṅgirasaḥ, in the latter passage in expressed contrast with *udgātar, hotar,* and *adhvaryu* of the *trayī.* At GB. 1. 2. 18 (end) the Brahman is described with the words, *eṣa ha vai vidvān sarvavid brahmā yad bhṛgvaṅgirovid,* indicating the identification of the AV. with the *sarvavidyā* which stands above the *trayī* (below, § 33); GB. 1. 3. 1, 2 describes vividly the futility of the sacrifice without a Brahman skilled in the *bhṛgvaṅgirasaḥ*; as a cow, horse, mule, or chariot cannot proceed with less than four feet, so the sacrifice must have four feet: the four Vedas and the four priests. Cp. especially GB. 2. 2. 13 with its source, TS. 3. 5. 2. 1, where the GB. demurs at the statement of the TS., *tasmād vāsiṣṭho brahmā kāryaḥ,* the GB. being committed emphatically to the *bhṛgvaṅgirovid.*

§ 32. The office of the Purohita in the ritual texts. — Even more energetic are the demands of the liturgic texts in the matter of the office of the *purohita* (*brahman, guru*): 'The king who rules the country shall seek a wise Brahman (*brahmāṇam*). He verily is wise that is skilled in the *bhṛgu* and *aṅgiras*; for the *bhṛgu* and *aṅgiras* act as a charm against all ominous occurrences, and protect everything' (Kauś. 94. 2—4; cp. 126. 2). The equivalence of *brahman*, *purohita*, and *guru* is guaranteed by comparing Ath. Pariś. 3. 1, *kulīnaṃ śrotriyaṃ bhṛgvaṅgirovidaṃ . . . guruṃ vṛṇīyād bhūpatiḥ*; and 3. 3, *tasmād bhṛgvaṅgirovidaṃ . . . kuryāt purohitam*. Cp. also 2. 2, *brahmā tasmād atharvavit*. Conversely, 'The gods, the Fathers, and the twice-born (priests) do not receive the oblation of the king in whose house there is no *guru* skilled in the Atharvan' (2. 3)[4]. Kauś. 17. 14 ff.; 140. 4 ff. exhibit king and Purohita in active cooperation. The Pariśiṣṭas are not content with such strong recommendations of the adherents of their Veda; they would have the adherents of the other Vedas, yea even of certain branches (*śākhā*) of the AV. itself, excluded from the *purohiti*: 'The Atharvan keeps off terrible occurrences, and acts as a charm against portentous ones ... not the Adhvaryu, not the Chandoga, and not the Bahvṛca ... The Bahvṛca destroys the kingdom, the Adhvaryu destroys sons, the Chandoga dissipates wealth; hence the *guru* must be an Ātharvaṇa .., A Paippalāda as *guru* increases happiness, sovereignty, health, and so does a Śaunakin who understands the gods and the mantras ... The king whose *purodhā* is in any way a Jalada or a Mauda is deposed from his kingdom within the year, (Ath. Pariś. 2. 2—5)[5]. The last four names are alike representatives of Atharvan schools (above, p. 11 ff.): the passage shows how eager was the scramble for the office of Purohita. That the Atharvans finally succeeded in making heard their clamorous demand for this office (see below, § 34), is probably due to their superior, if not exclusive, knowledge of witchcraft, which was doubtless regarded in the long run as the most practical and trenchant instrument for the defence of king and people.

§ 33. Causes leading up to the exaltation of the Atharvan and its priests. — In order to estimate these claims of the Atharvanists at their correct value the following needs to be considered. In the Vedic religion, or perhaps better religious evolution, three literary forms and correspondingly three liturgic methods of application of these forms to the sacrifice, were evolved at a time prior to the recorded history of Hindu religious thought and action. They are the well-known types *ṛcaḥ*, *sāmāni*, and *yajūṃṣi*, and their priestly exponents, *hotar*, *udgātar*, and *adhvaryu*. These literary forms taken individually are mere fragments of religious activity; these priests are only individual actors, not qualified each by himself to shoulder the burden of the literary knowledge or liturgic technique. The Hindus were at all times aware that these religious forms are fragmentary and phases of a whole. The RV. contains countless expressions indicating the insufficiency of the *ṛcaḥ* to fulfill alone the scheme of religious action: the absence of *sāmāni* would in principle leave Vedic religion just as much mutilated as the absence of *ṛcaḥ*; the categories are the three parts of a trio whose melody is carried by each in turn. A comprehensive vision was never wanting, though the search for a word for 'religion', or religious practice as a whole was at first not very successful. The Brāhmaṇa-texts[6] use *sarvavidyā* for knowledge of all the Vedas, but the most successful attempt at describing the religious literature and action as a whole is the word *bráhma*, and, correspondingly, he that knows the religion as a whole is a *brahmán*. Each of these words appears occasionally in the fourth place, *bráhma* after the *trayī*; *brahmán* in company with the priests of the *trayī*. Thus the TS. (7. 3. 1. 4) can say: *parimitā vā ṛcaḥ, parimitāni sāmāni, parimitāni yajūṃṣi; athāi 'tasyāi 'vā 'nto nā 'sti yad brahma*. In a sense the *bráhma* is a fourth Veda, but it is not coordinate with the other three: it embraces and comprehends them and much else besides; it is the religious expression and religious action as a whole, and the learned esoteric understanding of the nature of the gods and the mystery of the sacrifice as a whole (*brahma* in *brahmodya* and *brahmavādin*). In the Upaniṣads this *brahma*, frequently contrasted with the ordinary Vedas, is extolled above all other knowledge, and in a way personified, becoming one of the main conceptions which finally precipitate themselves in the pantheistic Brahman-Ātman. The knowledge of this *brahma* there constitutes the »*brahmavidyā*«. Needless to say this fourth Veda, if we may so call it, in all its aspects has primarily no connection with the AV., not even in the Saṃhitā (11.8.23; 15. 3. 7; 6. 3; cp. AB. 1. 22. 15), nor in the Upaniṣads of that Veda (e. g. Nṛsiṁhapūrvatāpanī 5. 2): the claim that the Atharvan is the Brahma-Veda belongs to the Atharvan ritual[7].

This broader religious knowledge exists again from earliest times, not only in the abstract, but centres in persons who grasped it as a whole, in distinction from the technically qualified priests devoted to some specialty. What the *bráhma* is to the *trayī*, that the *brahmán* is to *hotar*, *udgātar*, and *adhvaryu*. RV. 10. 71. 11 depicts the activity of the four priests, the first three handling their respective literary productions (*ṛcaḥ* etc.). The fourth priest is described in the words, *brahmā́ vadati jātavidyām*[8]: he has no special Veda, certainly there is no allusion to the AV. In RV. 7. 7. 5 the god Agni appears chosen as a Brahmán at a sacrifice which suggests the later *sattra* (*agnír brahmā́ nṛṣádane vidhartā́*). In the expression, *brahmā́ vadati jātavidyām*, the 'own wisdom' is the *bráhma* (neuter), and *vadati jātavidyām* foreshadows the *brahmodya* 'the holy, or theological mystery, or riddle', as well as the ritualist refinements which the Śrauta-texts introduce so often with the related expression, *brahmavādino vadanti*. In the non-Atharvanic Vedic texts it is never suggested that the Atharvan is of all other things the specific equipment which shapes the faculties of this all-around Vedic theologian. On the contrary the KB. raises the one-sided claim that a RV. scholar is the proper Brahman; Āpastamba, Yajñaparibhāṣāsūtra 19, more liberally, permits the Brahman to perform with all three Vedas, yet even he ignores the AV.[9] Vasiṣṭha was a celebrated Brahman and Purohita, and these qualifications were said for a time (probably by the descendants of Vasiṣṭha themselves) to be hereditary in this family. But the Brāhmaṇas say explicitly that this is an obsolete custom, every one properly equipped may be a Brahman[10]. Anyhow there is no original connection between Vasiṣṭha and the AV.[11], and it is not going too far to assume that the distinguished abilities demanded by the theory of this office were rare enough to admit everyone that had intrinsically valid claims upon it.

Doubtless the Atharvanists, plea that the Brahman must be one of themselves, and that, consequently, the AV. was the Brahma-Veda was suggested by an obvious schematic proportion. As the Hotar, etc., is to the RV., etc., so the Brahman is to the fourth Veda, and as the AV. is the fourth Veda, or rather a fourth Veda, it required no too violent wrench to identify it with that other comprehensive fourth Veda, the knowledge of the *bráhma*. Thus the Atharvan became the Brahma-Veda, and GB. 1. 2. 18, end, can say: *eṣa ha vai vidvān sarvavid brahmā yad bhṛgvaṅgirovid* (cp. 1. 5. 11, 15, 19, always with the idea of the *sarvam*). The fact that there was no systematic, sharply defined place for the Atharvanist in the scheme of the hieratic (*śrauta*) religion — witchcraft formulas at the sacrifice being handled as *yajus* by the Adhvaryu — must have been galling in the long run, until this arrangement was completed to their own satisfaction. They may have, though we do not know that they did, gathered courage for this *tour de force* from the frequent mention in the AV. itself of the word *bráhma* in the sense of charm, prayer, e. g. 1. 10. 1; 14. 44; 23. 4, etc. If this was done it was a proceeding both arbitrary and superficial: the word has in the AV. the meaning of charm only in so far as the hymns of that Veda happen to be charms; the RV. employs the term freely to designate its own *sūktāni* (e. g. 5. 85. 1; 7. 28. 1). One misses, too, in the AV. the plural *brahmāṇi* as the true Vedic type of designation for a special class of compositions, on a level with *ṛcaḥ*, *sāmāni*, *yajūṃṣi*, *atharvāṅgirasaḥ*, or, *atharvāṇaḥ* (*bheṣajāni*), and *aṅgirasaḥ* (*ābhicārikāṇi*). The Atharvanists doubtless also remembered that the AV. of all Saṃhitās contains the largest collection of theosophic hymns which deal explicitly (10. 2), or implicitly (10. 7), with the divine Brahman and the *bráhma*[12]; hence, to some extent at least, the later association of the superabundant Upaniṣads with Atharvan schools. In the Upaniṣads, as we have seen, the knowledge of just such theosophic relations is styled *brahmavidyā*.

§ 34. Connection of the Purohita with the AV., and interrelation of Purohita and Brahman. — To these Atharvanic pretensions there came from another quarter a measure of substantiality, probably at a comparatively early time, in this instance with the passive support of all Vedic schools. The matter concerns the office of the Purohita, the spiritual and temporal aid of the king, his chaplain and chancellor. To be sure the non-Atharvanic Saṃhitās, Brāhmaṇas, and Sūtras do not mention the AV. in this connection any more than in connection with the office of the Brahman at the *śrauta*-sacrifice. Yet it seems very unlikely that the knowledge of Atharvan practices should not at all times have been considered a very valuable adjunct, if not a *conditio sine quâ non*, of the *purohiti*. Purohitas, whether they are formal adherents of the AV. or not, are always engaging in Atharvanic practices, even against one another[13]. The interests of the king and his sovereignty (*kṣatriya* and *kṣatram*) are too obviously dependent upon magic rites to admit the likelihood that the pretensions to this office on the part of him that knew them should have been ignored. At all periods the safety of the king, the prosperity of his people, his ascendency over hostile neighbors, must have depended upon his Purohita's skill in magic. The description, AB. 8. 24—28, of the Purohita, his functions, and his relation to the king, transfers the reader to the sphere and spirit of the AV.; the same text (8. 25) describes a magic rite, called *brahmaṇaḥ parimāra*, designed to kill hostile kings, which might be an extract from the ritual of the Atharvan[14]. In later texts (GDh. 11. 15, 17; Yājñav. 1. 312; cp. also Manu 11. 33), as a matter of fact the rule is laid down formally that the Purohita should be an Atharvavedin. SĀYAṆA, Introd. to AV., p. 5, 6, makes the same claim outright (*paurohityaṃ cā 'tharvavidai 'va kāryam*); he is able to cite in support not only the rather hysterical dicta of the Atharvan writings themselves, but also ślokas from the Purāṇas, the Nītiśāstra, etc.[15]. In the Daśakumāracarita the marriage ceremony, as well as magic rites, are in fact performed at the court of a king with Atharvan rites, *ātharvaṇena* (*ātharvaṇikena*) *vidhinā*: the statement is the more valuable as it is incidental[16].

Not quite so well-defined are the practical realities in favor of the claim that the Brahman (fourth priest) must be an Atharvavedin, but we may assume that the growing affinity between the AV. and the *purohiti* contributed at least something to the partial success which doubtless attended that claim. It is not necessary for the purpose in hand to establish at all points the original relation between the Purohita and the Brahman whose identity is baldly assumed in many passages of the earlier Hindu literature[17]. A complete survey of the character of each, as well as their respective names establishes *a fortiori* genuine differences in their character. There is, however, one striking point of similarity between them, namely this, that they have in charge, each in his own way, the general interests of their noble employers. On the other hand all priests having other names, at a very early period, certainly at a period prior to the Atharvanic assumption, had in ordinary practice only subordinate charges, because of the technical character of their knowledge and occupation. RV. 10. 71. 11 (cp. 7. 7. 5) expresses clearly the existence of broader theological interests than mere expertness in the recitation and chanting of hymns, and the mechanical service of the sacrifice (*hotar*, *udgātar* and *adhvaryu*). This is the Brahmanship which later forks into two directions, on one side the general knowledge of the procedures at the sacrifice (the Brahman as fourth priest), and the theological speculations attaching (*brahmavādin*); on the other, the higher theosophy which ultimately leads to the *brahmavidyā* of the Upaniṣads. It is natural that a divine thus qualified should at a very early time have assumed permanent and confidential relations to his noble *rājanya*-employer, in all matters that concerned his religious and sacrificial interests. His functions are those of a high-priest. It seems unlikely that this Brahman was in all cases, too, competent to attend to those more secular and practical needs of the king connected with the security of his kingdom, the fealty of his people, and the suppression of his enemies. These activities, *rājakarmāṇi*, as the Atharvan writings call them[18], must have called for different training and different talents — they represent rather the functions of a chancellor and fighting chaplain, than those of a high-priest — and there is no reason to believe that every Brahman possessed these necessary qualifications in addition to his expertness in systematic theology. On the other hand, conversely, there must have been Purohitas incapable of assuming intelligent charge of the more elaborate Vedic performances (*śrauta*), unless we conceive that in such cases the Brahman was a mere figure-head and his office a sinecure. Yet precisely here is to be found the measure of truth which we may suspect in the Atharvanist claim that the supervising Brahman shall be an adherent of the AV. In many cases the tribal king, or *rājā*, might have had but one body-priest, well capable of attending to the kingdom's needs in all manner of charms and sorcery, and thus filling the *paurohitya* creditably with the entire armament of the Veda of charms and sorcery, himself an Atharvavedin. If the king had about him no systematic theologian resplendent in his *jātavidyā*, if there was no adept in that ideal fourth Veda, the *sarvavidyā* that looms above the *trayī vidyā*, the remoter applicability of the *śrauta*-practices to real life, or confidence in the ability of *hotar*, *adhvaryu*, etc., to perform their duties correctly of themselves, would lead him to entrust the general supervision of the *śrauta*-performances to his trusty Atharvan Purohita. Thus the sweeping claim of the Atharvan priests may be founded at least upon a narrow margin of fact; later the Atharvan priests are likely to have equipped themselves with enough external and mechanical knowledge to perform the function of Brahman with a show of respectability, witness the activity of the Brahman in the Vait. In very late times the ability of the Atharvans to practise *śrauta*-rites, and the canonicity of the Vait. were recognized by other Vedic schools, if the matter-of-fact references to that Sūtra on the part of the commentators to KŚ. be regarded as normal[19]. However the entire question of the relation of the AV. to *śrauta*-practices is a rather obscure point in the history of Vedic literature, it being assumed generally that the AV. had originally nothing to do with the larger Vedic ritual. The assumption in this broad form is at any rate too sweeping. The existing Saṃhitās of the AV. contain mantras which could have had no sense and purpose except in connection with *śrauta*-performances. A series of formulas, e. g. like AV.

6. 47 and 48, has no meaning except in connection with the three daily *savanas*: Vait. 21. 7 exhibits them, properly no doubt, as part of the *agniṣṭoma*. Or AV. 6. 114 is evidently an expiatory formula for faults committed at the sacrifice [20]. This last is the special sphere of the Brahman. The GB., more frequently than other Brāhmaṇas, refers to defects in the sacrifice (*viriṣṭa*, *ūna*, *yātayāma*) which are to be corrected (*saṃdhāna*) by mantras (1. 1. 13 and 22), and there are mss. of the Vait. which add six *prāyaścitta*-chapters to the body of that text [21]. Some knowledge of *śrauta*-matters, though not very extensive perhaps, the Atharvans must have had at a very early time, and thus the germs of the correlation of the Atharvan and Brahman may even rest upon some slender basis of very ancient tradition.

1 Abstract of the essay on this subject, SBE. XLII, p. LVII ff. — 2 Cp. above, § 26, and below, § 34. — 3 See below § 66, and note especially GB. 2. 2. 14, where the *atharvāṅgirasaḥ* are added every time in liturgical formulas to the *ṛcaḥ*, *yajūṃṣi*, and *sāmāni*. — 4 Cp. WEBER, Omina und Portenta, p. 346 ff.; IS. X, 138; SĀYAṆA, Introd. to the AV., p. 6. — 5 WEBER, IS. I. 296; BLOOMFIELD, JAOS. XI. 378, note. — 6 TB. 3. 10. 11. 4; TA. 10. 47; cp. ŚB. 14. 6. 7. 18; 9. 4. 17. — 7 SBE. XLII, p. XLIII. — 8 Cp. ibid. p. LIV, note 1. — 9 The commentary admits that the AV. may be included: MHASL., p. 470; ZDMG. IX, p. XLVII; SBE. XXX, p. 321; cp. ibid. XLII, p. LXV, note 2. — 10 WEBER, IS. X. 34, 35, 137. — 11 SBE. XLII, p. LV, note 1; LXV, note 3. Cp. also ROTH, Abhandlung, p. 9; MUIR, OST. I, 395. — 12 Cp. the mantra, GB. 1. 1. 9; SĀYAṆA, Introd. to AV., p. 4; Viṣṇu-Purāṇa 6. 5 (WILSON's translation, vol. V, p. 210). — 13 MHASL., p. 486. — 14 Cp. AV. 3. 19; Kauś. 14. 22—23; RV. 4. 50. 7—9. — 15 Cp. DEVA at KŚ. 15. 7. 11. — 16 See above, § 28; SBE. XLII, p. LXVIII. — 17 E. g. RV. 4. 50. 7 ff., where the Purohita is called Bṛhaspati, i. e. the divine *brahmán*. For the literature on the subject see SBE. XLII, p. LXVIII, note 3. — 18 See below § 55. — 19 GARBE in the preface to the edition of Vait., p. VI. — 20 See the analysis of these two classes of hymns, below, § 58 and 60. — 21 See GARBE, ibid. p. V; WEBER, Verz. II, p. 83; Kauś. Introd. p. XXXIII.

PART II. THE REDACTION AND EXTERNAL FORM OF THE ATHARVA-VEDA IN THE SCHOOL OF ŚAUNAKA.

A. DIVISION AND ARRANGEMENT OF THE HYMNS.

§ 35. The division of the Saṃhitā into 20 books. — The AV. in the Śaunakīya-śākhā is divided into 20 books, a number which is upheld to some extent by tradition. Thus GB. 1. 1. 5 and 8 speaks of 20 mythical sages descended from Atharvan and Aṅgiras, and Patañjali in the Mahābhāṣya to Pāṇ. 5. 2. 37, cites the example, *viṃśino 'ṅgirasaḥ* [1]. General statements of this sort cannot, however, be regarded as conclusive for the original number of the Śaunakīya-books, because AVP. also has 20 books whose genuineness is unimpeachable [2]. Indeed it would seem as though the original collection of the Śaunakins consisted of a lesser number of books, and that it was later swelled by the addition of a number of books sufficient to bring it into accord with the traditional number, that is, to assimilate it to AVP., or to some other redaction in 20 books. There is no doubt that the 20th book is a late addition compiled for the most part from the RV. for ritualistic purposes of an advanced character (see below, § 62). The concluding prayer at the end of book 19 (hymn 72) shows in fact that the collection was at some time conceived as having come to a full stop with book 19. But the latter book is hardly less doubtfully a secondary appendage, for the following reasons: It is exceedingly corrupt; it does not harmonize with the plan of arrangement of the hymns in the first 18 books, which, in spite of certain obscurities, or even puerilities, is on the whole a consistent one[3]; AVP. contains the 72 hymns of book 19 (with the exception of about a dozen) scattered throughout that collection, making it seem probable that the supplementary book 19 of the vulgata is in the main gathered from that very source[4]; AV. 19. 7 and 8 are repeated in full in Nakṣatrakalpa 10 and 26, which would seem to show that at the time of the composition of that text these hymns did not belong to the vulgata, as in the contrary case they would have been quoted by their pratīkas[5]; AV. 19. 22 and 23, a fanciful catalogue, or table of contents, of the Saṃhitā, are of obvious Pariśiṣṭa-character[6], and certainly do not refer to book 19[7], although they seem to refer continously (19. 23. 23—28) to books 13—18; the Kauś., by quoting only a few mantras of book 19 by *pratīka*, and presenting others in full (*sakalapāṭha*), seems to assign to it something like an intermediate position between a collection fully established within the Saṃhitā of its school, and a body of mantras conceived as belonging to another school[8]; finally both books 19 and 20 are not treated in the Prātiśākhya of the AV., or included in the analysis of the Saṃhitā as given by the Pañcapaṭalikā[9], a fact which is perhaps self-explanatory as regards book 20, but which stamps book 19 as a stranger at the time of the composition of the Prātiśākhya. Remarkable but not finally significant is the reference of the Uttamapaṭala, Ath. Pariś. 46. 4—6, to the constituency of the AV. According to this text the Śaunakīya ended with book 16, unless it were assumed that reference is made in it to another *śākhā*[10]. Inasmuch however as this tract indulges in oddities in connection with the remaining Vedic Saṃhitās, and because its account has in view specific ritualistic purposes, it is not necessary to assume that books 17 and 18 were added after the composition of this Pariśiṣṭa, or are in any sense the product of a later redaction than that of books 1—16. Book 18, to be sure, is wanting in AVP.; book 17, however, is for the most part included in it[11].

The AV. is divided into *kāṇḍa* 'books', *anuvāka* 'lessons', and *sūkta* 'hymns'. Another continuous division into *prapāṭhaka* extends in ROTH and WHITNEY's edition through the first 18 books (38 in all), but does not continue through books 19 and 20. In addition to *sūkta* there is also a parallel division of each *kāṇḍa* in *arthasūkta* 'hymns divided off according to sense', and *paryāyasūkta*, briefer subdivisions into groups of verses, usually ten a group. The latter subdivision is to be compared with the Rigvedic *varga*, beside the *sūkta*. Beginning with book 7 SHANKAR PANDIT's divisions in accordance with his authorities differ somewhat from those of the vulgate edition[12]. In Sāyaṇa's commentary the briefer hymns are combined into larger hymns in accordance with the traditional recitation; e. g. in the case of book 6 two hymns (*tṛca*) are fused into one[13]. The Kauś. is acquainted with the terms *adhyāya* (= *kāṇḍa*), *anuvāka*, *sūkta* and *paryāya*[14]. ŚB. 13. 4. 3. 7, 8 mentions the term *parvan* in connection with the recital of sections from the *atharvāṇaḥ* on the one hand and the *aṅgirasaḥ* on the other; the statement is on the face of it exoteric and fanciful, similar to the loose use of *parvan* in RV. 7. 103. 5; PG. 2. 10. 20[15]. The entire collection as printed in the vulgate numbers 731 hymns, aggregating about 6000 stanzas.

§ 36. Arrangement of the books according to hymns of different length. — Leaving aside book 20 whose arrangement like that of the *śrauta*-collections of the Yajus-saṃhitās is liturgical, and the supplementary book 19 whose arrangement is apparently hap-hazard, and at any rate not to be discussed without reference to AVP., the first 18 books disclose the following redactorial scheme[16]. The first seven books consist each of numerous hymns (respectively 35, 36, 31, 40, 31, 142, and 118) of not very many stanzas each, 18 at the utmost (5. 17). The hymns of each book are regulated by a lower limit in the number of their stanzas. First, ascendingly, the hymns of books 1—5, each containing about the same number of hymns, have respectively at least 4, 5, 6, 7 and 8 stanzas; this ascending scale seems to be repeated in a way inside of book 5, the norm of whose first two anuvākas (hymns 1—10) seems to be 8 or 9 stanzas followed in the rest of the book by hymns consisting at least of 11, and rising as high as 18 stanzas (hymn 17). After book 5 there is an obvious break in the arrangement: the number of hymns increases vastly but the scale of stanzas descends; book 6 contains 142 hymns of at least 3 stanzas each; book 7 contains 118 hymns of two, or even as low as one stanza each. The lower limit of stanzas in the hymns of each book may therefore be regarded in a certain sense as the normal number of stanzas of that book[17], suggesting critical operations in connection with those hymns that have more than the normal number. In such cases the question arises whether stanzas were not added by a later hand. It is also possible to surmise that certain hymns which originally fell short of the normal number of a given book were brought up to the norm by later additions. Systematic investigations of this sort have been carried on by BERGAIGNE and OLDENBERG on the RV. with interesting side-glimpses at the AV[18]. Thus the normal number of stanzas in the first book is 4, interrupted only by hymns 3 (9 stanzas), 7 (7 stanzas), 11 (6 stanzas), 29 (6 stanzas), and 34 (5 stanzas). Hymn 3 suggests the throwing out of the liturgically repeated stanzas 2—5, leaving 5 stanzas, but there is no reason further to suspect any of the remaining. In hymn 7 the first four stanzas are anuṣṭubh, interrupted by a triṣṭubh (stanza 5); it is therefore possible to imagine that the stanzas 5—7 were added later. Yet these stanzas are original, and there is no reason to suspect them on intrinsic grounds. In hymn 11 of 6 stanzas the last two may be suspected because they repeat the pāda, *ava jarāyu padyatām*, as a refrain. Hymn 29 suggests by comparison with RV. 10. 174 a critical manipulation which shall do justice to the original diaskeuastic intention of both collections. By cutting out AV. 29. 4 and 5 we have left 4 stanzas = RV. 10. 174. 1—3 and 5, and if we assume that RV. 10. 174. 4 = 10. 159. 4 is also secondary we obtain the original 4 stanzas of the hymn in both RV. and AV[19]. Finally AV. 1. 34 has 5 stanzas, of which the last may possibly be later, since its second hemistich is formulaic; then the first 4 stanzas might be looked upon as a debating charm, turned into a love charm by the appendage of stanza 5[20]. Conversely it is no less easy to breed in one's mind distrust of certain final stanzas of the hymns of four stanzas as indeed of the final stanzas of many Vedic hymns in general. This is so not only because additions are naturally made at the end, but also because final stanzas frequently disclose the true point of a hymn to which the initial stanzas, themselves of a preparatory, or ornamental character, as it were, work their way. E. g. in RV. 7. 103, a prayer to the frogs for rain, or AV. 4. 16, an imprecation against an enemy, or AV. 3. 13, a charm to conduct a river into a new channel, the initial stanzas work their way to the climax (or rather anti-climax) in the last stanza of each hymn[21]. Therefore there is quite frequently a break in the sense just before the last stanza. Thus, unless we be warned by these considerations, AV. 1. 2 may be plausibly regarded as a battle-charm consisting of the first 3 stanzas, but adapted later to a charm against diarrhœa by the added fourth verse[22]. Next AV. 1. 5 and 6 contain 4 stanzas each, together 8 stanzas; the corresponding hymn, RV. 10. 9, consists of 9 stanzas. Seven stanzas are common to both texts. Now the scheme of the RV. favors 7 stanzas for 10. 9: shall we say that RV. 10. 9. 8 and 9, as well as AV. 1. 6. 4 are later appendages, and that the last-mentioned stanza was added in the AV. to bring the hymn 1. 6 up to the normal number of 4 stanzas? The same question may be asked anent AV. 1. 17. 4 which looks a bit patchy (pāda c=RV. 1. 191. 6[c]), and differs in metre from the rest. Certainly according to the ritual stanza 4 is important, and contains the very point of the practices connected with the hymn. Then what is the meaning of the diaskeuastic manœuvre in AV. 1. 20 and 21? The two hymns are patchwork: stanza 20. 1 = TB. 3. 7. 5. 12 (ApŚ. 2. 20. 6); stanza 20. 2 occurs with variants AŚ. 5. 3. 22; the next, stanza 20. 3, seems original. From that point on the two hymns (20. 4—21. 4) are the same as RV. 10. 152, in 5 stanzas. Shall we say that a single hymn of 5 stanzas was inflated by the Atharvanist into two hymns of 4 stanzas each, in order to fit it to the external scheme of his arrangement? This would accord in principle with the previous critical acts. Once again, 5 stanzas of the two hymns 1. 23 and 24, dealing with the same subject (leprosy), are repeated TB. 2. 4. 4. 1—2. Has the AV. taken once more a hymn of 5 stanzas, and swelled it out to two of 4 stanzas each, in order to pamper its scheme? The danger and difficulty of such operations may be seen best in hymn 1. 4 = RV. 1. 23. 16—19. According to OLDENBERG, l. c., p. 225, RV. 1. 23 consists of 6 tṛcas (stanzas 1—18) which form a ritual series, stanzas 19—24 being an appendix. Now, unless the AV. borrowed its four stanzas (= RV. 16—19) directly from the redactorially finished RV. — a very unlikely assumption — these criteria lose something of their force as applied to the RV. itself; if their stringency in the RV. is not above suspicion, little confidence can be placed in similar operations in the AV., because they are in general dependant upon Rigvedic data. Without going so far as to say that the verse-norms of the Atharvanic books should be ignored in judging the historical make-up of the hymns, extreme scepticism is for the present the proper frame of mind. I say, for the present, because the prospect of having the other Atharvan Saṃhitā, the Paippalāda, in our hands soon is now very good: certainly even the most enthusiastic believer in these studies will be in favor of deferring them until the Śaunakīya's sister-saṃhitā discloses its treasure of facts. Hence similar observations for the remaining books will not be here undertaken: they would indeed require the freedom and space of an independent essay[23]. We must not, however, fail to draw attention to the fact that the ritual of the Atharvan, as that of the RV., generally recognizes hymns that are clearly composite by employing each part independently with a true sense of its proper value. HILLEBRANDT has discussed and illustrated this point for the RV.[24]; the present writer for the AV.[25]. Composite hymns of this sort are 4. 28 in two parts; 7. 56 in two parts, stanzas 5 ff. wanting in AVP., and rubricated separately Kauś. 139. 8; the two hymns 7. 74 and 7. 76 are tripartite and consist of heterogeneous stanzas which are employed properly in the Sūtra[26]; finally the checkered *kuntāpa*-hymns are divided properly in the ritual tradition of all schools that take occasion to introduce them (see below, § 63).

We have seen that the first seven books are arranged on the basis of the number of stanzas in the hymns; the numbers ascend from book 1—5, descend from book 6—7. Books 8—18, with the exception of 15 and 16, consist of long hymns; the shortest hymn (8. 1) in these is longer than the longest in the first seven books (hymn 5. 17 of 18 stanzas). We may note also that the shortest hymn, again barring books 15 and 16, stands at the beginning of the entire series; the longest at the end (hymn 18. 4 with 89 stanzas). Further, books 8—11 consist of 10 hymns each; after that the numbers descend in book 12 (5 hymns), 13 (4 hymns); 14 (2 hymns), and 17 (one hymn); cf. the arrangement according to anuvākas, below. Again, book 8 has the shortest hymns with an average of 25. 8 stanzas to a hymn; next, book 9 with an average of 30. 5 stanzas to a hymn; next, book 10 with an average of 35 stanzas to a hymn. But book 11 interrupts this ascending scale with an average of 31. 3 stanzas to a hymn, and after that this criterion, if it be more than an accident, is no longer applicable. Instead, another element of division rules the arrangement of the books, namely the division into anuvākas: the books are arranged from 8—17 according to the number of anuvākas in a descending scale. Books 8—13 have 5 anuvākas each; book 13 has 4; books 14—16 have two each; and book 17 has 1 anuvāka. Book 18, to be sure, again disturbs this descending scale with its 4 anuvākas. As far as books 13—18 are concerned, the prominence of the anuvāka-arrangement which plays no rôle in the first 7 books at all, is brought into view by the plural, duals, singular, and then again plural in the catalogue of these books, AV. 19. 23. 23—28: *rohitebhyaḥ svāhā*, plural (book 13); *sūryābhyāṃ svāhā*, dual (book 14); *vrātyābhyāṃ svāhā*, dual (book 15); *prājāpatyābhyāṃ svāhā* (why this designation?), dual (book 16); *viṣāsahyai svāhā*, singular (book 17); and, *maṅgalikebhyaḥ svāhā*, plural (book 18)[27].

§ 37. Arrangement of the hymns within the books. — Within a given book the hymns are on the whole not arranged at all, but seem to follow one upon the other pell-mell, with little reference to their subject matter, or any other discernible criterion. The numerical scheme of each book, to begin with, prevents the grouping of all related hymns. Thus 7. 65 is too short to take its place by the side of the hymns to the *apāmārga*-plant, 4. 17—19; the hymn 12. 5, on the other hand, is too long to figure by the side of 5.17—19, though they are all curses against the oppressors of Brahmans. Similarly 5. 23 is prevented by its length from joining the charms against worms (2. 32, 33). Yet a considerable amount of the material is obviously arranged according to subject matter: two, three, four, and rising from that to as high as twelve hymns, dealing with quite or nearly the same theme, are grouped in the same place. The last-mentioned number is the highest, being exhibited by 6. 110—121, all of which deal with expiation (*prāyaścitta*) of sins[28]. The next largest number, seven, is represented by the so-called *mṛgāra*-hymns, 4.23—29 (see §§ 45, 57); the group 2.18—23 contains 6 imprecations against enemies. Book 3 begins with an anuvāka in 5 hymns connected with royal practices (1—5); in a certain sense the five hymns of entire anuvāka 4.16—20, dealing with witchcraft, are made of the same stuff. Four groups of 4 hymns each are 7. 35—38 (women's charms); 7. 46—49 (divinities of the moon and heavenly wives); 19. 40—43 (*brahma, tapas, dīkṣā*); and 19. 47—50 (Night). Very much more frequent are groups of three: 1. 4—6 (water-charms); 1. 19—21 (battle-charms); 1. 22—24 (skin-diseases); 2. 15—17 (prose-formulas to secure long life); 4. 17—19 (charms with the *apāmārga*-plant); 5. 17—19 (against oppressors of Brahmans); 6. 22—24 (water); 6. 27—29 (ominous birds); 6. 34—36 (Agni-hymns); 6. 39—41 (*havis*-hymns: see § 60, end); 6. 65—67 (battle-charms); 6. 86—88 (rulership); 6. 97—99 (battle-charms); 6. 130—132 (love-charms); 7. 14—16 (Savitar); 7. 17—19 (Dhātar); 7. 79—81 (lunar); 12. 3—5 (in the interest of Brahmans); 19. 9—11 (*śānta* and *śam*); 19. 14—16 (freedom from danger); 19. 17—19 (prose litanies for protection); and 19. 28—30 (amulet of *darbha*). And then there are in addition some sixty or more pairs of hymns more or less allied in subject-matter: in general their connection is too obvious to require special statement; at times it needs to be watched for rather closely, as, e. g. in the case of 2. 1, 2 (Vena and Gandharva); 4. 1, 2 (*brahma* and *ka*); 7. 1, 2 (*manas* and *vāc*); 7. 8, 9 (journey and road); 6. 47, 48 (the three *savanas*); 7. 27, 28 and 98, 99 (ritualistic pairs); 7. 76 (end) and 77 (Indra and Maruts); 11. 7, 8 (both theosophic, sharing the pādas: 7. 25^{ab} = 8. 4^{ab}, 26^{ab}, and 7. 26^{ab} = 8. 24^{ab}). Of special importance for the future final history of the Saṃhitā is the undoubted prehistoric and organic connection of some of the groups; they appear together many times not only because they deal with the same theme, but because a given group in an earlier period of mantra-production made up one and the same hymn, or two or more hymns bearing upon the same theme and the same occasion. Thus the *mṛgāra*-group (4. 23—29) is undoubtedly built up on a rather slender tradition of *yajus*-materials; the first and last stanzas are almost always directly derived from some Yajus-collection, the interior five stanzas are the original product of the Atharvanist's muse[29]. Of the group 2. 19—23 the first seems also originally *yajus*-matter (MS. 1. 5. 2; ApŚ. 6. 21. 1): out of these passages the entire litany is produced by a kind of Atharvanic inflation[30]. There is a similar historic and organic connection between the four hymns 7. 46—49; the three hymns 1. 4—6; 6. 27—29; 7. 39—41; and 7. 79—81; the two hymns 1. 20, 21; 24, 25; 2. 32, 33; 4. 31, 32; 6. 87, 88; 125, 126; 9. 9, 10; 19. 7, 8; 22, 23 and 60, 61. A more complete sifting of the mantras will disclose other groups of this kind, and on the other hand the record of some connections of this sort is sure to have perished (e. g., perhaps, in the case of 1. 7, 8; 6. 103, 104; 10. 7, 8; 11. 9, 10, etc.). Not infrequently the hymns are grouped for reasons that are far more superficial and hap-hazard than those just mentioned. The present writer drew attention to facts of this sort in connection with the first book, as did later HENRY in connection with the seventh book[31]; they appear sporadically throughout the Saṃhitā. In the first place, just as the introductory hymn 1. 1 and the closing hymn of book 19 hold their places because of their subject-matter, so there is design in the opening-hymns of books 2, 4, 5, and 7, all of which begin with a theosophic or *brahmodya*-hymn in loftier diction. The grouping of 9. 5—7 seems to be due to the large patch of *brāhmaṇa*-prose contained in them. Hymns 1. 2, 3 and 7. 6, 7 (Aditi and Diti) deal in each pair with opposite rather than same themes. Above all verbal correspondences, at times so vague as to cast doubt upon one or the other of the following observations, seem to be the sole cause of the juxtaposition of hymns. Thus 1. 9, 10 are not connected by theme, but each contains the word *varuṇa* in the opening hemistich. Hymns 11—13 are linked by subtle correspondences: hymn 11 is a charm for easy delivery in childbed, ending with the refrain, *ava jarāyu padyatām*; hymn 12 begins with the word *jarāyujaḥ*, its theme being the 'cloud-placenta-born' lightning; then follows hymn 13 also addressed to lightning (root *stan* in 12. 1 and 13. 1)[32]. The word *vajra* links externally 6. 134 and 135; the words *stana* and *stanayitnu* 7. 10 and 11; *ava mṛj* and *apa mṛj* 7. 64 and 65; *prajāvantaḥ* and *prajāvatīḥ* 7. 74 and 75; *vṛkau* and *vṛkkau* 7. 95 and 96; stem *ka*, felt to be the same as *prajāpati*, 7. 100 and 101; stem *rakṣohan* 8. 2. 28 and 3. 1; stem *prāṇa* 11. 3. 54 ff. and 11. 4; *sam* and *śam* (as occasionally in parallel versions of the same mantra) 19. 1, 2; *śānta* and *śam* 19. 9—11. The group 7. 88—90 seems to be linked by a cumulation of verbal correspondences: they begin respectively with the words *api, apo*, and *api*; 88 and 89. 1 contain the root *pṛc*; and *śepe* in 89. 3 is perhaps correlated with *śepo* in 90. 3. In the group 7. 113—115 such an external correspondence can be made critically helpful: 7. 113 and 114. 1 obviously treat the same subject, whereas 114. 2 is foreign to their theme, and may have gotten this berth because its words *preto yantu*, as well as its sense, concatenate plausibly with 7. 115. 1 which begins, *pra patetaḥ*; cp. below, § 40.

The Saṃhitā-text of the AV. in the Śaunakīya-school was published in 1855 by R. ROTH and W. D. WHITNEY under the title, Atharva Veda Sanhita: the edition is occasionally spoken of as the vulgate by the present and other writers. This was followed by a number of subsidiary publications by WHITNEY: an alphabetic list of *pratīkas*, or verse-beginnings, in IS. IV. 9 ff.; the edition of the Atharva-Veda-Prātiśākhya, or Śaunakīyā Caturādhyāyikā in JAOS. VII. 333—615 (addenda, JAOS. X, 156 ff.); and an Index Verborum to the published text which at the same time reproduces the readings of the pada-text (JAOS. XII). WHITNEY's posthumous work, containing other indexes, critical notes to the text, and a translation is now in the press of the Harvard Oriental Series (ed. C. R. LANMAN): see JAOS. XV. CLXXI ff. Another edition of the same Veda in both *saṃhitā* and *pada*-form, with a fragmentary commentary ascribed to Sāyaṇa, is partly published and wholly in the press, under the title Atharvavedasamhitā (Bombay 1895); it is from the pen of the late SHANKAR PĀNDURANG PANDIT. The value of the commentary is stated critically by WHITNEY, Festgruss an Rudolf von Roth, p. 89 ff. For the Kashmirian version of the AV., the so-called Paippalāda-Śākhā (above p. 11), see ROTH, Der Atharva-Veda in Kaschmir (Tübingen 1875): it is now proposed by the present author to publish a photographic reproduction of the unique manuscript of that Veda; see the circular to that effect issued by the Johns Hopkins University in 1898, and JAOS. XX. 184 ff.

1 WEBER, IS. XIII. 433; WL.2, p. 161, note. The statements of both GB. and Mahābhāṣya refer in this matter to an Atharvanic tradition broader than that of the Śaunakīya, since both texts present *śaṃ no devī* (1. 1. 6) as the initial stanza. This probably suits the AVP.; see Kauśika, Introduction, p. XXXVII ff. — 2 The beginnings of the books of AVP. and their relation in general to the books of the Śaunakīya are stated above, p. 14, on the authority of ROTH, Der AV. in Kaschmir, p. 15 ff., 18. — 3 See below, §§ 36 and 37. — 4 ROTH, ibid. p. 18. AV. 19. 56—58 are directly designated as *paippalādamantrāḥ*, Ath. Pariś. 8. 2: see above p. 12. — 5 WEBER, IS. IV. 433, note 2. — 6 They occur, in fact, in full text, at the end of the Uttamapaṭala, Ath. Pariś. 46; cp. WEBER, ib. 433. — 7 The expression, *brahmaṇe svāhā*, which WEBER, ib. 433, note 3, suspects as referring to book 19, is a mere general ending to both lists 19. 22. 20 and 23. 29: it invokes *brahma*, prayer, in general; cp. the metrical sts. at the end of each chapter. — 8 See Kauś. Introd. p. XL, and cp. PISCHEL, GGA., April 1891, p. 283. — 9 WHITNEY, JAOS. VII. 334, 581; SHANKAR PANDIT's edition, vol. I, Critical Notice, p. 24. — 10 WEBER, IS. IV. 432. — 11 ROTH, ibid. p. 18. — 12 SHANKAR PANDIT, ibid. p. 16 ff. — 13 *asmin kāṇḍe prāyeṇa sarvāṇi sūktāni tṛcātmakāny eva tathāpi adhyāpakasaṃpradāyānurodhena tṛcadvayam ekīkṛtya sūktatvena vyavahriyate* (SĀYAṆA, vol. II, p. 2). — 14 See Indexes, p. 382. The *paryāya* are also alluded to in the late Pariśiṣṭa-hymn 19. 22. 7. The date of AV. 19. 22 and 23 can be fixed as later than the Kauśika. In 22. 11—13 the formulas *upottamebhyaḥ svāhā*, *uttamebhyaḥ svāhā*, and *uttarebhyaḥ svāhā* allude without doubt to the frequent citations in Kauś. of hymns and stanzas which have been previously stated in groups. See for *upottama*, Kauś. 26. 34; for *uttama*, Kauś. 26. 40; 41. 15; 50. 14; for *uttara*, Kauś. 48. 36. — 15 Differently WEBER, IS. I. 295; II. 396; IV. 434; V. 22, 77; SPAW. 1891, p. 770, note 1; WL.2 137, 165; cp. SBE. XLII, p. XXI. — 16 Cp. BERGAIGNE, Recherches sur l'histoire de la Samhitā du Rig-Veda, I, p. 4 and 75 (JA. 1886); WEBER, IS. XVII. 178; XVIII. 1, 154. — 17 The Anukramaṇī of the AV. designates this lower limit as the norm (*prakṛti*) of the books, the deviations as *vikṛti*; see WEBER, l. c. — 18 BERGAIGNE, l. c.; OLDENBERG, Die Hymnen des Rig-Veda, p. 243 ff. — 19 OLDENBERG, l. c. — 20 Cp. SBE. XLII. 274 ff. — 21 BLOOMFIELD, JAOS. XVII. 178; WEBER, IS. XVIII. 66; SBE. XLII. 348. — 22 Cp. SBE. XLII. 233 ff. — 23 As further specimens of hymns that invite such criticism we may mention 2. 3, 4 (last sts.); 2. 10 (cp. TB. 2. 5. 6. 1; HG. 2. 3. 10; ApMB. 2. 12. 6); 2. 12 (last 3 sts.; cp. SBE. XLII. 297); 2. 14 (st. 4; cp. ibid. 301); 3. 15, 19, 29 (last two sts.); 3. 30 (the irregular st. 6 interrupts the concatenation of 5 and 7; but see SBE. XLII. 363); 4. 2 (last st.); 4. 16 (last two sts.); 4. 17 (st. 5, rather extraneous = 7. 23); 5. 17 (BERGAIGNE, l. c., p. 22; OLDENBERG, l. c., p. 244). — 24 BB. VIII. 195 ff.; ZDMG. XL. 708 ff.; cp. WEBER, SPAW. 1891, p. 798. — 25 Kauśika, Introduction, p. XLI. — 26 SBE. XLII. 554, 557, 559. — 27 Cp. BERGAIGNE, l. c., p. 75, note. — 28 In a less specific way all the hymns 19. 26—39 deal with amulets of some sort, and therefore represent a still larger group of 14 hymns. — 29 See below, §§ 45 and 57. — 30 In accordance with notions very prominent in GB. The Rig-Vedic cosmic triad, Agni, Vāyu, Sūrya, is there

swelled out to a tetrad by the addition of Candra and Āpaḥ (the moon with the waters) to provide for the AV., the other three being correlated with the members of the *trayī vidyā*; see § 45. — 31 Seven Hymns of the AV., AJPh. VII. 470ff.; Le Livre VII de l'AV., p. IX. — 32 The first 13 hymns of book 1 seem to be arranged continuously in groups; after that the regularity of the scheme breaks down; cp. Seven Hymns, ibid.

B. THE METRES OF THE ATHARVAN AND THEIR RELATION TO THE CRITICAL RESTORATION OF THE TEXT.

§ 38. The metres, with special reference to the Atharvanic (popular) anuṣṭubh. — The metres of the original parts of the AV. are in the main still the common Vedic metres, gāyatrī, anuṣṭubh, paṅkti, in short metre; triṣṭubh, and jagatī, in long metre. A considerable part of the Śaunakīya-text, notably book 15 and most of book 16, are in prose[1]; metrical and prose matter are a good deal mixed up[2], so that it is frequently difficult to determine whether a passage is merely cadenced prose, or doggerel metre, or originally good metre spoiled by interpolations and additions which at times distinctly betray themselves as glosses. The Bṛhatsarvānukramaṇī, in the course of its struggles with these defective metres, enriches the metrical terminology with new varieties: the words, *nicṛt, bhurij, -garbhā* (e. g. *virāḍ-garbhā bhurik*), *ārṣī*, etc. figure frequently[3]. The metres vary in the same hymn more than is customary in the RV.: it would seem as though this variation was in a measure felt to be a stylistic or literary device[4]. E. g., it is hardly mere accident that many hymns open with a (to our feeling) livelier anuṣṭubh stanza (short metre), and continue with triṣṭubh-stanzas (long metre); see 1. 13; 1. 18; 2. 29; 4. 16; 6. 3. 1^{ab}; 6. 49; 7. 68; 7. 72 (cp. RV. 7. 103). Occasionally an anuṣṭubh-hymn opens in still livelier gāyatrī: 2. 32; 4. 12. Conversely some effect, perhaps the opposite effect of solemnity, seems also to be intended when a short-metre hymn is introduced by a triṣṭubh: 2. 4; 3. 5; 5. 7; 6. 111. It is perhaps no accident that the Vedic wedding-stanzas are prevailingly anuṣṭubhs, the funeral-stanzas triṣṭubhs. The metres of the AV. are on a level with those of the Gṛhyasūtras. Aside from the greater freedom and irregularity of all types this is shown by applying OLDENBERG's test of the anuṣṭubh[5]. The original Atharvanic anuṣṭubh stanzas, i. e. those that do not coincide with the hieratic RV. stanzas, differ from the Rig-Vedic anuṣṭubh on the one hand, and from the Epic and Buddhistic śloka on the other. Whereas in the RV. the first pāda of the anuṣṭubh hemistich regularly ends in a diiambus, or second pæon (◡ — ◡ ⏓), and in the Epic and Buddhistic śloka still more regularly in a first epitrite or antispast (◡ — — ⏓), the first pāda of the Atharvan and Gṛhya hemistich permits these as well as all other possible feet of four syllables. The hymns that were tested for this purpose are: 1. 1; 1. 2; 1. 7; 1. 8; 5. 19; and 12. 4. 1—20, in addition to single stanzas of many other hymns. The Atharvanic and Gṛhya anuṣṭubh may be designated as the popular anuṣṭubh in distinction from the hieratic anuṣṭubh of the soma-hymns in the RV.: a hymn like RV. 10. 85 is, of course, in popular anuṣṭubh. Considering the absolute quantitative freedom of the eight-syllable line of the Younger Avesta[6], we have reason to assume that the popular and freer anuṣṭubh is structurally and chronologically earlier than the better regulated hieratic (somic) anuṣṭubh, an assumption which is no wise disproved by the parallel grammatical and lexical criteria of the two types of literature (see below, § 42). The theory that the development of the popular foot took place from ◡ — ◡ ⏓, through ⏓ ⏓ ⏓ ⏓ to ◡ — — ⏓ is on its face implausible: in the light of the trend of all Hindu metrical development the change from the regulated type ◡ — ◡ ⏒ to the free type ⏒ ⏒ ⏒ ⏒ is unparalleled and unintelligible. Instead we may assume that the Aryan free octosyllabic lines, grouped into two hemistichs of 16 syllables developed the iambic cadence at the end of each hemistich in prehistoric Vedic times, and continued so in the more popular poetry until the beginnings of the Epic and Buddhistic śloka. At the same time a more exquisite treatment at the hands of the hieratic poets developed the Rig-Vedic anuṣṭubh on a parallel line, by repeating the final cadence of the hemistich before the cæsura in the middle of it[7].

§ 39. On the critical restoration of Atharvan metres. — Atharvan metres are so generally capable of improvement that we are in danger of singing our own rather than Atharvan hymns, when we apply ourselves to the task of improving them. An uneasy sense is left that we all know how to make better verse-lines than those that have somehow got to be in vogue among the Atharvan writers; carried out to its full consequences this would eliminate one of the more marked peculiarities that render the Atharvan what it is[8]. Yet it is impossible to abstain entirely: such abstemiousness would suggest the equally mistaken view that all Atharvan stanzas are before us in the form in which they were originally composed. Great tact and a keen sense of where to draw the line are particularly required in amending the text: in any case the critic upon whom this task is forced may not hope to escape error altogether. In the very opening hymn (1. 1. 4[b]) it seems necessary to throw out the entirely unmetrical *hvayatām*, although what remains is by no means perfect. But there are far more certain cases: in 2. 3. 6[d] *rakṣasām* is surely a gloss; so also *krimīn* in 2. 31. 4[c]. In 2. 33. 5[cd] *bhāsadam* is certainly superfluous, being derived from the parallel version, RV. 10. 163. 4. Quite certain are the following cases of interpolations and glosses: *devān* in 3. 15. 5[d]; *brahmajyasya* in 5. 19. 7[d]; *takmaṁs* in 5. 22. 5[c]; *haviṣā* in 6. 40. 1[d]; *svasti* in 6. 40. 2[d]; *diśo* in 6. 98. 3[b] (cf. TS. 2. 4. 14. 1; MS. 4. 12. 2); *dantau* in 6. 140. 3[c]; *puru* in 7. 21. 1[d]; *devā* in 7. 70. 2[c] (cf. TB. 2. 4. 2. 2); *amitrā* in 8. 8. 2[cd]; *arṣaṇīr* in 9. 8. 21[c]; *viśvasya* in 9. 10. 14[c] (cf. RV. 1. 164. 35[b]; VS. 23. 62[b]; LŚ. 9. 10. 14[b]); *duṣkṛte* in 10. 1. 23[c]; *vār ugram* in 10. 4. 3[d], 4[d] (cf. 7. 56. 3[d], 7[d]); *mātariśvā* in 10. 9. 26[c]; either *ubhe* or *ime* in 11. 5. 8; *pṛthivyāṃ* in 11. 5. 12[cd]; *catasraḥ* in 19. 1. 3[c]. Less certain is the disposition of *patir* in 3. 4. 1[b]; *gṛhāṇāṃ* in 3. 12. 6; *gandharvān* in 4. 37. 8[c]; *amūṃ* in 5. 8. 8[c]; *sacetasaḥ* in 6. 68. 1[cd]; *manasā* in 6. 83. 4[c]; *adharo* in 6. 134. 2[a]; *kalaśaḥ* in 9. 1. 6[b]; *bhikṣām* in 11. 5. 9[b]. And there are, of course, cases in which corrections of other sorts strengthen the impression that the metres may be improved by critical restorations. Thus the defective pāda 9. 2. 4[d] is followed in the same hymn, pāda 9[d], by what reads like its own correction; or, the temptation to make over into good metre 9. 5. 1[ab] so as to read, *ā naya etam anv ā rabhasva, sukṛtāṃ lokaṃ gachatu prajānan*, is very great. Similarly 11. 2. 2 may be much improved by transferring *aviṣyavaḥ* at the end of the first hemistich (so also AVP.) to the second hemistich[9]. On the other hand there are not wanting instances in which inferior metre is on second thought proved to be just what the Atharvavedin wrote. Thus 9. 4. 22[cd] consists of two defective pādas; the first being short, the second ending in a wrong cadence: *āyur asmabhyaṃ dadhat prajāṃ ca, rāyaś ca poṣair abhi naḥ sacatām*. All attempts to better this hemistich are wasted, because it is nothing but a secondary transfer from the plural to the singular of the perfectly good hemistich 18. 4. 62, *āyur asmabhyaṃ dadhataḥ prajāṃ ca, rāyaś ca poṣair abhi naḥ sacadhvam*. Or, one might be tempted to amend the short pāda 2. 4. 6[b], *atho arātidūṣiḥ*, especially as it is repeated in a metrically preferable form in 19. 34. 4^b, *atho arātidūṣaṇaḥ*. But the entire character of the last hymn is inferior and its version of the pāda is probably in the nature of a secondary *lectio facilior*: the catalectic line, 2, 4. 6^b, had best be left undisturbed, as such lines must be in many other instances[10]. Anyway there are almost countless cases in the AV. in which corrections at the hand of the metre would really amount to independent composition, cases like 3. 28. 1; 4. 11. 4^b, 6^d; 4. 17. 3^{cd}; 5. 7. 1^{cd}; 6. 134. 3; 7. 76. 5^a; they not only point out the need of extreme caution in general, but tend to shake confidence in all but the most unavoidable emendations.

§ 40. Order of stanzas and concatenation as critical aids. — Of distinct strophic arrangement of stanzas there is little or nothing in the AV.; the arrangement of the hymns in the various books according to the number of their stanzas is also carried out in a very crude and superficial manner[11]. Hence there is very little basis for a critique of the arrangement of the stanzas in a given hymn, or the distinction between original stanzas and such as may have been added by a later hand. Nevertheless the existing text is open to improvement in these respects, although subjective impression is here more easily than in other forms of criticism confounded with historical reality. To begin with, some hymns are certainly composite, as may be readily gathered from their context and their employment in the ritual books; e. g. 4. 38; 7. 74; 7. 76[12]. For no visible reason, but yet certainly, 6. 48. 2 and 3 have changed places: Vait. 17. 10 and the parallel versions have them in the right order[13]. The long hymn 12. 4 shows traces of confusion in the order of its stanzas: the fourth may be suspected of having stood originally after the fifth, because the second hemistich of st. 4 seems to summarize the statements made in the remaining three hemistichs of the two stanzas. Similarly there seems to be considerable confusion in the order of stanzas 43—47: cf. the rearrangement proposed by the author[14]. When we find in the midst of the wedding-stanzas of the *sūryā-sūkta* (14. 1. 1 ff. = RV. 10. 85. 1 ff.) the stanza 14. 1. 17, which is evidently RV. 7. 59. 12 in a form adapted to the marriage-rites (*aryamaṇam* substituted for *tryambakam*), we may judge at least that it did not belong to the original stock of the wedding-stanzas; on the other hand the concatenation of its second hemistich with 18^{ab} would seem to show that it was adapted to serve in the very place where it occurs in the AV. Similar considerations will show that the stanza 14. 1. 43, in concatenation with 44, although also of secondary workmanship — it occurs nowhere else — yet holds its place by rights in the AV. Concatenation is a very common feature in the AV.[15], and to a certain extent guarantees the order of stanzas in the Saṃhitā. Thus all three stanzas of 6. 42 and 6. 118 concatenate, so that we may feel fairly sure that the Atharvan composer placed them in this order, whatever may have been their pre-history, whether they were original with the Atharvanist, or first composed in another quarter of Vedic activity. So also the first two stanzas of 6. 118 occur again MS. 4. 14. 17; TA. 2. 4. 1 (cp. TB. 3. 7. 12. 3), the third seems original with the Atharvanist; yet it is not therefore in any sense a stranger to the Atharvan redaction. The same rhetorical device of concatenation may at times point to the exclusion of one of the connected stanzas; e. g. the irregular stanza 5. 14. 11, containing the expression *mṛgīva*, may have slipped in because of *mṛgam iva* in stanza 12; or 5. 4. 6, also irregular, containing the words *ā vaha*, may have been placed where it is, because of *nirāvahan* in stanza 5. Again, a verse that interrupts two concatenating stanzas may be suspected; e. g. 3. 30. 6, interrupting stanzas 5 and 7; or 2. 3. 4, interrupting stanzas 3 and 5; cp. also our remark on 7. 114. 2, above, § 37, end. In the commentary to our translation, SBE. XLII, we have never treated such cases as anything more than possibilities: such criteria rarely seem coercive, as we have no reason to rely much on the conscious directness of purpose, or certainty of touch of the Atharvan poets in any such matters.

1 A compact list of the prose passages is printed by WHITNEY, Index Verborum, p. 5 ff. — 2 Cp. e. g., 4. 3. 7^{cd}; 4. 11. 7^{d}; 4. 12. 6; 5. 29. 14; 6. 16. 3; 6. 76. 3^{c}; 7. 81. 4, 5; 7. 82. 2; 8. 2. 11; 10. 6. 35. — 3 Cp. the extracts from the Anukramaṇī in WEBER'S translations of AV. 3—5, IS. XVII. 177 ff.; XVIII, 1 ff. — 4 BLOOMFIELD, JAOS. XVII. 176, note. — 5 ZDMG. XXXV. 181 ff.; XXXVII. 62 ff.; Die Hymnen des Rig-Veda, p. 26 ff.; SBE. XXX, p. XI fg., XXXV ff.; cp. JACOBI, IS. XVII. 442 ff. — 6 GELDNER, Metrik des jüngeren Avesta, p. VI ff., 60 ff. — 7 Cp. WINTERNITZ, The Mantrapāṭha, Introd. p. XLIV. — 8 BLOOMFIELD, SBE. XLII, p. 296, 584; OLDENBERG, DLZ. March 1897, p. 370. — 9 SBE. XLII. 619. — 10 Cp. WHITNEY, Index Verborum, p. 5. — 11 See above, § 37. — 12 Kauś. Introd., p. XLI ff.; cp. above, § 36. — 13 See BLOOMFIELD, Contributions. Fifth Series. JAOS. XVI. 5, note 3; cp. in the Saṃhitā itself the proper arrangement of the corresponding stanzas 6. 47. 2 and 3. — 14 SBE. XLII, p. 660. — 15 E. g. 1. 23. 1, 2; 4. 1. 4^{b}, 4^{c}; 4. 8. 4, 5, 6; 4. 29. 1, 2; 4. 36. 3, 4; 4. 37. 9, 10; 5. 11. 7, 8, 9; 5. 14. 1, 2; 5. 20. 1, 2; 5. 22. 3, 4, 5; 5. 22. 8, 9; 5. 29. 2, 3; 5. 29. 12, 13; 5. 30. 8, 9; 6. 15. 1, 2; 6. 63. 2, 3; 6. 99. 2, 3; 6. 117. 2, 3; 6. 123. 1, 2; 6. 138. 1, 2; 8. 2. 7, 8; 9. 2. 9, 10; 9. 5. 21, 22; 9. 5. 23, 24; 10. 8. 22, 23; 12. 3. 5, 6; 12. 3. 41, 42; 12. 3. 43, 44; 13. 1. 6, 7; 13. 1. 53, 54.

C. THE RELATION OF THE ATHARVA-VEDA TO THE REMAINING HYMN-COLLECTIONS.

§ 41. **Special features of the Atharvan collection; its connection with ApŚ. and TB.** — The relation of the text of the AV. in the Śaunakīya-version to the other collections of Vedic mantras is both intimate and intricate. A complete survey of these relations can be obtained only by means of such a concordance of these mantras as has been gathered up by WHITNEY for his posthumous work on the AV., now passing through the press in the Harvard Oriental Series[1]. A yet more perfect insight into the relationships of the Atharvan mantras will result from the pāda-concordance of the entire body of Vedic mantras which is being compiled by the present writer[2]. The Atharvan is very reminiscent: in unexpected places, often in hymns that are on the whole original with the AV., a shorter or longer passage, frequently only a single pāda, appears to have been borrowed from another connection, or, to state it more cautiously, to coincide with another collection. Thus in the very first hymn pāda 3^{b} = RV. 10. 166. 3^{b}; in the second hymn pādas 2^{ab} are variants of RV. 6. 75. 12^{ab}, pāda 2^{d} = RV. 3. 16. 5^{d}. Other instances of fragmentary correspondences are AV. 1. 17. 4^{c} = RV. 1. 191. 6^{c}; AV. 1. 26. 1^{c} = RV. 1. 172. 2^{c}; AV. 2. 2. 2^{b} = RV. 8. 48. 2^{b}; AV. 2. 12. 4^{b} = RV. 7. 44. 4^{d}; AV. 4. 4. 4^{a} = RV. 10. 97. 8^{a} (et al.); AV. 4. 5. 7^{e} = RV. 10. 166. 2^{b}; AV. 4. 10. 6^{e} (formulaic appendage = 2. 4. 6^{d}; 12. 2. 13^{d}; 14. 2. 67^{d}) is common in the entire mantra-literature; AV. 5. 20. 8^{b} = RV. 10. 103. 10^{a} (cp. 10^{b}); AV. 5. 21. 11^{ab} (= 13. 1. 3^{ab}) = TB. 2. 5. 2. 3^{ab}; AV. 6. 80. 1^{ab} = RV. 10. 136. 4^{ab}; AV. 8. 7. 27^{a} = RV. 10. 97. 3^{b}; AV. 10. 1. 6^{a} = RV. 10. 164. 4^{c}; AV. 10. 8. 40^{cd} = RV. 8. 101. 14^{cd}; AV. 10. 9. 27^{e} = RV. 4. 50. 6^{d} (et al.); AV. 10. 10. 32^{ab} = RV. 10. 154. 1^{ab}; AV. 11. 1. 3^{d}, 11^{d} = RV. 4. 50. 10^{d}; AV. 13. 1. 11^{d} = RV. 10. 123. 8^{d}; and many other instances. These correspondences fade out into mere reminiscences or echoes, as when, e. g., AV. 3. 1. 2 is made up from a variety of RV. motives (AUFRECHT, KZ. XXVII. 219; BLOOMFIELD, SBE. XLII. 326). Similarly AV. 3. 3. 2^{b}, 5^{d} reminds one of RV. 10. 103. 6; or AV. 4. 7. 2, 3 of RV. 10. 187. 10; or AV. 5, 23 of RV. 10. 191; or AV. 1. 26 of RV. 1. 172; or AV. 2. 3 of TB. 2. 5. 6. 4.

In this connection are to be mentioned a number of interesting or curious points of contact of the Atharvan mantras with the remaining body of the Vedic hymns and formulas. AV. 1. 17. 1 is quoted by Yāska, Nirukta 3. 4, in a variant form which is not derived from AVP.; Durga to Nir. 6. 12 quotes AV. 12. 2. 28 with variants (perhaps those of AVP.): see ROTH, Erläuterungen, p. 80. The JB. quotes in full AV. 5. 19. 1 with variants. AV. 4. 16 is unknown in the other collections, except that its sixth stanza is modulated interestingly ŚS. 1. 6. 3. A formula LŚ. 3. 5. 15 reproduces AV. 9. 1. 9, and a mantra in Vait. 36. 27 contains marked features derived from AV. 13. 1. 23. The prose formula AV. 19. 55. 5[a] is a variant form of MS. 3. 9. 4 (p. 120, l. 17), and the formulas AV. 20. 2 are somewhat independent versions of ĀpŚ. 11. 9. 8; KŚ. 9. 8. 9 ff. The fifth st. of AV. 3. 4 is quoted with a variant pratīka, *ā prehi paramasyāḥ parāvatā* (*iti yājyānuvākye*) at MS. 2. 2. 11 (p. 24, l. 3), but no such two stanzas are quotable elsewhere in the Maitrāyaṇī, or anywhere else in the literature: the pratīka at MS. is employed in connection with a royal rite similar to that at the base of the Atharvan hymn. Quite a number of those sts. of the SV. which are not derived from the RV. occur also in the AV., as may be seen readily in AUFRECHT's list of these sts. in the Introduction to the second edition of »Die Hymnen des Rig-Veda«, p. XLV ff. The correspondences of Atharvan and Gṛhya-stanzas are very extensive, and often disguised by corruptions and secondary manipulations of the original text: both varieties of mantras perform their share of these processes, but the mantras of the Gṛhyasūtras are even more corrupt than those of the AV. Cp. as examples AV. 5. 25. 8 with ŚG. 1. 19. 11; AV. 3. 10. 1 with SMB. 2. 8. 1; or AV. 8. 6. 26 with HG. 1. 19. 7. Noteworthy, above all, are the special correspondences of the ĀpŚ. with the AV., showing dependence of the Sūtra upon the AV.: the variants of the ĀpŚ. are generally of inferior quality. Thus AV. 2. 7. 1 is reproduced in a corrupt form ĀpŚ. 6. 21. 2; the two sts. AV. 3. 7. 1, 2 appear, with inferior variants, ĀpŚ. 13. 7. 16; the opening sts. of AV. 5. 6 recur secondarily ĀpŚ. 16. 18. 7; part of the formula AV. 5. 9. 8 occurs at the beginning of ĀpŚ. 6. 21; the st. AV. 7. 27 recurs with variants ĀpŚ. 4. 13. 4; AV. 8. 5. 19 appears with essential differences in ĀpŚ. 16. 19. 1, and similarly AV. 9. 5. 2 in ĀpŚ. 7. 17. 2, or AV. 12. 1. 55 in ĀpŚ. 5. 9. 11; the two sts. AV. 12. 2. 13, 14 are varied even more ĀpŚ. 9. 3. 22; especially noteworthy is the reproduction of the obscure formulas AV. 16. 2. 4 in ĀpŚ. 6. 20. 2 (end). We may also note that ĀpŚ. 16. 16. 1 reproduces with variants some of the ślokas in Kauś. 97. 8, as a sign of connection between the two spheres of mantra-tradition. Quite a considerable number of Atharvan hymns and stanzas recur in TB. and, apparently, nowhere else: e. g., AV. 1. 23, 24 in TB. 2. 4. 4. 1, 2; AV. 2. 10 in TB. 2. 5. 6. 1 ff.; AV. 4. 8 in TB. 2. 7. 15 and 16; AV. 4. 22 in TB. 2. 4. 7. 7 ff.; AV. 6. 38 in TB. 2. 7. 7. 1 ff.; AV. 6. 75 in TB. 3. 3. 11. 3 (ĀpŚ. 3. 14. 2); AV. 7. 70 in TB. 2. 4. 2. 1 ff.; AV. 7. 99 in TB. 3. 7. 6. 1; AV. 7. 110 in TB. 2. 4. 5. 7; AV. 13. 1 (in part) in TB. 2. 5. 2. 1 ff. Since the TB. is the Brāhmaṇa of ĀpŚ. this marked relationship of both these texts with the AV. may possibly not be without significance; it seems to reach decidedly beyond that general connection which may be expected in all mantra-collections: no such degree of intimacy exists, e. g., between the AV. and the corresponding texts attaching themselves to the White Yajur-Veda, namely the ŚB. and KŚ.

§ 42. **Relation of the language of the AV. to that of the RV.** — All discussions of the relation of the Śaunakīya-Saṃhitā to the other Vedic collections must be regarded as provisional as long as the text of the AVP. remains inaccessible. Still certain general statements as to the relationship of the Śaunakīya-collection with the RV. on the one hand, and the Yajur-Vedas on the other, are not likely to be subject to great change upon the accession of new materials. With the RV. the Śaunakīya shares about one seventh of its material, if we leave aside the hymns of book 20 that are borrowed directly from the RV.[3]. Considerably more than one half of the RV. sts. which correspond to the AV. belong to the tenth book of the RV., largely the last anuvāka of that book; about one sixth to the first book; about one tenth to the seventh book; about one eighth to all the other books put together[4]. In the overwhelming number of cases, aside from the wedding stanzas (AV. 14), and the funeral stanzas (AV. 18), the material common to the two Saṃhitās is Atharvanic in character, i. e. it consists of charms friendly or hostile; on the other hand the more general prayers which have for their theme the adoration of a given divinity, rather than the attainment of a specific object, are rarely shared by the two collections. The two styles of hymns may be conveniently designated as popular or Atharvanic on the one hand, and hieratic or ritualistic on the other. The language of the former class is related more closely to that dialect or dialects which are at the base of the language of the Brāhmaṇas, Sūtras, and the later literary forms in general. For reasons that are nearly always one-sided and subjective, sometimes patently erroneous, the language of the popular or Atharvanic hymns is generally regarded as chronologically later than that of the hieratic hymns, and thus every Vedic hymn that deals with popular matters is condemned on account of its language to a berth in the 'later Vedic period'. The scope of the present work does not permit the full discussion of this important question: suffice it to say that many linguistic forms that are looked upon as indications of late date are in reality as old, sometimes older, than the entire individual period of the Aryan language in India. Thus the dual in *-au*, and the instrumental plural in *-ais*, though dealt with in such discussions as signs of a later time are Indo-European forms (Goth. *ahtau*; Lith. *vilkais*); similarly the 'late' forms, stems, or roots *hvayāmi*, *karomi-kuru*, *panthānam*, *sarva* (as compared with *viśva*), *rajju*, *lubh*, *svap* for *sas*, which have been regarded as signs of late date are each of them prehistoric[5]. The question is therefore largely one of degree of closeness to the popular dialect or style of diction: this is the primary point of view from which the language of what we have called Atharvanic, or popular hymns can be compared with the hieratic hymns. A given form is not necessarily of recent origin because it begins to crop out in the tenth book of the RV., appears still more frequently in the popular Vedic collection of the AV., and is the regular form of the post-mantric language; nor, consequently, are hymns necessarily late because they abound in words and forms that are strangers to the diction of the hieratic hymns. A necessary preliminary to a final study of the relative chronology of the Vedic hymns is their separation into at least two classes which grew up along parallel lines, the hymns connected with the soma-worship and the hymns connected with popular practices. They are largely synchronous: each is addicted to its own dialect, differing from the other in lexicon, grammar, style, and metrical habits[6].

That the purely linguistic data alone are a broken reed in support of the chronological fixation of a given hymn may be illustrated by a comparison of AV. 3. 18 with RV. 10. 145. The second st. of the RV. ends in *kuru* for which AV. reads *kṛdhi*: now *kuru* is 'late', and *kṛdhi* is 'old', i. e. it belongs to the hieratic sphere of diction. To suppose therefore that the Atharvan form of the hymn is older than that of the RV. would at first sight be the orthodox conclusion, but in st. 5 AV. reads 'late' *bhūtvā* for RV. *bhūtvī*, and the RV.

readings, *parā dhama* for *parā ṇuda* (st. 2); *athā sapatnī* (RV. 3) for *adhaḥ sapatnī* (AV. 4); *gṛbhṇāmi* (RV. 4) for *jagrāha* (AV. 3); *atha tvam* for *atho tvam* (st. 5)[7] make a better impression, and a decidedly strong case for the RV., rather than for the AV., as representing the original version of the hymn at the back of both redactions. The AV. has slipped into the hieratic diction in the case of *kṛdhi*, whereas *kuru* was quite natural in a popular hymn from the very earliest times, although, of course, it is also possible that *kuru* in the RV. was substituted in a popular mood for *kṛdhi*. All this is as though a preacher in the pulpit glided in and out of biblical diction in the course of his sermon: at one moment he may be employing the language of Isaiah or the Psalms; at another the most forceful popular speech of the day. The proximity of the language of the genuine Atharvanic hymns to that of the Brāhmaṇas and Classical Literature is no chronological criterion: only when what we have called hieratic hymns are modulated over into Atharvanic diction does the presumption of late date stand justified. Especially desirable is cumulative evidence: bad metre, obvious adaptation to secondary purposes, disjointedness of stanzas, and the like: they are the true Atharvan characteristics.

With a view to all these considerations there can be no doubt that the redaction of the AV. is of later date than that of the RV.; that its external presentation by the diaskeuastae is less scholarly, or rather more ignorant than that of the RV.; that the secondary application of old hymnal material — a kind of popular etymology exercised upon the stanzas, as it were — is more common than in the RV.; that possibly some materials are directly derived from the ready made Rig-Vedic collection; and, finally, that a good part of the AV. was composed at a very late time. On the other hand it is equally certain that the main current of Atharvan tradition, the Atharvanic or popular hymns by distinction, goes back to a head-spring quite as far away and as high up in antiquity — if not more so — than the hieratic or ritualistic hymns. A hymn like AV. 4. 16, representing the better type of Atharvanic effort, is quite as archaic as any RV. hymn of related character; a hymn like AV. 4. 12 seems even to be rooted in prehistoric antiquity. The assumption, e. g., that none of the numerous medicinal charms of the AV., notably the charms against *takman* (fever), existed prior to the redaction of the RV. is not warranted, as we have seen, by linguistic criteria, and contrary to sound ethnological consideration. Precisely these and kindred hymns contain most abundantly the evidence of prehistoric origin: see, e. g., AV. 7. 116 (SBE. XLII, p. 4 and 565). That the RV. picked up quite a considerable number of Atharvanic charms (see AUFRECHT's edition, vol. II, p. 670 ff.) and passed by others, is due to its prevailing character of a Śrauta Mantrapāṭha, so to say. The hieratic hymns were the theme that really concerned the Rigvedin's interest: of other material he took what was conveniently at hand, without aiming at and without being able to reach exhaustiveness.

§ 43. The various readings of the RV. and the AV.—The following selection of examples may illustrate the interrelation of the materials common to RV. and AV. In AV. 1. 4. 4 the fourth pāda is an Atharvanic addendum as compared with RV. 1. 23. 19, and more particularly the other versions VS. 9. 6, etc.: the Atharvanist clinches the statement of pāda c, *aśvā bhavatha vājinaḥ*, by adding the otherwise unknown pāda, *gāvo bhavatha vājinīḥ*. In 1. 29 *maṇinā* for *haviṣā* in RV. 10. 174, and the substitution of *abhi vardh* for *abhi vart* seem to represent later Atharvanic intensity. In 2. 12. 6 *atīva* is inferior to *ati vā*, RV. 6. 52. 2. In 2. 33. 5^{cd} the metrically superfluous *bhāsadam* is certainly a gloss derived from the RV. version, 10. 163. 4.

AV. 6. 91. 3^{c} as compared with RV. 10. 137. 6^{c} has the variant *viśvasya* for *sarvasya*: it is possible therefore to conceive of the Atharvan version of the st. as the older, though a 'hieratic' reminiscence may be all there is at the bottom of *viśvasya*. But what is truly significant for the date of the Atharvan redaction is the occurrence of the same stanza in AV. 3. 7. 5 with the last pāda altered from, *tās te kṛṇvantu bheṣajam*, to, *tās tvā muñcantu kṣetriyāt*, indicating the adaptation of the stanza at an unquestionably later time to a secondary purpose. In AV. 3. 11. 3^{cd}, 4^{cd} we may safely assume a later handling of the pādas that appear RV. 10. 161. 3^{cd}, 4^{cd}; especially AV. 4^{c}, *śataṃ ta indro agniḥ savitā bṛhaspatiḥ*, must be later than RV. 4^{c}, *śatam indrāgnī savitā bṛhaspatiḥ*. AV. 3. 15. 3 occurs identically in its proper connection RV. 3. 18. 3: the word *ichamāno* suggested its adaptability for the Atharvanic mixtum compositum; the following hemistich of AV. is also secondary (RV. 1. 31. 16^{ab}), gathered in by the Atharvanist because it speaks of the 'far road which we have travelled', an expression too suitable to a merchant's charm not to be recruited into it[8]. In RV. 7. 41 we have pāda 1^{a} *havāmahe*, but in pādas 1^{d}, 2^{a} *huvema*; AV. 3. 16. 1, 2 flattens them all out to *havāmahe*: without any prejudice against the stem *hava-* as 'later' it may be safely assumed that this old hieratic hymn was by these changes brought nearer to the popular diction at a later time. In 3. 17. 2^{cd} *virājaḥ* for *girā ca*, and, *ā yavan* for *āyat* or *eyāt*, RV. 10. 101. 3 and the Yajur-versions, are both odd and secondary. AV. 3. 31. 5 is surely a mere mouthing over of RV. 10. 17. 1 (cp. AV. 18. 1. 53). The theosophic hymn (*hiraṇyagarbha*) AV. 4. 2 is described by Weber, IS. XVIII. 9, as a disguised, altered, and mutilated version of RV. 10. 121 (et al.), adapted by the Atharvanist to the very use in which it appears Kauś. 45. 1 ff.: when a *vaśā*, i. e., a supposedly sterile cow, is slain, and it turns out that she was pregnant, then this hymn is employed and adapted as a *prāyaścitta*. Similarly a comparison of AV. 5. 2 with RV. 10. 120; of AV. 5. 3 with RV. 10. 128; of AV. 6. 126 with RV. 6. 47. 29—31 will reveal every time better tradition on the part of RV. AV. 4. 9. 4 is an evident adaptation of st. 12 of the *oṣadhistuti*, RV. 10. 97 (et al.). In AV. 4. 21. 5^{a} *ichād* is a modern corruption of *achān* (3^{d} sg. of *s*-aorist from root *chand*), RV. 6. 28. 5; cp. *'śnute* for RV. *aśnute* in st. 4. The three hymns AV. 6. 27—29 represent RV. 10. 165 with interpolations and corruptions: AV. 27. 3^{c} is metrically inferior to RV. 3^{c}; AV. 29. 1^{c} to RV. 4 (*vā* in AV. is superfluous); AV. 28. 1^{d} has *prá padāt páthiṣṭhaḥ* for RV. 5^{d}, *prá patāt pátiṣṭhaḥ*: the false accent of AV. *páthiṣṭhaḥ* (it should be *pathi-ṣṭháḥ*, if it meant 'standing upon the road') betrays the secondary character of the Atharvan version; cp. also AV. 28. 1^{c}, *saṃlobhayanto*, popular, for RV. 5^{c} *saṃyopayanto*, hieratic, which are illustrated interestingly by the relation of AV. 12. 1. 29^{d} (*yup*) to Kāuś. 71. 19 (*lup*). In AV. 6. 92. 3^{b} *dhāvatu* for *dhātu*, RV. 10. 56. 2^{b}, is a sign of secondary adaptation: the Atharvan version is part of a charm to endow a horse with swiftness. AV. 7. 39, as compared with RV. 1. 164. 52; TS. 3. 1. 11. 3 (cp. also Suparṇākhyāna 17. 4), is secondary in it readings, and in pāda d exhibits adaptation to a practical purpose. The pāda, AV. 7. 89. 1^{a} (10. 5. 46^{a}), *apo divyā acāyiṣam*, is scarcely to be recognized as the opening of that well-known stanza which begins in other Vedic texts (RV. 1. 23. 23^{a} et al.) with the pādas, *āpo* (or, *apo*) *adyānv acāriṣam*, and, *apo anv acāriṣam*: there can be no doubt about the secondary character of the AV. reading. In AV. 7. 91. 1^{c} *naḥ* is metrically superfluous, and wanting in all other versions of the st., RV. 6. 47. 12; 10. 131. 6; AV. 20. 125. 51, etc. The st. AV. 7. 97. 2 is full of changes from the hieratic to popular diction as compared with RV. 5. 42. 4, and partly also with the Yajur-versions (VS. 8. 15, et al.): *no* for *ṇo*; *neṣa* for *neṣi*; *harivan* for *harivaḥ*; *svastyā* for *svasti*; cp. also the corrupt *brahmaṇām* in pāda c, assimilated to *devānām* in pāda d, for the correct *brahmaṇā* of the parallel texts. AV. 8. 7. 28 is a secondary working over of RV. 10. 97. 16, notwithstanding that AV. has in pāda d the more hieratic *viśvasmād* for RV. *sarvasmād*. To these examples may be added those pointed out by OLDENBERG, especially from the 14th and 18th books of the AV.[9]: they also show the constant removal of the Atharvan stanzas from the more archaic hieratic form and thought sphere to the plainer habits of speech and thought of the people. Of especial significance for the chronology of the AV. seem to me to be certain cases in which that Veda employs one or more stanzas that coincide with the RV. as a theme which is expanded or beaten out, either into several stanzas, or into an entire hymn. Thus the two sts. AV. 1. 19. 3, 4 seem to be nothing more than RV. 6. 75. 19 spun out, and rendered more typically Atharvanic by introducing Rudra and his arrows. AV. 1. 22 corresponds in its first and fourth stanzas to RV. 1. 50. 11, 12: the interior stanzas, absolutely original, seem to modulate and expand the theme set by sts. 1 and 4. Similarly AV. 3. 24. 1 = 10. 17. 14 (et al.) looks as though it had been picked out as the theme which a later poet might fitly develop into a song of the harvest. Again AV. 14. 2. 17, representing RV. 10. 85. 44, is followed by the similar st. 18 which is original with the Atharvanist, is linked verbally with 17, but does not add anything of consequence to the thought. A diaskeuastic performance like AV. 7. 50 in which the anuṣṭubh stanzas are original, the triṣṭubhs common property, with distinct signs of adaptation to the aim in hand (gambling-charm), lends support to such analyses. The force of these necessarily subjective observations is increased a good deal by the unquestionable fact that the AV. handles stanzas seemingly original in the Yajus-Saṃhitās in the same way, the most notable instances being the two chains of hymns 2. 19—23, and 4. 23—29 (the so-called *mṛgāra*-hymns). See below, § 45.

§ 44. Traces of superior tradition in the AV. as compared with the RV. — As regards direct evidence that the AV. reaches in some respects behind the tradition of the RV. to that floating mass of mantra-materials from which all redactions flowed, it must be admitted to be weak in force in comparison with the evidence just presented. BERGAIGNE and OLDENBERG have assumed that such evidence may be gathered from certain groupings of stanzas, and arrangements of hymns in both Vedic schools, and we have felt compelled, without denying the possible force of their observations, to suspend judgment upon them, at least until the evidence of the Paippalāda is in[10]. Such inferences as may be gathered from the metres, sense, and linguistic forms are rarely of such a nature as to prove the superior tradition of the AV. Occasional instances like AV. *kṛdhi* for RV. *kuru*; AV. *viśva* for RV. *sarva*, noted above, are almost forceless. An archaism (attraction) such as is contained in AV. 14. 1. 46d, *mayaḥ patibhyo janaye pariṣvaje*, where RV. 10. 40. 10d reads *janayaḥ*, looks a little affected, because the plural to match *patibhyo* seems really to be demanded by the sense, and the general form of the obscure stanza seems more trustworthy in RV. than AV. In AV. 6. 27. 3b the form *āṣṭrī* (padap. *āṣṭrī iti*), for *āṣṭryām*, RV. 10. 165. 3, is an archaic locative (Ath. Prāt. I. 74) which seems to indicate a certain superiority of the Atharvan text: this is, however, not borne out by pādas 2b and 3c whose Rigvedic form is metrically preferable. Again AV. 8. 3. 7ab, *utārabdhān spṛṇuhi jātaveda utārebhāṇām̐ ṛṣṭibhir yātudhānān*, as compared with RV. 10. 87. 7ab, *utālabdhaṃ spṛṇuhi jātaveda ālebhanād ṛṣṭibhir yātu-*

dhānāt, contains twice the 'old' form *rabh* where the RV. has 'late' *labh*, but pāda b is metrically superior in RV., and the sense of the RV. is also more compact (see LUDWIG'S translation, nr. 430). Less assailable is the superiority of the reading AV. 3. 1. 4[c], *viṣvaksatyaṃ kṛṇuhi cittam eṣām*, 'deprive their schemes of fulfilment', for the senseless version, RV. 3. 30. 6[d], *viśvaṃ satyaṃ kṛṇuhi viṣṭam astu*, even though pāda a in RV. is distinctly superior to AV.[11]. And so the reading *aviśvavinnām*, in contrast to *viśvavidam*, AV. 9. 9. 10[d], is not only superior to *aviśvaminvām*, RV. 1. 164. 10: it is of the kind that cannot be explained as due to later correction, but represents the original tradition of the stanza[12]. Cp. also *pariṣkṛtā*, AV. 14. 1. 7[d], better than *pariṣkṛtam*, RV. 10. 85. 6[d]; *janām̐ anu*, AV. 14. 2. 10[b], for the senseless *janād anu*, RV. 10. 85. 31[b]. Occasionally, too, there are to be found here, as in the inter-relation of all Saṃhitās, independent variants whose language and general impression seems equally good in both sources. Thus the little hymn AV. 6. 2 is related to RV. 7. 32. 6, 8, but its character is so independent and archaic, as to suggest original workmanship of no mean quality and age. Or the subtle modulation of RV. 6. 11. 4 (MS. 4. 14. 15) in AV. 3. 3. 1, in spite of certain adaptive traits in AV. (*āmuṃ naya*, in pāda d), is not easily accounted for as a working over of the RV. form; it represents rather an independent effort in the same sphere of ideas, whose language and date as compared with RV. cannot be said to be inferior. And there are, of course, throughout the AV., hymns and stanzas of a totally independent character that suggest very old workmanship, not only such as are of purely Atharvanic character and popular diction, but such as are written in good hieratic language. Thus the hymn to the battle-drum, 5. 20, may be later than the oldest parts of the RV., but there is in it nothing that suggests late composition, later, e. g., than the stanzas addressed to the drum, RV. 6. 47. 29—31 (AV. 6. 126, et al.). Or the language of the theosophic hymn 5. 1, which is original with the exception of stanza 6 = RV. 10. 5. 6, is not of such a character as to justify the belief that a later versifex might have so completely immersed himself in the style and mode of thought of the early Rishis as to be able to produce stanzas as good — or as bad, according to the point of view. Cf. also such a hymn as 6. 61. On the whole therefore the AV. is the bearer of old tradition not only in the line of the popular charms; but also to some extent, albeit slight, its hieratic materials are likely to be the product of independent tradition that has eluded the collectors of the other Vedas, the RV. not excepted[13].

1 Cp. JAOS. XV, p. CLXXII. — 2 Cp. ibid., p. CLXXIII ff. — 3 See below, § 62. — 4 Cp. WHITNEY'S tables, IS. II. 347. — 5 *hvayāmi* is Avestan *zbayemi*; for the dissyllabic roots in *u* see BLOOMFIELD, JAOS. XVI, p. CLVIII ff.; BB. XXIII. 107 ff.; *panthānam* is Avestan *pañtānem*; *sarva* is Avestan *haurva*, etc.; *rajju* is not separable from Lith. *rezgù* 'braid'. Cp. HILLEBRANDT, GGA. 1889, p. 401; BLOOMFIELD, JAOS. XVII, p. 175, note 5. — 6 For the literature on this subject see ARNOLD, JAOS. XVIII. 204 ff.; cp. ROTH, Abhandlung, p. 22 ff. — 7 *atho* at the beginning of pādas is a favorite Atharvan expression. — 8 Cp. SBE. XLII. 353. — 9 Die Hymnen des Rig-Veda, p. 320 ff. — 10 See above § 36. — 11 SBE. XLII. 326. — 12 OLDENBERG, l. c. 323, following LUDWIG, V. 447. — 13 Cp. HILLEBRANDT, GGA. 1889, p. 404 ff.

§ 45. Adaptation and expansion of Yajus-themes for Atharvanic purposes. — The preceding analysis of the relation of the AV. to the RV. has been on the whole in the nature of support to existing views on the subject: it does not seem at all likely that these will ever be materially changed. As regards the relation of the AV. to the Yajus-Saṃhitās the impression exists among scholars — to what extent it is not easy to say, because of the absence of definitive statements — that the AV. is entitled to a prior position and date of final redaction as compared with the collections of mantras in the YV. Such a view, if it exists at all[1], is not sustained by the facts in the case: on the contrary an extended comparison of the two classes goes to show that the redaction of the AV. holds much the same place compared with the redactions of the YV. as when compared with the RV. The materials common to the two Vedas appear in the main in better form and more original application in the Yajus than in the AV.; the special habit of the AV. to adapt and to group stanzas for secondary purposes is fully in evidence. Here again the Atharvan redactors may, in fact are likely to have gathered up some materials that escaped the scrutiny of the Yajus-redactors, or that had passed out of active use before the conclusion of these redactions, but the Atharvan redaction cannot well be assumed to have preceded the Yajus. The best evidence for this is not so much the general superiority of the readings of the Yajus as certain drastic methods by which the AV. forces purely liturgical stanzas into its own service of low folk-lore and witch-craft. The Atharvan in such cases has not in view incidental features of larger aims and performances, as is the case with the sorcery stanzas and formulas of the Yajus, but it makes the Yajus-stanzas in question the basis of an independent, self-centred act of the usual Atharvanic sort. It will be worth while to dwell in detail upon a few cases of this kind by way of establishing the presumption that this habit exists in the AV. on a larger scale.

In MS. 1. 5. 2; ApŚ. 6. 21. 1 we have five formulas addressed to Agni in which he is implored to attack with his manifold fiery qualities 'him that hates us and whom we hate'. These same five formulas appear AV. 2. 19, but this is followed by four other hymns in which Vāyu, Sūrya, Candra, and Āpaḥ (the waters) are addressed in the same terms. To speak of the fiery qualities, *tapas*, *haras*, *arcis*, *śocis*, *tejas*, of Vāyu or the waters is of course possible in the course of the development of the later liturgic litanies, where everything is possible on a pinch. Yet it may not be doubted that the restriction in the *śrauta*-texts of these five appeals to Agni marks the original status: out of this the AV. has developed a formidable pentad in the second degree (25 formulas) which are prescribed, correctly no doubt, Kauś. 47, at the introductory oblations in *āṅgirasa*-practices (hostile sorcery). But further, the pentad of divinities is most characteristically Atharvanic. Whereas the Brāhmanical texts in general present times without end a cosmic-Vedic triad: Agni-Pṛthivī-Rigveda, etc.; Vāyu-Antarikṣa-Yajurveda, etc., Sūrya-Dyu-Sāmaveda, etc., the Atharvan writings, craving a cosmic base for their Veda, expand this into a tetrad or pentad, by the addition of Candramas, or Candramas and the waters[2]: Kauś. 119. 2, 3; GB. 1. 1. 17—20, 29; 2. 16, 24; 3. 24, etc. There can be no doubt that the old fire-formulas were an original stock of Yajus, and that the AV. has expanded them to accord with notions of its own whose date cannot have been as early as that of the existing Yajus-collections.

Closely and characteristically similar is the history of the so-called *mṛgāra-sūktāni*, AV. 4. 23—29[3]. In the first place we may note that this litany consists of seven hymns of seven stanzas each, i. e., a heptad in the second degree; this numerical symmetry, in itself suspicious, points to secondary handling, just as in the preceding pentads. The entire litany aims, as its refrain-pādas clearly show, to drive out calamity (*muc aṁhasaḥ*). The structure of these hymns is as follows: barring 4. 28, the first and last stanza of each hymn consists of Yajur-mantras which are employed in the Yajus-saṃhitās as *yājyāpuronuvākyās*, TS. 4. 7. 15; MS. 3. 16. 5; KS. 22. 15; on the other hand the intervening stanzas in the AV. are in the main original. Now it were possible to imagine that the Yajus-stanzas were picked out of longer hymns, though there is no special reason for such a supposition. That they were not gathered from the Atharvan hymns in question may be regarded as certain: why should the choice have fallen every time upon stanzas 1 and 7? More important, nay conclusive, however, is the fact that the intervening stanzas (2—6) in the AV. are obviously secondary padding. This may be seen best in 4. 29: stanzas 1 and 7 are of ordinary mantra-character, praising Mitra and Varuṇa in language that does not arrest attention. Stanza 2, on the other hand, in its first hemistich chews over pādas b and d of stanza 1, adding nothing but the beginning of a list of old Rishis whom Mitra and Varuṇa are supposed to have helped out of difficulties in the days of yore: they are the traditional worthies Babhru, Aṅgiras, Agasti, Jamadagni, Atri, etc. The dulness of the epigonal author betrays itself throughout: in stanzas 3 and 4 he repeats Atri's name, the whole is veritable clap-trap. It will not require close inspection of the intermediate stanzas of the remaining hymns to convince one that there also the outer stanzas are the 'leitmotiv', the rest the muse of a late author who relies in the main upon his own mediocrity, but occasionally gathers in some existing mantra or pāda. On the other hand the one altogether original hymn of the series, 4. 28, is addressed to Bhava and Śarva: these popular divinities must not be wanting in the AV. in any continuous invitation of *nivid*-character, addressed to the Vedic pantheon (cf. AV. 11. 2). Along with its originality 4. 28 exhibits also its particular Atharvanic character (*kṛtyākṛt* and *mūlakṛt* in stanza 6; *kimīdin* in stanza 7): the hymn is clearly an intruder in the sphere of ideas from which these *mṛgāra*-stanzas are derived, lending itself conveniently to the building out of the numerical scheme, as well as to the Atharvanic idea of the proper way of making an exhaustive appeal to the most important members of the pantheon of that time.

We may in fact safely present the statement as the outcome of the preceding analysis, that the AV. handles the prose formulas of the YV. in a decidedly secondary fashion, and that both Yajus-formulas and Yajus-stanzas are frequently used as themes to which the Atharvanist has added new matter to suit his own devices. For instance 10. 5 is an incantation to the waters, being a long and weary litany, partly in Yajus-prose, partly in poor metre. In it occur as themes that are beaten out beyond endurance such formulas as, *indrasyauja stha* (VS. 37. 6), or *viṣṇoḥ kramo 'si* (TS. 4. 2. 1). There is not the slightest chance that these formulas were borrowed by the YV. from the AV., nor can there be any doubt that the AV. got hold of these themes at a time when they were already perfectly familiar in their liturgical application to special acts of the *śrauta*-sacrifice. Similary AV. 5. 24 is an overlong litany engaging the help of the pantheon, *asmin brahmaṇy asmin karmaṇy asyāṃ purodhāyām* etc.: according to Kauś. 17. 30 the piece is recited on entering upon the duties of the *purohiti*, a rather secondary and Atharvanic restriction. Anyhow, the Atharvanic handling of this theme is secondary to that of the YV.: TS. 3. 4. 5; MS. 2. 6. 6; TB. 3. 11. 4; ŚS. 4. 10. 1—3; PG. 1. 5. 10; HG. 1. 3. 10, 11; if nothing else, *asmin brahmaṇy* of the AV., as against *asmin brahmann* of the YV., points to later redaction and the passage out of the hieratic sphere to the popular. Similarly a prose hymn like AV. 2. 17, consisting of formulas of the type, *ojo 'si, ojo me dāḥ svāhā*, presupposes existing Yajus-formulas, developed into a litany for specific purposes; cf. VS. 19. 9; TB. 2. 6. 1. 5, etc. As regards the use of one or two Yajus-stanzas as a theme for an entire hymn there are quite a number of unquestionable cases. Thus AV. 1. 31 begins with the well-known stanza, *āśānām āśāpālebhyaḥ*, TB. 2. 5. 3. 3; 3. 7. 5. 8; AŚ. 2. 10. 18; ApŚ. 4. 11. 1, etc., but the remaining stanzas of the hymn do not occur outside of AV. One needs but look at the stanza 2^{ab} to eliminate the possibility that the YV. borrowed its stanzas from the AV: it is the latter that beats out the theme of the first stanza in good stupid Atharvan fashion. And the others are no better: the case is most convincing. Similar, though not quite so certain, is the structure of AV. 1. 35, addressed to the *dākṣāyaṇa*-amulet: the first two stanzas occur VS. 34. 51, 52; RV. Khila 10. 128. 8, 9; the last two are original, except that 4^{cd} is formulaic (AV. 8. 2. 21). Here also it would seem as though the Atharvanist had borrowed an existing theme in order to build up a more substantial hymn suitable to his own devices. Again AV. 3. 19 begins with a stanza that occurs also VS. 11. 81; TS. 4. 1. 10. 3; MS. 2. 7. 7 (et al.), followed in the sequel, stanza 3^{cd}, by two pādas that represent the continuation of the Yajus-texts. The very mixed character of the Atharvan stanzas makes at once for the supposition that the hymn is a mere elaboration of a pair of well-connected Yajus-stanzas: stanza 2 is hackneyed; stanza 3^{ab} substitutes a triṣṭubh, whose metre disturbs, and whose tone is secondarily Atharvanic, for the regular anuṣṭubh Yajus-pādas; above all the introduction of *idam* in pāda 1^{a} which makes the pāda falsely regular, ending in ⏑——⏓, and changes the sense (*idaṃ brahma* 'this charm', for *brahma* 'brahmanhood') — all these points are well accounted for if we regard the AV. hymn as a compilation, with the Yajus-stanzas as the main motive; it would be a total perversion to assume that the Yajus-texts selected and varied the two stanzas 1 and 3. The same kind of theory is applicable to AV. 6. 62 whose first stanza = MS. 3. 11. 10; TB. 1. 4. 8. 3, may have served as the theme: the other two stanzas seem to occur nowhere else, and they are not of such a kind as to exclude the notion of late origin by way of variations to the theme, even though they fall very well into the tone of the hieratic language. Or again, AV. 7. 20 begins with two anuṣṭubh stanzas that are familiar in the Yajus, TS. 3. 3. 11; MS. 3. 16. 4; the hymn continues with four triṣṭubh stanzas that are original. Again it would seem as though the Yajus-stanzas were the theme: the variant *mama* in AV. 1^{d} for *mayaḥ* of the Yajus favors the assumption. A little different is the case of AV. 1. 20 and 21, two battle-charms which are built up in the main upon mantra-stock that occurs also RV. 10. 152. The circumstances are as follows: the two hymns making together 8 stanzas coincide in their last 5 stanzas with the RV. hymn. The first three stanzas are patchwork, stanza 1 = TB. 3. 7. 5. 12; ApŚ. 2. 20. 6; stanza 2 = AŚ. 5. 3. 22; one can not say here exactly that the first stanza is the theme of the entire hymn, but certainly when the Atharvan compilation took place its first stanza existed as a Yajus: whencesoever the Yajus-text derived it, it was not borrowed from Atharvan sources; the reverse is altogether more likely.

§ 46. The various readings of the AV. and the Yajus-Saṃhitās. — Extensive comparison of the readings of AV. as compared with the Yajus show the former to be on the whole inferior to the latter: the tradition of the AV. is less pure in every way. The metres are more irregular, the grammatical forms and constructions less intelligible, the adaptive touches very frequent. Thus AV. 2. 6. recurs VS. 27. 1 ff.; TS. 4. 1. 7. 1 ff.; MS. 2. 12. 5, on the whole with insignificant variants, until we arrive at st. 4. Here AV. has in the middle of a triṣṭubh the non-descript pāda c, *sajātānāṃ madhyameṣṭhā*, for which MS. has, *sajātānāṃ madhyameṣṭheyāya*, in good metre and excellent sense; the AV., in addition to the metrical irregularity, places *madhyameṣṭhāḥ* into agreement with Agni whom it does not fit nearly as well as the person making the prayer: it is he that wishes to stand (superior) in the midst of his rivals. The other Yajur-versions have *sajātānāṃ madhyamasthā edhi* which is also possible metre, though not absolutely convincing; pāda b is superior in all the Yajus. In AV. 2. 28. 5^{a} *naya* for *kṛdhi* of all other versions marks the popular strain: see, TS. 2. 3. 10. 3; MS. 2. 3. 4; TB. 2. 7. 7. 5; TA. 2. 5. 1. The st. AV. 2. 29. 3, quoted Vait. 22. 16, is repeated with variants MS. 4. 12. 3; KS. 5. 2; TS. 3. 2. 8. 5; KŚ. 10. 5. 3. In all these the difficult duals *dhattam* and *saçetasau* are replaced by singulars, *dadhātu* and *savarcasam* (KS. *suvarcasam*); and they all regard *āśīr* as the nom. sg. of the stem *āśir* 'milk added to soma'; see especially Vait. and KŚ. (*āśiram*). This construction fails in the AV. where *āśīr* is the nom. sg. of *āśis* 'prayer'. The dual *dhattam* in pāda b seems to refer proleptically to *dyāvāpṛthivī* in st. 4, as Sāyaṇa assumes unhesitatingly. Note also *sauprajāstvam* (AV.) for *suprajāstvam* (YV.); the former is a monstrosity. The entire st. of AV. is adapted secondarily to two persons who are engaged in the practice of transmitting disease one from the other: the Yajur-version has nothing of the kind, and its originality is not to be doubted[4]. In AV. 2. 34. 1, *ya īśe paśupatiḥ paśūnām* is metrically inferior to *yeṣām īśe*, TS. 3. 1. 4. 1, as also in st. 2, *pramuñcanto bhuvanasya reto*, to TS., *pramuñcamānaḥ* etc. AV. 3. 13 adapts a number of fanciful stanzas to the practice of conducting a river into a new channel: the first six sts. recur in TS. 5. 6. 1. 2—4; MS. 2. 13. 1 in connection with certain oblations of water (*kumbheṣṭakāḥ*, or *apāṃ grahāḥ*), being evidently at home in the Yajur-ritual. As frequently elsewhere in the AV., the body of the hymn is mere ornamentation or solemn verbiage, the seventh and last st. is original, turning forth the point of the hymn and the practice. Accordingly pāda 5^{d}, *ā mā prāṇena sahā varcasā gamet*, a jagatī in the midst of triṣṭubhs, is more modern and inferior to *ā mā prāṇena saha varcasā gan* (*varcasāgan*) of the Yajus. The version of AV. 3. 14. 2, 3 seems inferior to that of MS. 4. 2. 10, where the gāyatrī-form instead of the anuṣṭubhs of AV. and sundry readings, *poṣā* for *pūṣā*, *avihrutāḥ* for *abibhyuṣīḥ*, and *purīṣiṇīḥ* for *karīṣiṇīḥ*, make a better impression. No hymn illustrates better the impurity, one might say the stupidity, of the rendering of Yajus-material in the AV. than the *āprī*-hymn, 5. 27, which is repeated in all Yajus-saṃhitās, VS. 27. 11—22; TS. 4. 1. 8; MS. 2. 12. 6; KS. 18. 17; KapS. 29. 5. Whereas these texts agree in the main, the Atharvan version is verbally and metrically so corrupt as to be scarcely translatable. Notably the first pāda of the second st. appears in the AV. as the fourth pāda of the first st., thus depriving the second st. of its necessary *āprī*-divinity, *tanūnapāt*, and overloading st. 1 with two, the *samidh* and *tanūnapāt*; sts. 10—12 are mere hodge-podge as regards metrical arrangement. The version of AV. 6. 38 in TB. 2. 7. 7. 1 presents on the whole more primary readings in TB.: *āgan* for *etu* in the refrain; *krandye* for *vāje* in 4^{b}, the former being the archaic *lectio difficilior*, and in close parallelism to *māyau*; AV. 2^{b}, *tviṣir apsu goṣu yā puruṣeṣu*, is an obvious verbal and metrical corruption as compared with TB., *tviṣir aśveṣu puruṣeṣu goṣu*: to be sure contrariwise AV. 4^{a}, *rājanie* seems better than *yā rājanye* of TB. The sense and the wording of AV. 6. 74. 3 is inferior to TS. 2. 1. 11. 3: the entire AV. hymn is patchwork; especially 3^{d} exhibits the usual adaptive touches, to make the st. directly and practically serviceable. AV. 6. 98. 3^{ab} reads, *prācyā diśas tvam indrāsi rājotodīcyā diśo vṛtrahaṃ chatruho 'si*, for TS. 2. 4. 14. 1; MS. 4. 12. 2, *prācyāṃ diśi tvam indrāsi rājotodīcyāṃ vṛtrahan vṛtrahāsi*: not only is *diśo* in AV., pāda b, metrically superfluous, but the AV. version is altogether slipshod. AV. 7. 3. 1^{d}, *svayā tanvā tanvam airayat*, is a miserable pāda in a triṣṭubh st.; all other versions, TS. 1. 7. 12. 2; MS. 1. 10. 3; AŚ. 2. 19. 32; ŚS. 3. 17. 1; KŚ. 25. 6. 10, are better. In AV. 7. 4 *suhūte* is inferior to *svabhūte* of all other versions, and especially *viyugbhir*, in the sense of 'unhitching', replacing *niyudbhir*, and coined for the nonce to match *vi muñca*, exhibits the stanza in a corrupt and adapted form: see VS. 27. 33; MS. 4. 6. 2; ŚB. 4. 4. 1. 15; TA. 1. 11. 8; AŚ. 5. 18. 5; ŚS. 8. 3. 10. In the triṣṭubh st. AV. 7. 6. 2 pāda b is a jagatī, because AV. has substituted popular *havāmahe* for hieratic *huvema* of all other versions: VS. 21. 5; TS. 1. 5. 11. 5; MS. 4. 10. 1; AŚ. 2. 1. 29; ŚS. 2. 2. 14. The fondness of the AV. for *havāmahe* in place of *huvema* has beguiled it elsewhere into the same irregular proceeding: e. g. in 7. 40. 1[d], compared with TS. 3. 1. 11. 3; MS. 4. 10. 1 (cp. also RV. 1. 164. 52[d]); or, compare AV. 7. 63. 1[b], *ukthair havāmahe paramāt sadhastāt*, with the parallel pādas, *agniṃ huvema* etc., TA. 10. 2. 1 (68)[b], and *ugraṃ huvema* etc., Mahānārāyaṇa Up. 6. 6.[b]. In AV. 7. 14 2[b] the reading *kṛpāt* of both published editions and the mss. in saṃhitā and padapāṭha is nonsensical: Sāyaṇa reads and comments upon *kṛpā* in accordance with all the other numerous versions, SV. 1. 464; VS. 4. 25; VSK. 4. 8. 3; TS. 1. 2. 6. 1; MS. 1. 2. 5; ŚB. 3. 3. 2. 12; AŚ. 4. 6. 3; ŚS. 5. 9. 7. The comparison of AV. 7. 15 with the parallel versions, MS. 2. 10. 6, et al., reveals secondary readings and adaptation in AV.; in 7. 16 the AV. reads *vardhaya* for *bodhaya* of the other texts (MS. 2. 12. 5, et al.), and to *bodhaya*, curiously enough, the ritual, Kauś. 59. 18; Vait. 5. 9, responds with its verb *bodhayati*[5]; in AV. 7. 47. 1[b] *suhavā* is inferior to *suhavāṃ* of the other versions, MS. 4. 12. 6, et al. That the AV. version of the *rohita*-stanzas at the beginning of book 13 is inferior to that of TB. 2. 5. 2, and the result of adaptation has been shown by the writer, Contributions, Fourth Series, AJPh. XII. 430 ff.

§ 47. The various readings of the AV. and the Śrautasūtras. — The comparisons just stated have shown incidentally that the mantras in the Śrauta-sūtras share in general the superiority of the Yajus-saṃhitās as compared with the AV. This seems to be true also of those cases in which AV. and Śrauta-sūtras present materials of the hieratic quality which do not occur in either RV. or Yajus-saṃhitās. As early as 1856 ROTH did not shrink from exposing the secondary manipulations and inferior readings of AV. 2. 5 as compared with AŚ. 6. 3. 1[6]; he might have added, if the text had been accessible, ŚS. 9. 5. 2. The liturgical form of these sts. in the Śrauta-sūtras, manifest from the insertion of secondary phrases, is disregarded and corrupted in the AV. to such an extent that the sts. are in reality untranslatable in its version. A detailed comparison of AV. 6. 1 with AŚ. 8. 1. 18 (= SV. 1. 177; AB. 5. 13. 8) exhibits the little hymn in what may be regarded as at least a more original form in AŚ. both in sense and metre. The hymn begins AŚ., *doṣo āgād bṛhad gāya*, 'now evening hath arrived, sing thou merrily'; for this AV. reads, *doṣo gāya bṛhad gāya*, 'now sing in the evening, sing thou merrily': the first *gāya* seems a mere repetition of the second. Pāda 2[a] in AŚ., *tam u ṣṭuhy antaḥsindhum*, is corrupted metrically in AV., *tam u ṣṭuhi yo antaḥ sindhau*; and pāda 3[b] in AŚ., *sāviṣad vasupatiḥ*, is also more trustworthy than AV., *sāviṣad amṛtāni bhūri*. Again AV. 6. 33 whose first two sts. are scarcely translatable in our version appears ŚS. 18. 3. 2 in a form which at least makes a show of intelligibility; cf. also ĀA. 5. 2. 1. 2—4; ArS. 1. 3. Similarly compare AV. 6. 35 with AŚ. 8. 11. 4; ŚS. 10. 9. 17, especially the senseless pāda 2[c], *agnir ukthеṣv aṃhasu*, with, *agnir ukthena vāhasā* of the Śrauta-texts. The distinction between hieratic and popular mantras is to be observed here as elsewhere: we may expect popular stanzas in as good or better form in the AV.; see especially the parallels between ApS. and

AV. grouped together above, § 41; or cf. the corrupt version of AV. 10. 3. 5 in TA. 6. 9. 2.

§ 48. Traces of superior tradition in the AV. as compared with the Yajus-texts. — Here and there, but rarely, the AV. seems to present superior readings; more frequently, the Atharvan readings seem no better and no worse than those of the Yajus-texts. PISCHEL[7] has made out a good case for the superiority of AV. 6. 22. 3 over TS. 3. 1. 11. 7: especially pāda b in AV. is superior to TS. which seems to be borrowed from RV. 5. 58. 3. In AV. 3. 4. 2 the first pāda, *tvāṃ viśo vṛṇatāṃ rājyāya,* is almost certainly superior to the adapted, *tvāṃ gāvo 'vṛṇata rājyāya,* TS. 3. 3. 9. 2; MS. 2. 5. 10, although the Yajur-version of the remaining pādas is at least as good as the Atharvan. In AV. 6. 5. 3ª *kṛṇmo* is an instance of an occasional hieratic form for popular *kurmo* of the Yajus (VS. 17. 52; TS. 4. 1. 1. 2; MS. 2. 10. 4[8]), but this instance of superiority is at once reduced to the proper proportion on observing that pāda 2ᵈ in AV., *jīvātave jarase naya,* is unmetrical, and the result of adaptation to *āyuṣya*-purposes, as compared with the Yajus-pāda, *sajātānām asad vaśī.* AV. 2. 10, notwithstanding the secondarily introduced refrain, is based upon a quite as good or better source than TB. 2. 5. 6. 1 ff.: see pādas 1ª, 3ª, and pāda 2ᵇ, *śaṃ somaḥ sahauṣadhībhiḥ,* which is also better than TB., *śaṃ dyāvāpṛthivī sahauṣadhībhiḥ;* in the latter *dyāvāpṛthivī* is out of keeping, borrowed from the preceding stanza, apparently to equalize the metre. AV. 3. 10. 1 impresses one as at least as good as its parallel, TS. 4. 3. 11. 5; in fact *duhām* in pāda 3 is an archaism as compared with *dhukṣva* in TS. Nevertheless the entire hymn in the AV. is a mixtum compositum, as may be seen especially in st. 7 which consists of an original gāyatrī-pāda, followed by a rather formulaic, imitative triṣṭubh-pāda[9], and concludes with a common anuṣṭubh-hemistich (VS. 3. 49; TS. 1. 8. 4. 1; MS. 1. 10. 2). Instances in which the quality of the readings seems equally good as those of the Yajus are AV. 6. 47. 1, as compared with TS. 3. 1. 9. 1; KŚ. 9. 3. 21 (MS. 1. 3. 36 is inferior); or AV. 6. 55. 1, as compared with TS. 5. 7. 2. 3, where indeed pāda c in AV. is smoother, though probably not more original than TS. And in a case like the little hymn AV. 6. 79, as compared with TS. 3. 3. 8. 2, it seems equally impossible to establish chronological relation on the ground of the variants. Neither these nor other sporadic instances of intelligent handling of mantra-themes are likely ever to change the main proposition, namely that the collection and redaction of the AV. took place at a time when the main body of Yajus-stanzas and formulas were in existence in essentially their present forms and present application. The fuller knowledge in the future of the Yajus-tradition likely to come especially with the publication of the Kāṭhaka and Kapiṣṭhala Saṃhitās will not change this, even granted that here and there an inferior reading regarded at present as of Atharvanic origin may in reality have come from a source outside of that Veda: in the majority of cases the Atharvan variants of the hieratic mantras are original with that Veda and inferior to the tradition of the Yajus, no less than to that of the Rig-Veda.

1 Cp. WHITNEY, JAOS. XII, p. 3, bottom. — 2 In the latter case Candramas is the divinity, corresponding e. g. to Agni; the waters are the element, corresponding e. g. to Pṛthivī. — 3 See below, § 57. — 4 Cp. SBE. XLII. 309. — 5 Cp. HENRY, Le Livre VII, p. 58. — 6 Abhandlung über den Atharva-Veda, p. 11 ff. — 7 Ved. Stud. I. 84 ff. — 8 Cp. also *kṛdhi,* AV. st. 2ª, for *naya* in YV. — 9 Cp. AV. 6. 47. 2ᵈ; TS. 3. 1. 9. 2ᵈ.

PART III. CONTENTS OF THE ATHARVA-VEDA IN THE ŚAUNAKĪYA-SCHOOL.

§ 49. Classification of the hymns. — The classification of a body of 731 Vedic hymns is not an altogether easy matter. The question what a given hymn is about is not always to be answered in certain tones, even in the case of Atharvan hymns, although prayer and action are more closely allied in this than in any other Veda. All scholars are agreed now that the Sūtra of Kauśika frequently furnishes valuable hints towards making out the situation within which many hymns were conceived, by furnishing the *mise-en scène*, as it were, of a given hymn; but all scholars are also agreed that the Sūtra draws in a large measure upon the independent tradition of folk-customs and practices in general, interweaving the Atharvan hymns as prayers applicable to the situation with more or less fitness. The Atharvan hymns themselves, as the hymns of the Veda in general, are open to the charge of secondary adaptation of the floating body of Vedic stanzas to purposes different from those which were in the mind of the original composers; see SBE. XLII, Introduction, p. LXIII ff., and the Index under, 'adaptation of mantras'. In such cases, of course, the Atharvanic view is the one that primarily concerns the interpreter of the AV. A large number of hymns are hard to classify because of the variety of themes and objects presented in them. The arrangement of the hymns into ten classes, attempted for the first time by the author in his 'Hymns of the Atharva-Veda', SBE. XLII, has upon closer inspection proved quite tenable; it is made the basis of the following analysis. But in addition the materials that did not come within the scope of that volume had to be taken into account here; the result altogether is stated under 14 heads: 1) Charms to cure diseases and possession by demons (*bhaiṣajyāni*). — 2) Prayers for long life and health (*āyuṣyāṇi*). — 3) Imprecations against demons, sorcerers, and enemies (*ābhicārikāṇi* and *kṛtyāpratiharaṇāni*). — 4) Charms pertaining to women (*strīkarmāṇi*). — 5) Charms to secure harmony, influence in the assembly, and the like (*sāṃmanasyāni*, etc.). — 6) Charms pertaining to royalty (*rājakarmāṇi*). — 7) Prayers and imprecations in the interest of Brahmans. — 8) Charms to secure prosperity and freedom from danger (*pauṣṭikāni*). — 9) Charms in expiation of sin and defilement (*prāyaścittāni*). — 10) Cosmogonic and theosophic hymns. — 11) Ritualistic and general hymns. — 12) The books dealing with individual themes (books 13—18). — 13) The twentieth book. — 14) The *kuntāpa*-hymns. —

The only complete translation of the AV. is that of the Anglo-Indian scholar R. T. H. GRIFFITH, entitled, Hymns of the Atharva-Veda (Benares, Lazarus & Co.). WHITNEY'S posthumous translation of the entire collection is going through the press, to be published in the Harvard Oriental Series (ed. C. R. LANMAN). A large number of hymns have been translated by A. LUDWIG in the third volume of his great work, Der Rig-Veda, p. 428 ff., as also scatteringly through the same volume; cp. the Index to the entire work, vol. VI p. 57 ff. A hundred selected hymns were translated by JULIUS GRILL under the heading, 'Hundert Lieder des Atharva-Veda', in the 'Programm des Seminars Maulbronn', Tübingen 1879; published in a second edition as an independent volume, Tübingen 1888. About one third of the hymns were selected by the present author for his volume 'Hymns of the Atharva-Veda, together with Extracts from the Ritual Books and the Commentaries', SBE. XLII (ed. MAX MÜLLER). A considerable quantity of Atharvan matter is treated by ROTH, Abhandlung über den Atharva-Veda, Tübingen 1856; and in the 'Festgruss an Otto von Böhtlingk', p. 95 ff.; by J. MUIR in OST. (see the indexes to vols. I, IV, and V); by H. ZIMMER, Altindisches Leben (see the indexes p. 453); by SCHER-

MAN, Philosophische Hymnen aus der Rig- und Atharva-Veda-Samhitā, p. 41 ff.; by BLOOMFIELD, in 'Seven Hymns of the AV.', and the six series of 'Contributions to the Interpretation of the Veda' (the places of publication are stated AJPh. XVII, p. 399, note); by PAUL DEUSSEN, Allgemeine Geschichte der Philosophie, vol. I, part 1; and scatteringly by many authors throughout the Oriental and Philological Journals and treatises. Many translations of individual books exist: Books 1—5 by WEBER, IS. IV. 393 ff., XIII. 129 ff., XVII. 177 ff., XVIII. 1 ff.; book 6, hymns 1—50 by C. A. FLORENZ, BB. XII. 249 ff.; books 7—13 by VICTOR HENRY (Paris, Maisonneuve, 1891—96); book 14 by WEBER, IS. V. 195 ff.; book 15 by AUFRECHT, IS. I, 130 ff.; book 18 by WEBER, SPAW. 1895, p. 815 ff.; 1896, p. 253 ff. — A translation of the AV. into Persian is said to have been made by Brahmans for the emperor Akbar, but it has not as yet turned up; see Abu Fazl's Aīn-i-Akbarī in BLOCHMANN's translation, Bibliotheca Indica, 1868, p. 105 (A.D. 1575). Cp. WEBER, SPAW., 1890, p. 787, note.

§ 50. Class 1). Charms to cure diseases and possession by demons (bhaiṣajyāni). — The medicinal charms of the AV. go by the name of *bheṣajam* 'remedy', the healing plant is *bheṣajī*, the waters are *bheṣajīḥ*. The term is not restricted altogether to medicine; it includes also exorcism of demons, and approaches closely to the conception of *śānti* in distinction from *abhicāra*, embracing thus everything that comes under negative, defensive, pious magic[1]. The derivative *bhaiṣajya* occurs neither in RV. nor AV; it appears later in connection with the more advanced and technical medicinal practices as laid down in the *bhaiṣajya*-chapters of the Kauśika-sūtra (25—32), and found scatteringly in the Brāhmaṇas and Sūtras[2]. The practices there involve a more extensive materia medica and more elaborate therapeutics, but it is difficult to define in detail the extent to which practices similar to those of the Sūtras must be presupposed from the start with the charms of the AV. Action of some sort is likely to have accompanied nearly all of them; frequently otherwise unintelligible statements of the hymns are clarified by the practices in the Sūtras[3]. At any rate the charms of the AV. along with such practices as went with them represent quite the most complete account of primitive medicine preserved in any literature. The limited number of RV. hymns which deal with the same subjects are of essentially the same character and period (RV. 10. 137, 161, 163; cp. also 1. 191; 7. 50; 8. 91; 10. 57—60, and other sporadic utterances). The existence of such charms and practices is guaranteed moreover at least as early as the Indo-Iranian (Aryan) period by the stems *baeṣaza* and *baeṣazya* (*mañthra baeṣaza*, and *baeṣazya*; *haoma baeṣazya*), and by the preeminent position of water and plants in all prayers for health and long life[4]. ADALBERT KUHN has pointed out some interesting and striking resemblances between Teutonic and Vedic medicinal charms, especially in connection with cures for worms and fractures. These may perhaps be mere anthropological coincidences, due to the similar mental endowment of the two peoples. But it is no less likely that some of these folk-notions had crystallized in prehistoric times, and that these parallels reflect the continuation of a crude Indo-European folk-lore that had survived among the Teutons and Hindus. The opposite view is now ordinarily asserted with a degree of dogmatism not at all warranted by the evidence[5].

The connection of the Atharvanic medical charms with the later Hindu medicine of classical times (Āyur-veda) has never failed to impress itself both upon the Hindus themselves who regard the Āyur-veda as an *upaveda* ('after-Veda') of the Atharvan; Western scholars also were not slow to correlate the two strata of medical literature — to the advantage of the understanding of both. The diagnosis of fever (*takman* in the AV., *jvara* in the later medicine), especially of intermittent fever; of wasting pulmonary diseases (*yakṣma*), and of a considerable number of other diseases is almost the same in both. The present author has more recently identified the *āsrāva* of the AV. with later *atisāra* 'diarrhœa'; the *apacit* of the AV. with later *apacī* 'scrofulous sores', and the Atharvanic disease which is described (AV. 6. 25) as *manya* and *skandhya* with the 'Manskunder' (also a scrofulous affection), as reported upon the basis of the classical Śāstras by WISE, Hindu Medicine, p. 316[6]. From the other side the gap between classical and Atharvanic medicine, still a wide one, has also narrowed very materially. The early views of European scholars as to the fabulous antiquity of the Āyur-veda (1000 B. C.) was criticized especially by HAAS and ZIMMER, but their disposition of the chronology of classical medicine seems to have erred almost as much in the direction of too great a modernness as the earlier view in the direction of an impossible antiquity[7]. The recent discovery of the Bower ms. exhibits medical science at about the the fifth century A. D. in much the same condition and the same degree of development as in the medical Śāstras of Suśruta and Caraka, presupposing an evolution which must have lasted some centuries when compared with even the later Atharvanic medicine of the Kauśika[8]. The presence of foreign, especially Greek, influence in Hindu medicine has also been assumed on the ground of rather sparse points of resemblance[9], whereas on the other hand the influence of Hindu medicine upon early Arabic medicine, and through it upon European medicine in general, is guaranteed beyond peradventure. JOLLY's forthcoming elaboration of Hindu Medicin in this Encyclopedia will doubtless throw additional light on these and kindred questions[10].

The classification of the medical hymns of the AV. is difficult for various reasons: the meaning of the names of the diseases is often obscure; a great variety of unrelated diseases are often grouped in the same charm; the line between disease and possession by demons and demoniac influences is not drawn sharply; and the curative influences that are employed are either of the symbolic order, or consist of amulets instead of healing substances. These amulets are largely derived from the vegetable kingdom, the designation of the plants being again generally quite obscure. Good illustrations of the symbolic treatment are offered by the charm to cure jaundice (1. 22), and the brief charm against *takman* 'fever' (7. 116). In the former the yellow color of the patient is sent where it naturally belongs, to the yellow sun and yellow birds, the red color of the cow being substituted for the yellow; in the latter the hot fever is sent to the cool frog who may be supposed to find it enjoyable. On the other hand the *kuṣṭha*-plant that is implored to help against fever (5. 4; 19. 39), or the pepper-corn that is employed in the quaint charm against wounds (6. 109) cannot be supposed to owe their presence in these surroundings to any real medicinal properties. For all that a classification of the hymns yields a picture in vague outline of that same Hindu medicine that is treated so bulkily in the Śāstras and their descendant works. Clearest in expression are the hymns against *takman*, or fever, the *jvara* of the later medicine. The word *takman* does not occur outside of the AV. Four hymns, 1. 25; 5. 22; 6. 20; and 7.116, are devoted to its cure; two others, 5. 4 and 19. 39, are addressed to the plant *kuṣṭha* with special reference to the cure of this disease. Just as Suśruta designates fever as 'the king of diseases' so the *takman* seems in Atharvanic times to have been the most dreaded ailment. Its diagnosis seems to have been fairly searching and exact: the chief symptom is the alternation between heat and chills; it is intermittent, arriving either every day at the same time, every third day, or omitting every third day; and it is accompanied by jaundice which suggests true malarial fever, especially during the rainy season. It is associated with a variety of other diseases, headache, cough, *balāsa, udyuga,* and *pāman* 'itch' (also in the Avesta), the *takman's* 'brother's son'. Its most salient symptom, heat, suggests Agni 'fire' as the cause. It is generally cured by prayer and conjuration to which the Kauśika adds symbolic practices; the plant *kuṣṭha* and the tree *jaṅgiḍa* furnish amulets against it. Once (7. 116. 2) the cooling frog is suggested in the mantra, and applied in the corresponding practice of the Sūtra[11]. Closely associated with the *takman*-hymns is 1. 12, an interesting charm addressed to lightning (Agni) conceived as the cause of fever, headache, and cough[12]. To the cure of jaundice, frequently mentioned along with fever, 1. 22 is devoted independently; the symbolic proceedings indicated above are executed energetically in the practices of the Sūtra[13].

The ancient Vedic disease dropsy (*jalodara*, 'water-belly'), the infliction of Varuṇa in punishment of moral delinquency (*anṛta*), is represented by three hymns, 1. 10; 7. 83; and 6. 24. In the latter it seems coupled with heart-disease, an instance of good diagnosis. The cure indicated both in the hymns and sūtras is water which is used symbolically and with a touch of homœopathy[14]. Again, in another disease which suggests the presence of overabundant humors, water and water-procuring ants ('piss-ants') figure as the remedy, in the same symbolic-homœopathic way (attractio similium) as in the case of dropsy. The disease in question, *āsrāva*, is treated in 1. 2; 2. 3; and 6. 44; the commentators define it as *atisāra* 'diarrhœa' which is correct in the main, although perhaps excessive micturation and other excessive discharges may have been included primarily. One of these charms (1. 2) seems to have been originally a battle-charm, adapted by adding st. 4 to its present use[15]. Another (6. 44) appeals for help to an object called *viṣāṇakā*, either a plant or a horn (at any rate with punning intention: *vi ṣā* 'loosen')[16]. The converse of excessive discharges, namely constipation and retention of urine, is cured by 1. 3, and is accompanied by an interesting medical practice in Kauś. 25. 10—19. A disease whose vague description suggests either rheumatism or colic, due to the missiles of Rudra, is driven out with 6. 90: to this Kauś. 31. 7 adds homœopathically a spear-amulet to counteract the pains that seem as if from a spear. Diseases of the pulmonary order are exorcised in 6. 14, addressed to *balāsa*[17], and to cough (*kāsa*) in 6. 105; 7. 107. The terms *yakṣma, rājayakṣma*, and *ajñātayakṣma* (also *pāpayakṣma* in TS.) are in the later medicine applied to pulmonary diseases[18]; for the Vedic period this definition seems too narrow: AV. 2. 33 (RV. 10. 163); 3. 11; 9. 8; 19. 36; 44, etc. point to the more general meaning 'wasting disease', or 'disease in general'. Very curious and problematic is 6. 80, accompanying an oblation (*havis* in the technical sense: see below, § 60, end) to the sun, conceived as one of the two heavenly dogs. In the ritual this is treated as a cure for paralysis (*pakṣahata*, hemiplegia)[19]. Three charms are directed against *kṣetriya* 'inherited disease' (2. 8; 10; 3. 7); the symptoms of the *kṣetriya* are not described: the disease may have been of the scrofulous or syphilitic order. Other internal diseases are alluded to incidentally, or grouped in the panaceas (*sarvabhaiṣajya* of the commentators), especially in 2. 33; 9. 8; and 19. 44: cf. for these ZIMMER, p. 378 ff., and the item 'diseases' in the Index to SBE. XLII. 697.

To the cure of ills of a more external character, especially skin-diseases, a considerable number of charms address themselves. Leprosy (*kilāsa*) is cured in 1. 23 and 24 by applying black plants, *rajanī* and *śyāmā*, (allopathic symbolism); abcesses (*vidradha*) are mentioned with other diseases in 6. 127. 1;

9. 8. 20[20]. Of particular interest are the charms directed against scrofulous sores called *apacit* (later *apacī*), and related diseases: 6. 25; 6. 57; 7. 74. 1, 2; 7. 76. 1, 2; 7. 76. 3. Their character was misunderstood prior to the author's essay on this theme[21]. The sores, tumors, and pustules apparent in this disease are conjured in the hymns themselves to fall off, or fly away, because in the naive view of the folk they were supposed to have settled like birds upon the afflicted person. The Sūtra, however, treats the disease by drastic applications, and in one instance (6. 57) the famous remedy of Rudra, the *jālāṣa* (urine), is indicated as the remedy by the mantras themselves[22]. The cure of wounds and fractures is accomplished by two hymns (4. 12; 5. 5) which appeal to the plant called variously *arundhatī*, *lākṣā*, or *silācī*: the name *arundhatī* points towards a punning symbolic connection between the disease (*arus* 'wound') and the simple. The first of these two hymns has been compared by A. KUHN with the Merseburg charm, and many other similar productions from various Teutonic and Slavic sources[23]. The pepper-corn (*pippalī*) curiously figures in 6. 109 as a cure or preventive of the same trouble. Flow of blood is charmed to a stop by the pretty hymn 1. 17 which seems (st. 4) to indicate the use of a bandage or compress filled with sand[24]. The Brāhmaṇas and Sūtras mention types of Vedic lore designated as *sarpavidyā* and *viṣavidyā* 'science of serpents and of poisons'[25]. These so-called sciences similarly to *yātuvidyā*, *rakṣovidyā*, etc., are referable in the main to the AV. which presents many charms not only to keep serpents from the premises (below, § 57), but also for the cure of their poisonous bites. Such charms are 5. 13; 5. 16; 6. 12; 7. 56; and 7. 88; of these 5. 13 is of especial interest as containing many words founded upon the bed-rock of folk-lore, among others the word *tābuvam* which WEBER has identified with 'taboo', not, however, failing to recognize the attendant difficulties[26]. The importance of this particular phase of witchcraft is shown by the existence of the Gāruḍa-Upaniṣad which is nothing more than a charm against snake-bites, put into the mouth of Brahman, and elevated to the position of *brahmavidyā*[27]. In the Bengal Presidency alone the number of deaths from serpents bites in 1876 amounted to 11 416[28]. And there are also charms directed against poison not derived from serpents, 4. 6 (poisonous arrows); 4. 7; and 6. 100. In these cases water seems to be depended upon as a cure; of especial interest is 6. 100 in which the water-producing ants (*upajīkā*) yield the healing fluid[29]. The ritual reinforces these poison-charms with appeals to Takṣaka (Vaiśāleya), the serpent-good[30]. To the cure of worms (*krimi*) three charms are devoted: 2. 31 (worms in general); 2. 32 (worms in cattle); and 5. 33 (worms in children). Identical, or similar stanzas appear in many other texts, especially TA. and SV. Mantrabrāhmaṇa: A. KUHN has shown that the greatest variety of diseases are regarded in the naive view of folk-medicine as due to the presence of worms. This accounts for 'worms in the head' (2. 31. 4) 'the variegated worm, the four-eyed' (2. 32. 2), and the like[31]. The Sūtra presents complicated practices. The charm 6. 16, addressed to a substance called *ābayu*, which Kauśika identifies with mustard, is directed against ophthalmia; a disease of the eye, *alaji*, known in the later medicine[32], is mentioned 9. 8. 20. In the same hymn and elsewhere diseases of the ear are also mentioned (9. 8. 1, 2). Three lively, picturesque charms, 6. 21; 136; 137, cause hair to grow luxuriantly: 'With reins they had to be measured, with outstretched arms they had to be measured out. May thy hair grow as reeds, may it (cluster), black, about thy head!' (6. 137. 3). One of these charms (6. 136) is performed with the otherwise unknown plant *nitatnī*, 'she that takes root'; all three are accompanied in the Sūtra by fanciful symbolic

practices. Three charms, 4. 4; 6. 72; and 6. 101, in language not at all veiled, profess to promote virility (*śepaharṣaṇa*).

A maniac 'who, bound and well-secured, loudly jabbers' is exorcised in 6. 111. Insanity is due to possession by demons, especially the mind-bewildering Gandharvas and Apsaras[33]. At this point especially Atharvanic medicine passes over into demonology: the boundary-line between the two is rarely well-defined[34]. This class of hymns, therefore, is in close contact with those treated here in the third category. The rather romantic charm 4. 37 appeals to the plant 'goats-horn' (*ajaśṛṅgī*: comms., *meṣaśṛṅgī*, and *viṣāṇī*) to drive Rakṣas, Apsaras, and Gandharvas out of a possessed person. The choice of this particular plant is probably due in part or entirely to its meaning (etymological symbolism). Rakṣas and fits (*grāhi*) are driven out in 2. 9 with an amulet made from ten different kinds of holy (*śānta*) wood; demons and diseases in 19. 36 with another composite hundred-fold amulet. The last three charms have suggested analogies from Teutonic folk-lore[35]. Rakṣas and Piśācas are also exorcised in 4. 36 and 6. 32. The plant *pṛśniparṇī* is conjured, 2. 25, against the demon of disease called *kaṇva*, conceived especially as the devourer of the embryo in the womb. Suśruta still recommends the *pṛśniparṇī* as a preventive against miscarriage (*garbhasrāve*)[36]. Three charms, 2. 4; 19. 34; 35, addressed to an amulet derived from the *jaṅgiḍa*-tree, are directed against diseases and demons.

At another point the remedial charms pass over by imperceptible degrees into the class of the 'life-giving' charms (*āyuṣyāṇi*) of our second category. Special substances, or water and the plants in general, are implored for complete exemption from sickness (*sarvarogabhaiṣajya*, i. e., panaceas). Thus the *varaṇa*-tree (*var* 'protect') in 6. 25; the plant *kuṣṭha* in 6. 95; the *cīpudru*-tree in 6. 127; bdellium in 19. 38; barley and water in 6. 91; an amulet of salve (*āñjana*) in 19. 44. Or Soma and Rudra are appealed to in 7. 42 (RV. 6. 74. 2, 3); Vāta, the wind, in 4. 13 (RV. 10. 137), the so-called *śaṃtātīya*-hymn. Hymns and stanzas addressed to the waters, often not original in the AV., are used as panaceas (1. 4—6), or against some special disease, e. g., 6. 22, which the Sūtra prescribes against dropsy. Plants are similarly appealed to in 6. 96, and especially in the long hymn 8. 7 which counts upon the virtue of all possible magic and medicinal plants (analogous to the so-called *oṣadhi-stuti*, RV. 10. 97). Or, again, a hymn or stanza of general character is adapted as a *bhaiṣajyam*, as e. g. 7. 10 (RV. 1. 164. 49) which is prescribed for a child seized by the demon Jambha (convulsions) as it is being nursed by its mother (note the word *stana* in the st.). And there are hymns which aim to secure immunity from all diseases, real or fanciful, by simply driving them out by conjuration, naming them one after another, until the list is exhausted: 2. 33 (RV. 10. 163 = AV. 20. 96) and 9. 8 (cp. also 19. 44). We may finally note 2. 29, a charm for securing long life (*āyuṣya*), which Kauś. 27. 9—13 employs in a practice designed to transmit the disease of one seized by thirst (*tṛṣṇāgṛhīta*) upon another person. St. 6 seems to accord with this transference, vaguely suggesting modern transfusion[37].

Roth, Zur Litteratur und Geschichte des Weda, p. 37; Grohmann, IS. IX. 381 ff.; WL.[2], 33 (cp. 283 ff.); Weber, Die Griechen in Indien, SPAW., 1890, p. 924 ff.; Ludwig, Der RV., III. 343; Zimmer, p. 374 ff. (cp. Kaegi, Jahrbücher für classische Philologie, 1880, p. 464 ff.); Bloomfield, SBE. XLII, p. 1—48, and the notes corresponding; Winternitz, Folk-Medicine in Ancient India, Nature, vol. LVIII, p. 233 ff. (July 7, 1898).

1 This definition touches upon the important division of the Atharvan into two Vedas, Ātharvaṇa (*śānta, bheṣaja*), and Āṅgirasa (*ghora, ābhicārika*): see above, p. 8 ff.;

SBE. XLII, p. XVIII ff.; HILLEBRANDT, Ritual-Litteratur, p. 169, 177. Good and evil magic are distinguished at all times, e. g., in the Mahābhārata: HOPKINS, JAOS. XIII. 312, 365. By the side of this stands the three-fold distinction of the ritualistic manuals: *ābhicārika*, *śāntika*, and *pauṣṭika*; see MADHUSŪDANASARASVATĪ, IS. I. 16; BLOOMFIELD, Seven Hymns, AJPh. VII. 477; HILLEBRANDT, ibid. p. 169; cp. Rig-vidhāna 1. 1. 3, and, MEYER, Introduction, p. XII. — [2] HILLEBRANDT, l. c. 181. Cp. MEYER, Rig-vidhāna, Introduction, p. XIII. — [3] BLOOMFIELD, Seven Hymns, AJPh. VII. 467 ff.; Contributions. Second Series, AJPh. XI. 320 ff. — [4] See Vend. 20—22 (especially 20. 4; SBE. IV. 221, note); SPIEGEL, Die Arische Periode, p. 97, 155, 170, 204; GEIGER, Civilization of the Eastern Iranians, p. 215 ff. Avestan *pāman* = Ved. *pāman* 'itch' is the apparently solitary instance of the identical nomenclature of a disease. — [5] A. KUHN, KZ. XIII, pp. 49—74, and 113—157; L. v. SCHROEDER, Indien's Litteratur, p. 175 ff.; SBE. XLII, p. 313, 386, 454; cp. PICTET, KZ. V. 337 (antiquated). The use of the frog against fever may also reach back to prehistoric beginnings; see GROHMANN, IS. IX. 386, 414; SBE XLII. 565 ff.; JAOS. XVII. 173. — [6] AJPh. VII. 467 ff.; XI. 320 ff. — [7] HAAS, ZDMG. XXX. 617 ff.; XXXI. 647 ff.; ZIMMER, 374 ff.; WL.[2], 286 (and, Nachtrag, p. 13 ff.); L. v. SCHROEDER, l. c. 730 ff.; WEBER, SPAW., 1890, p. 924 ff. — [8] HOERNLE, PBAS., April 1890; JBAS., 1891, p. 139 ff.; ROTH, WZKM. V. 303; BÜHLER, ibid. 102 ff., 302 ff.; JOLLY, Festgruss an Roth, p. 18; WZKM. XI. 164 ff. — [9] ROTH, ZDMG. XXVI. 448; WEBER, SPAW., 1890, p. 29. — [10] Connected treatises on classical Hindu Medicine: WL.[2], p. 283 ff.; v. SCHROEDER, l. c. 729 ff. The most convenient digest of Hindu Medicine based upon native literature is still, WISE, Commentary on the Hindu System of Medicine[2], 1860 (regrettably without an index). For purposes of comparison see the list of diseases and plants (many medicinal) in the index of SBE. XLII, p. 697 and 702. — [11] WEBER, IS. IV. 119; GROHMANN, IS. IX. 381 ff.; ZIMMER, p. 379 ff.; HARDY, Die Vedisch-Brahmanische Periode, p. 198; BLOOMFIELD, SBE. XLII, p. 441 ff., 565 ff.; cp. WISE, p. 219 ff. — [12] AJPh. VII, p. 469 ff.; SBE. XLII. 7, 246 ff. — [13] SBE. XLII. 263 ff. — [14] SBE. XLII. 11 ff., 241, 471, 562, and cp. Index, under 'attractio similium', and, 'homœopathy'. — [15] SBE. XLII. 233 (cp. AJPh. VII. 467). — [16] AJPh. XII. 426 ff.; SBE. XLII. 481. — [17] SBE. XLII. 450 shows that the exact nature of *balāsa* is not defined by the texts. — [18] WISE, p. 210, 321 ff.; GROHMANN, IS. IX. 400; ZIMMER, p. 376 ff. — [19] JAOS. XV. 163 ff.; SBE. XLII. 500 ff. — [20] ZIMMER, p. 386; WISE, p. 210. — [21] Contributions. Second Series, AJPh. XI. 320 ff. Cp. the commentary on these stanzas in SBE. XLII. — [22] Contributions. Fourth Series, AJPh. 425 ff.; SBE. XLII. 489. — [23] See note 5. — [24] St. 1 with interesting variants occurs in Yāska's Nirukta 3. 4. — [25] ŚB. 10. 5. 2. 20; 13. 4. 3. 9; ŚŚ. 16. 2. 15; AŚ. 10. 7. 5; Chānd. Up. 7. 1. 2 ff. Cp. RV. 7. 50, and, Rig-vidhāna 1. 2. 5; 27. 1; 28. 1—3. — [26] SPAW. 1896, p. 681—4; 873—5; Festschrift für A. Bastian, p. 361—6. Cp. now IS. XVIII. 215. — [27] JACOB, Eleven Ātharvaṇa-Upaniṣads, p. 83—88; WEBER, IS. XVII. 161 ff.; DEUSSEN, Sechzig Upanishad's, p. 627 ff. — [28] WEBER, ibid. p. 167. — [29] BLOOMFIELD, Seven Hymns of the AV., AJPh. VII. 482 ff.; SBE. XLII. 511. — [30] SBE. XLII. 374; WEBER, SPAW., 1896, p. 684 note, 875. — [31] A. KUHN, KZ. XIII. 49 ff., 113 ff.; ZIMMER, p. 393; SBE. XLII. 22 ff., 313 ff.; cp. WISE, p. 307, 348 ff. — [32] WISE, p. 296; ZIMMER, p. 390. — [33] See the note on 6. 111. 4, SBE. XLII. 520. Cp. IS. I. 217, note. — [34] Cp. Suśruta 1. 89. 19, *daivabalapravṛttā ye devadrohād abhiśastakā atharvakṛtā upasargakṛtāś ca* (*vyādhayaḥ*). — [35] SBE. XLII. 409 and 291. — [36] Ibid. 302. — [37] Ibid. 308, 310.

§ 51. Class 2). Prayers for long life and health (*āyuṣyāṇi*). — The second class of hymns to which tradition fittingly assigns the name *āyuṣyāṇi* (sc. *sūktāni*)[1] is not separated by hard and fast lines from the medicinal charms. Thus 19. 44, though it exhibits in the main the characteristics of an *āyuṣyam*, mentions specifically a considerable list of diseases; or 3. 11 which also mentions diseases is employed, Kauś. 27. 32—33, in an interesting symbolic practice directed against *grāmya vyādhi*: the commentators pretty consistently explain this as venereal disease[2]. Throughout the *śrauta* and *gṛhya*-texts are found in enormous quantity formulas and stanzas which pray for life (*āyus*), life's breath (*prāṇa*, etc.). and incidentally for all other desiderata, such as *varcas*, *bala*, *yaśas*, *kīrti* (strength and glory), cattle and other property. In the forthcoming Vedic Concordance the formulas and pādas beginning alone with the words *āyus* and *dīrgha* (*āyus*), or derivatives from these words, number 200 or more[3]. The characteristic feature of such formulas, as also of the *āyuṣyāṇi* in the AV., is not so much prayer for the cure of disease as the eager endeavor to secure life unto the ideal old age of a hundred years[4] for a person, either a sacrificer, or still more frequently, a boy entering adult life through the various ceremonial stages attendant upon the development of the young Hindu from birth to confirmation (*upanayana*). Hence these hymns are employed very properly in the Atharvan ritual under the rubric of *āyuṣyāṇi* (sc. *karmāṇi*), beginning Kauś. 52. 18, and containing the ceremonies of tonsure (*cūḍākarman*), shearing of the beard (*godāna*), and the *upanayana*. The Gṛhya-sūtras exhibit them in much the same way on the same occasions: the Atharvan materials show little originality and frequently coincide with the mantras of the other Saṃhitās. A survey of one or two of these charms, e. g. 2. 28 or 3. 11, discloses at once the very familiar catch-words of the entire class: they ask for life (*āyus, jīvana, asu, prāṇāpānau*); it shall last a hundred years (*śataśārada, śataṃ himāḥ, śatāyus*); death shall not come until old age (*jaras, jarā, jariman, jarāmṛtyu, jaradaṣṭi*); the charm shall protect against the regrettably large number of deaths, 100 or more (*mṛtyavo ... śataṃ ye*, 2. 28. 1; *anye mṛtyavo yān āhur itarāṃ chatam*, 3. 11. 7; *ekaśatam*, 8. 2. 27): 101 deaths are still remembered by Suśruta (Āyur-veda 1. 122. 10) as a characteristic conception of the AV., *ekottaraṃ mṛtyuśatam atharvāṇaḥ pracakṣate* (cp. SBE. XLII, p. 307); finally, Yama, Mṛtyu, Antaka, Nirṛti, etc. are cajoled with politenesses and obeisance. Of course this technique is by no means restricted to the *āyuṣyāṇi*; not only is it exhibited *a fortiore* by the medicinal charms, but also the charms for prosperity in general and the witchcraft-charms naturally avail themselves of it. Yet it is unmistakably the specialty of this class: the Sūtra and the Atharvan scholiasts deserve credit for defining it schematically and presenting the employment of the hymns in question in the very situations to which they owed their composition at least in a large measure.

A noteworthy characteristic of these hymns is the special prominence of Agni, whereby hangs a bit of ancient mythological history. Agni himself is Āyu 'alive'; the personal Āyu of the myths and legends, notably Āyu, the son of Purūravas and Urvaśī, is not likely ever to divulge his true nature without the same naturalistic back-ground[5]. Hence the *āyuṣya*-hymns place life in the special charge of Agni, without, of course, excluding other divinities. In the Yajus-texts, Gṛhya-sūtras, and Upaniṣads also Agni is frequently associated with life's breaths[6]. Typical for the AV. is 7. 53. 6, *āyur no viśvato dadhad ayam agnir vareṇyaḥ*. The hymns 2. 13; 28; 29; 7. 32 and other scattered stanzas furnish illustrations of this point. Otherwise the absence of salience of these hymns is relieved only by the association with them of life-bestowing, and life-protecting amulets which are in the main truly Atharvanic. The golden amulet which the Dākṣāyaṇas, rich in the possession of gold, fastened upon Śatānīka (1. 35) is such a one[7]; an amulet of gold is used also with 19. 26. Salve (*āñjana*) figures in 4. 9; 19. 44; 45; the pearl and its shell in 4. 10; the *pūtudru*-tree in 8. 2; an amulet addressed as *astṛta* 'unconquered'[8] in 19. 46. Similarly the sacred girdle (*mekhalā*) furnishes the basis of an *āyuṣyam* in 6. 133; and the shearing of the beard is turned into a life-giving ceremony in 6. 68. Quaintly does the hymn 3. 31 solder together a mixtum compositum to the same end out of a variety of psycho-physical and mythological reminiscences[9]. The hymns 8. 1 and 2, employed Kauś. 58. 3, 11 in special ceremonies called *brāhmaṇoktam* and *ṛṣihasta* (parts of the *upanayana*), are Atharvanesque by virtue of their impassioned fervor and great length. The relationship of this type with the prose formulas of the Yajus and the

Gṛhyas betrays itself in the so-called hymns 2. 15—17; 5. 9; the prose formulas that go to make up 19. 51; 60; 61; 67 occur in these texts also[10]. The remaining *āyuṣya*-hymns are devoid of either mythological or antiquarian interest (1. 30; 3. 11; 5. 28; 30; 6. 41; 53; 19. 24; 27; 58; 70), and glide over imperceptibly into a style of hymn which is not strictly *āyuṣya*, being regarded otherwise (*pauṣṭika*: our class 8, § 57) by the Sūtra. They are in reality not different in their general purpose (1. 31; 4. 13; 6. 5; 13; 16. 4; 19. 30; 32; 33; see also the long so-called *viṣāsahi*-hymn, book 17).

[1] See SBE. XLII. 49 ff., and notes; Kauśika, Index B, p. 383[n], s. v. *āyuṣyāṇi*; cp. MEYER, Rig-vidhāna, Introduction, p. XII, under the heading 'longa vita'; Svidh. 2. 1; PG. 1. 16. 5 ff. — [2] SBE. XLII. 341. — [3] We refer to the formulas of the type, *āyur me dehi*; *āyuḥ prāṇaṃ me dhukṣva*; *āyuṣpā agne 'sy āyur me pāhi*; *dīrghāyutvāya śataśāradāya*; etc. — [4] WEBER, IS. XVII. 193 ff.; Festgruss an Rudolf von Roth, p. 137. — [5] BERGAIGNE, La Religion Védique, I. 59 ff.; II. 91 ff.; RV. 4. 2. 18, *martānāṃ cid urvaśīr akṛpran vṛdhe cid arya uparasyāyoḥ* 'for mortals even many Urvaśīs ('fire-sticks') were prepared (root *kṛp* = *klp*) unto the production of the noble Āyu ('fire') below'. Purūravas and Urvaśī suggest the fire-sticks; Āyu is their son: VS. 5. 2; TS. 1. 3. 7. 1; 6. 3. 5. 3; MS. 1. 2. 7; 3. 9. 5; ŚB. 3. 4. 1. 22; KŚ. 5. 1. 30; ĀpŚ. 7. 12. 13; Kauś. 69. 20. The expression *bahavo me samānāḥ*, used by Āyu, MS. 1. 6. 12, refers to the many individual productions of fire; cp. the brothers of Agni. See now BLOOMFIELD, JAOS. XX. 180 ff. Differently GELDNER, Ved. Stud. I. 243 ff., especially 283. — [6] E. g. VS. 3. 17; TS. 1. 5. 5. 3; 7. 4; ŚB. 2. 3. 4. 19; ŚŚ. 2. 11. 3; PG. 2. 4. 8; Praśna Up. 1. 7; Maitri Up. 6. 5, 9, 33; cp. SBE. XLII. 366. — [7] ŚB. 6. 7. 4. 2; WEBER, IS. IV. 358, 430. Cp. Rvidh. 4. 9. 1. — [8] Sāyaṇa, *astṛtanāmākhyamaṇi*. — [9] JAOS. XV. 181 ff.; SBE. XLII. 364 ff. — [10] Hymns 19. 60 and 61 in TS. 5. 5. 9. 2; GB. 2. 1. 3; TA. (Āndhra) 10. 72; ĀpŚ. 3. 20. 3; PG. 1. 3. 25; Vait. 3. 14. Hymn 67 frequently in the Gṛhya-sūtras.

§ 52. **Class 3). Imprecations against demons, sorcerers, and enemies (*ābhicārikāṇi* and *kṛtyāpratiharaṇāni*).**—The third class of hymns is directed against demons, sorcerers, and enemies[1]: between hostile human sorcerers and dangerous demons the Atharvanic Hindu knows no distinction, as may be seen from 2. 18, where the *bhrātṛvya*, *sapatna*, *arāya*, *piśāca*, and *sadānvā* are successively placed under the same ban. The delimitation of this class is again somewhat uncertain and subjective. On the side of demonology it touches upon the first class, because the remedial charms are not unfrequently directed against possession by demons. In so far as it is composed of imprecations and sorceries against enemies it concatenates with the royal rites (class 6, § 55) whose battle-charms assail the enemy in essentially identical terms; with the imprecations of Brahmans against those that neglect and oppress them (class 7, § 56); with the love-practices of women, in so far as they are calculated to undermine rivals (class 4, § 53); and with the charms designed to secure influential position in the community and superiority in general (class 5, § 54), inasmuch as here also rivalry is expressed or implied. The present class covers however the central ground of what is known as *abhicāra* and *yātuvidyā* (*rakṣovidyā*), the terrible side (*ghora*) of this Veda. A wide-spread tradition reaching back to the Vedic hymns themselves associates this part of the Veda with the semi-divine race of the Aṅgiras: such charms are known as the *aṅgirasaḥ*, the second part of the old designation of the AV. (*atharvāṅgirasaḥ*); the term Āṅgirasa-veda also occurs[2]. All this in distinction from the *atharvāṇaḥ* (Ātharvaṇa-veda) which refers to the auspicious charms and practices (*bheṣaja*, *śānta*, and *pauṣṭika*)[3]. The term *abhicāra* is generic; the Atharvan and other Vedic texts know in addition *kṛtyā* 'spell', *valaga* 'secret spell', and *mūla-karman* (*-kriyā*) 'practices with the roots of plants', performances undertaken more drastically with tangible objects: magic or spells are placed or hidden in places where they may most injure. The hymn 10. 1 represents the *kṛtyā* as an elaborate effigy (bogey) with head, nose, and ears; the ritual is well acquainted with similar artful devices[4]. The Vedic texts, and more schematically the later Vidhāna-literature, present terms, which assume growingly a technical flavor, for a variety of special phases of sorcery: *sapatnabādhana, nairbādha, vināśana, pīḍana, māraṇa, vaśīkaraṇa, vidveṣaṇa, mohana, stambhana, cātana, uccāṭana,* etc.; these are grouped variously as the systematic subdivisions of *abhicāra*[5]. The Atharvan makes further the important distinction between sorcery which takes the initiative (*abhicāra*), and defensive, or retaliative sorcery; the latter merely repels the practices undertaken by others (*pratyabhicaraṇa, pratisara,* and *pratīvarta*). In the later systematization (e. g. Rig-vidhāna 4. 6. 4; 8. 3) the term *āṅgirasa* = *ābhicārika* is modulated similarly into *pratyāṅgirasa* = *pratyabhicaraṇa*[6].

All India is pervaded by sorcery from the RV. (7. 104; 10. 84; 128; 155) through the Yajus-literature, and, curiously enough, also the Upaniṣads[7], through the systematic Vidhāna-texts to the Tantras of the worshippers of Śakti. Especially the Yajus and Śrauta-texts frequently abandon for a moment their main theme in keen remembrance of 'him that hates us and whom we hate'[8]. This is done either by imparting to one or another sacrificial act a sinister turn by a conscious symbolic modification of the practice, or in the course of the so-called *kāmyeṣṭayaḥ*, many of which are directed against enemies. Thus the formulas of the ritual-literature are quite frequently identical with, or similar to prose passages of the *abhicāra*-hymns of the AV.: in addition to the formula, *yo asmān dveṣṭi yaṃ ca vayaṃ dviṣmaḥ*, we may mention especially those of the type, *idam ahaṃ taṃ valagam ut kirāmi*[9], or the very common form, *idam aham amum āmuṣyāyaṇam amuṣyāḥ putram* (etc., with sinister close)[10]. Thus the *abhicāra*-litany AV. 2. 19—23 is developed secondarily in accordance with specific Atharvanic cosmogonic ideas[11] out of formulas in MS. 1. 5. 2; ApŚ. 6. 21. 1. In judging the chronology of the Atharvan collection in its finished aspect it is important to note that these formulas certainly existed in Vedic literature outside of Atharvanic schools, and prior to any Atharvan redaction. The practice of sorcery, if not its imprecations, goes back at least to Indo-Iranian times (Avestan *yātu*)[12].

The class of *abhicāra*-hymns in which the offending power is rather of the demoniac sort is represented by the following: 1. 7; 8; and 28 are directed against Yātudhāna, Kimīdin (Atrin), Piśāca, etc.; in the first two the incantation endeavours especially to make the Yātudhānas come out and proclaim their true character: as soon as they reveal their nature they become innocuous. The demoniac brood is attacked 1. 16 with lead which is regarded as especially offensive to demons[13]. Lead figures also in the elaborate exorcism of Agni Kravyād, the funeral fire, personified as a demon, 12. 2. On founding a family, or when the domestic fire is lighted after the funeral of the father, Agni Kravyād is conjured by assigning to him his own proper substances: lead, reeds, a black sheep, and beans (Kauś. 71. 6 ff.). A similar rite is untertaken with sts. 13, 14 in a variant form at ApŚ. 9. 3. 22; cp. the use of beans, Ovid. Fast. 429—444[14]. Here belongs also the elaborate conjuration of numerous obscure evil demons (hocus-pocus of the lowest bathos) 8. 6, designed apparently to secure safe delivery of women (see below, § 53). Demons (or diseases) called *viṣkandha* and *kābava* are exorcised in 3. 9 with a certain amulet which Kauśika derives from the *aralu*-tree, and which is fastened by a reddish-brown thread. A variety of female demons (*sadānvā*; cp. RV. 10. 155), very obscure as to their individual designations, are conceived as hostile to men, cattle, and home; they are driven out by means of 2. 14. An amulet derived from a certain keen-sighted, keen-eyed plant in the nature of a sun-flower, known to the ritual as *sadampuṣpā*, makes visible, ergo impotent, all sorts of demons in 4. 20: it 'sees here, sees yonder, sees in the distance, sees'..., and therefore 'drags out from his retreat the sorcerer and the Kimīdin'[15]. The *apāmārga*-plant, by virtue of its superficial etymology (*apa marj* 'wipe out'), as well as certain peculiarities of its natural history, here as in the Śrauta-texts[16], is appealed to against the same uncanny powers: three charms, 4. 17—19 (cp. also 7. 65), are addressed to it. More conventional are 6. 2; 34; and 52, directed against Rakṣas: they recur for the most part in the RV. and elsewhere. The prose hymns 2. 18 and 2. 19—23 (see above) efface the hazy boundary-line between demons and human enemies.

Charms directed against human enemies are more numerous: they are at times quite general and colorless; more frequently they are specialized by addressing some definite divinity, or some plant or other substance in the nature of a protective amulet, or instrument of attack. Thus 6. 37; 7. 13 and 59 are mere curses; 5. 29; 7. 34; 8. 3 (= RV. 10. 87, to Agni Rakṣohan); 19. 65; 66 are addressed to Agni; 7. 110 to Indra and Agni (battle-gods); 7. 31 to Indra; 7. 91; 92 to Indra Sutrāman; 7. 51 to Indra and Bṛhaspati; 8. 4 to Indra and Soma (RV. 7. 104); 6. 6 to Bṛhaspati and Soma; 7. 75 to the Marut Sāṃtapanas (RV. 7. 59; TS. 4. 3. 13. 3): the sts. of these hymns recur largely in the other Saṃhitās and are conventionally Vedic, not especially Atharvanic. More pointed are those with amulets and other instruments: 1. 29, secondarily made up of sts. from RV. 1. 174 and 159, attacks the enemy *abhīvartena maṇinā*[17] 'with the victorious amulet'; similarly 6. 75 with *nairbādhyaṃ havis* 'the oblation of suppression'; and 3. 6 with an amulet of *aśvattha* which has the epithet *vaibādha* 'displacer'. A certain plant 'god-begotten, hated by the wicked, which wipes out the curses (of enemies)' is conjured in 2. 7; the *talāśā*-tree similarly in 6. 15; the *varaṇa*-tree (*var* 'defend'; cp. 6. 85) in the long hymn 10. 3; an amulet formed in the likeness of a plough out of the hard *khadira*-tree, which was used also in the manufacture of real plough-shares[18], is implored both for prosperity and destruction of enemies in 10. 6; and *darbha*-grass serves the same end, 19. 28; 29; 30; 32; 33. In 6. 134 a staff (*vajra*) is used in sorcery against enemies; and 6. 135 conjures one's own food and drink 'to drink away' and 'swallow up' the life's breath of the enemy. Very characteristic, though somewhat obscure, are the two imprecations 7. 95 and 96, directed against the two kidneys of an enemy: the point seems to be to stop their action so as to cause retention of urine. The second of these charms (7. 96) seems however to have been composed originally as a medical charm for the cure of a movable kidney, having been adapted secondarily to a hostile purpose[19]. Decidedly loftier in tone and original in the AV. is the famous, oft-translated hymn 4. 16, a prayer to Varuṇa for protection against treacherous designs, whose fervor and ethical coloring suggests irresistibly scriptural parallels, especially from the Psalms[20]; equally interesting is 2. 12, known in the ritual as 'the cleaver of Bharadvāja'. This was for a long time misunderstood as depicting a fire-ordeal, but it is in reality an imprecation against an enemy thwarting holy work[21]. Conversely, 5. 8 and 7. 70 engage in this very impious practice, namely the frustration of the sacrifice of an enemy: 'Nirṛti, allying herself with death, shall smite his offering before it takes effect' (7. 70. 1). Closely related with these is the so-called *vihavya*-hymn 5. 3 (= RV. 10. 128; TS. 4. 7. 14[22]): its name is derived from the word *vihava*, translated in the lexicons rather loosely by 'call'. It means 'call in different directions', 'conflicting call'; the hymn is a good specimen of an early witchcraft practice, designed to attract the gods away from others to one's own sacrifice. In the *śrauta*-ritual the same notion is present vividly in the conflict of sacrifices called *saṃsava*, or *vispardhā*[23]. An especially Atharvanic flavor attaches to 7. 5 which is devoted to the extravagant praise of this same (*vihavya*) hymn. The gods performed the human sacrifice (*puruṣamedha*), but mightier than that is the *vihavya*-sacrifice: in vain[24] did they sacrifice a dog, in vain the limbs of a cow, the *vihavya* alone availed them (sts. 4, 5). Very characteristic, too, is the blend of witchcraft with original theosophic conceptions in the hymn to Kāma, 'the bull that slays the enemy', 9. 2: *kāma* 'love' is originally a cosmic force (RV. 10. 129. 4 = AV. 19. 52. 1), but its personification as a supreme being suggests very soon his power to protect those who worship him, and to destroy the enemies of the worshipper (cp. below, § 59).

The class of 'counter-witchcraft' charms (*kṛtyāpratiharaṇa*)[25] is characterized especially by the word *prati* and derivatives and compounds from it, e. g. *pratyabhicaraṇa* 2.11.2; *pratisara* and *pratīvarta*, 8.5.1,4; *pratyañc* and *pratīcīna* 10.1.6. The persons against whom these defensive charms are directed are designated, 5. 31. 12, as *kṛtyākṛt* 'he that fashions spells', *valagin* 'he that digs for magic purposes', *mūlin* 'he that digs after roots', and *śapatheyya* 'he that emits curses' (cp. 4. 9. 5). A good specimen of the style of these defensive charms is 10. 1. 6: 'Pratīcīna ('Back-hurler'), the descendant of Aṅgiras, is our overseer and Purohita: do thou drive back (*pratīcīḥ*) the spells, and yonder fashioners of the spells!' Two of these charms (2.11; 8.5) are undertaken with the *srāktya*-amulet, derived from the *sraktya*-tree (schol. *tilaka*)[26]; another (5. 14) is addressed to a plant whose name is not stated; yet another, 2.24, names four male *kimīdin* and four female *kimīdinī* with curious, at times euphemistic designations, and calls upon their sorceries to turn against themselves, that is, against the perpetrators of these sorceries. Especially forceful is 5.31, containing a long catalogue of homely animate or inanimate objects within which spells were instituted: an unburned vessel, grain, raw meat; the cock, goat, and other animals; the *gārhapatya*-fire, house-fire, house, assembly-hall, gaming-place; the army, the drum, the arrow, and the weapon; the well, and the burial-place. A spell in the nature of a terrifying, evil-working figure (bug-bear, bogey, bogle; German popanz) 'endowed with nose, endowed with ears, and multiform', 'prepared by a Rāja, prepared by a woman, prepared by Brahmans', is driven out, under protestation of great loathing and fear, in 10. 1. Prose formulas similar to those enumerated Kauś. 49. 7 ff. are banded together as hymns for the same purposes in 4. 40 and 5. 10. Curse personified is invoked against him that curses in 6. 37 and 7. 59.

[1] LUDWIG, Der Rig-Veda, III. 338 ff.; BURNELL, Sāmavidhāna-Brāhmaṇa, Introduction, p. XXII ff.; MEYER, Rig-vidhāna, Introduction, p. XIII ff.; HARDY, Die Vedisch-Brahmanische Periode, p. 193 ff.; OLDENBERG, Die Religion des Veda, p. 262 ff.; 476 ff.; HILLEBRANDT, Ritual-Litteratur, p. 167 ff.; 174 ff.; BLOOMFIELD, SBE. XLII, p. 64 ff., and notes; MAGOUN, AJPh. X. 165 ff.; WINTERNITZ, Witchcraft in Ancient India, New World, September 1898. — [2] See the elaboration of this view, SBE. XLII, p. XVIII ff.; above, p. 8 ff.; cp. HILLEBRANDT, l. c. 169. — [3] The frequent legends in the Brāhmaṇas, narrating the conflict between the Aṅgiras and the Ādityas in connection with sacrificial performances, generally (not so AB. 6.34 ff.) represent the Ādityas as the pious, ultimately successful sacrificers, whereas the Aṅgiras appear in a light similar to the Asuras in the so-called *daivāsurāṇi* (sc. *ākhyānāni*), i. e. they are worsted in the conflict: WEBER, IS. I. 292; IStr. III. 80; SPAW, 1891, p. 811 ff. This also reflects perhaps, in a roundabout way, the wizard, impious character of the Aṅgiras, and correspondingly the connection of holy rites with the Ādityas. Cp. the *śuklāni yajūṃṣi* = *ādityāni* in the ŚB. (WEBER, l. c. p. 812, note 2). In the Yajus-formulas, however, both Aṅgiras and Ādityas are venerable: MS. 1. 6. 1 (86. 7); 1. 6. 2 (87. 3); ĀpŚ. 5. 11. 7; Kauś. 70. 6. — [4] See Kauśika, Introduction, p. XLVII, s. v. *āvalekhanī* (*pratikṛti*), and SBE. XLII, Index, under 'effigy'. Cp. HILLEBRANDT, l. c. 177. Practices with roots are ex-

pressly forbidden in the Dharma-texts, and execrated in the Mahābhārata; SBE. XLII, p. L, LIV (cp. above, § 26, 27). — 5 GOLDSTÜCKER, Sanskrit Dictionary, s. v. *abhicāra*; MEYER, Rig-vidhāna, Introduction, p. 13 ff.; WEBER, IS. III. 156; Verz. I. 270 ff.; II. 318, 1184; HILLEBRANDT, l. c. 177, note 1. — 6 See AV. 2. 11. 1; Kauśika, Index B, s. v. *kṛtyāpratiharaṇāni* (cp. AV. 5. 14). For *pratisara* and *prativarta* see SBE. XLII. 576; WEBER, APAW. 1893, p. 18; for *pratyāṅgirasa*, SBE. XLII, p. XIX, and above, p. 8. — 7 See ŚB. 14. 9. 4. 10 = Bṛh. Ār. Up. 6. 4. 12; and cp. the Gāruḍopaniṣad. — 8 BURNELL, l. c. XXIII; L. v. SCHROEDER, Indiens Litteratur, p. 121 ff. — 9 VS. 5. 23; TS. 1. 3. 2. 1; MS. 1. 2. 10; ApS. 11. 11. 8, etc. — 10 E. g. MS. 4 7. 9 (106. 3); ApŚ. 14. 6. 12. — 11 See above, § 45. — — 12 SPIEGEL, Die Arische Periode, p. 218 ff.; GEIGER, Civilization of the Eastern Iranians, I. 160 ff. — 13 SBE. XLII. 256. — 14 LUDWIG, Der Rig-Veda, III. 479; HENRY, Les Livres X—XII, p. 188 ff., 227 ff. Cp. SBE. XLII, Index, under 'beans' and 'sesame'. — 15 SBE. XLII. 68, 398 ff.; Contributions. Seventh Series, AJPh. XVII. 402 ff. — 16 VS. 35. 11; ŚB. 13. 8. 4. 4. Cp. e. g. the *apāmārga-homa* at the Rājasūya: WEBER, APAW., 1893, p. 17 ff., and the indexes to OLDENBERG, Religion des Veda (*apāmārga*), and SBE. XLII ('plants and trees'). — 17 RV. 1. 174. 1, *abhīvartena haviṣā*. It is not easy to decide which reading is older, as does WEBER, IS. IV. 423, note, in favor of *haviṣā*: both *maṇi* and *havis* are characteristically Atharvanic. See for the *havis*-hymns, below, § 60, end. The hymn is known as the *abhīvartam* (sc. *sūktam*), ApŚ. 14. 19. 6; 20. 1; AG. 3. 12. 12; Kauś. 16. 29. — 18 See the authorities for this construction, SBE. XLII. 608 ff. — 19 LUDWIG, Der Rig-Veda, III. 343, 344, 517; HENRY, Le livre VII, p. 38 ff., 109 ff. Differently, WEBER, IS. V. 247. — 20 SBE. XLII, p. 88, 389 ff. — 21 Contributions. Second Series, AJPh. XI. 330 ff.; SBE. XLII. 89, 244 ff. — 22 Also *vihavīya*, KŚ. 25. 14. 18. See TS. 3. 1. 7. 3; PB. 9. 4. 14; LŚ. 4. 10. 8. In Kauś. 38. 26 this hymn is recited secondarily but significantly by a father who is about to divide his property, so that no quarrels shall ensue. — 23 See HILLEBRANDT, Soma, p. 119 ff.; Ritual-Litteratur, p. 166; GARBE, Vaitāna, Translation, 16. 6; 17. 7, notes. Cp. TS. 2. 4. 1—3. — 24 HENRY's emendation of *mugdhā* to *mūrdhnā* (Le livre VII, p. 2, 49) thus becomes unnecessary. — 25 SBE. XLII. 70—80, and the notes on the hymns there rendered. Cp. Kauś. 39. 7, and HILLEBRANDT, Ritual-Litteratur, p. 178. — 26 Seven Hymns, AJPh. VII. 477 ff.; SBE. XLII. 575.

§ 53. Class 4). Charms pertaining to women (strīkarmāṇi). — The scheme of the Atharvan ritual makes provision for a class of practices aptly designated as 'womens' rites' (*strīkarmāṇi*): they are treated connectedly in the second half of the fourth book of Kauśika (32. 28 to the end of the book). The practices there work up very intelligently a quite considerable number of hymns scattered through the first seven books of the AV. (in addition only 8. 6); these are sufficiently marked to entitle them to treatment in a class by themselves[1]. In the centre of these hymns stand the wedding-stanzas of the *sūryā-sūkta* (RV. 10. 85) whose superior length and importance, however, calls for a separate presentation and a separate account of the practices connected with them, in the 14th book of the AV. and the 10th book of Kauśika[2]. The eventful life of women before, during, and after marriage has given rise to many practices and charms which are naturally ignored by the main current of Vedic tradition, the Śrauta-literature, but are fitly embodied in the Atharvan and the Gṛhya-sūtras. The RV. in addition to the wedding-stanzas (10. 85; also 10. 40, and elsewhere) has a number of such charms in the 10th book (145, 159, 162, 183); in the Śrauta-literature passages like TS. 2. 3. 9. 1; MS. 2. 3. 2; TB. 2. 3. 10 (love-charms), or ŚB. 14. 9. 4 = Bṛh. Ār. Up. 6. 4, devoted to women, attract attention by their rareness and comparative incompatibility with their surroundings. The Gṛhya-rites are also restricted in the main to the more normal auspicious feminine practices: wedding ceremonies, and the holy performances (*saṃskāras*) connected with pregnancy and child-birth. A sorcery-practice like ApG. 3. 9. 4 ff. (Mantrapāṭha 1. 15 = RV. 10. 145 = AV. 3. 18), designed to cut out the co-wives or rivals of a woman, is rare and has quite the Atharvanic flavor. Similarly HG. 1. 14. 7; ApG. 8. 23. 3. The later Vidhāna-literature, on the other hand, reproduces and systematizes the sorcery-rites of women, doubtless in direct continuation of practices especially common in the Atharvan schools. Pāṇini 4. 4. 96 still describes as *ṛṣau*, i. e. as Vedic, the kind of mantra which he calls *hṛdya*, according to the scholiast in the sense of *hṛdayasya bandhanaḥ* 'captivating the heart', or *vaśīkaraṇamantraḥ*: doubtless he has in view both the love-charms of the present category, and the more general conciliatory hymns of the following class[3]. The Rig-vidhāna employs the terms *hṛdya*, *saṃvanana*, and *vaśīkaraṇa* for both these kinds of charms: 1. 2. 5; 2. 35. 2; 3. 15. 2 ff.; 19. 3 ff.; 21. 4, etc.[4]; the Sāmavidhāna-brāhmaṇa treats the corresponding matters in 2. 5 and 6, where Sāyaṇa has also frequent occasion to employ the verb *vaśīkar*; they are also known in the Tantric sorcery-books (*strīvaśya*, *pativaśya*, etc.)[5].

The majority of the hymns in question are devoted to the relation of the two sexes. Especially common are philtres or love-charms performed by men as well as women: 1. 34; 2. 30; 3. 25; 6. 8; 9; 89; 102; 129; 130—132; 139; 7. 38; in these various plants and other substances, herbs, licorice, salve, *kuṣṭha*, spikenard, etc., are invoked to lend charm to the person performing the philtre. Or the activities of animal-life and nature in general that are analogous to the emotions of love, are called upon to reproduce themselves in the beloved object: 'I draw to myself thy mind as the leading stallion the female side-horse' (6. 102. 2); 'the cows who lick their young, in whose heart love is planted, shall make yonder woman bestow love upon me' (6. 9. 3); 'as the wind tears this grass from the surface of the earth, thus do I tear thy soul' (2. 30. 1); 'as the creeper embraces the tree on all sides, thus do thou embrace me' (6. 8. 1); 'thy heart shall parch with love of me, and thy mouth shall parch with love of me' (6. 139. 2); 'we inflame thy heart, we inflame thy mind' (6. 89. 2). With the last passage cf. 'ut feriatis et incendiatis cor et mentem N. in amorem meum'[6]. The arrow of the god of love figures 3. 25. 2: 'the arrow, winged with longing, barbed with love, whose shaft is unswerving desire, with that, well-aimed, Kāma shall pierce thee in the heart'[7]. The formulaic hemistich, or its second pāda, *yathā mama kratāv aso, mama cittam upāyasi*, 'in order that thou shalt be at my bidding, shalt follow my thought', recurs frequently: 1. 34. 2; 3. 25. 5; 6. 42. 3; 43. 3; similarly, *yathā māṃ kāminy aso, yathā man nāpagā asaḥ*, 1. 34. 5; 2. 30. 1; 6. 8. 1. These expressions are indicative of a certain mechanical technique in the production of these philtres: they must have had a considerable market, but they certainly are not the worst that the Atharvan has preserved. Closely related with these philtres is another group aiming at the discomfiture or destruction of rivals in love, or co-wives (*sapatnībādhana*, Rvidh. 4. 12. 1, 3). Two hymns of this sort are found RV. 10. 145 (AV. 3. 18; ApMB. 1. 15); and 10. 159 (ApMB. 1. 16)[8]. The Atharvan has 1. 14 (misunderstood by the earlier interpreters as a marriage hymn[9]); 3. 18; 7. 35; 113; and 114: with fierce denunciation and uncanny practices one woman endeavors to rob another of her attractiveness, her *bhaga* (luck in love), or her fecundity. Still more drastic are two charms to deprive men of their virility, 6. 138 and 7. 90: 'O herb, turn this man for me to-day into a eunuch that wears his hair dressed . . ., that wears a hood! Then Indra with a pair of stones shall break his testicles both! . . . A hood upon his head and a hair-net do we place' (6. 138). The converse of the preceding hymns are the charms to allay jealousy, aiming to quench the fire, the heart-burning of love: 6. 18; 7. 45; and 7. 74. 3. To the domain of romantic love belongs also 6. 77, a charm to cause the return of a truant woman, furnished with significant symbolic practices, Kauś. 36. 5—9; and 4. 5, a sleeping-charm preparatory to an assignation, working up (perhaps with secondary adaptation) a number of stanzas of RV. 7. 55.

The remaining hymns of this class belong to the calmer sphere of conjugal life. The charm 1. 18 (cp. 7. 115) aims to remove evil bodily characteristics and to drive out Arāti from a woman, apparently that she may afterwards bear offspring (st. 1[d]). These evil characteristics suggest those that are to be avoided when choosing a bride, in the Gṛhya-sūtras and Dharma-śāstras[10]: the present hymn seems to be in the nature of a *prāyaścitta* calculated to render such a woman fit for marriage. Next come the so-called *pativedanāni*, 'charms to obtain a husband (or wife)': 2. 36; 6. 60; and 6. 82. Here the serene, auspicious gods Aryaman and Bhaga figure especially: the coloring is that of the wedding-stanzas and ceremonies. Similar is the position of 6. 78, a blessing upon a married (royal) couple; of 7. 37, a stanza in which the bride says to the bridegroom: 'I envelop thee in my garment that was produced by Manu, that thou shalt be mine alone, shalt not even discourse of other women!'; and 7. 36, a love-charm spoken by the bridal couple: 'The eyes of us two shine like honey, our foreheads gleam like ointment. Place me within thy heart; may one mind be in common to us!' Finally the post-marital interests of conception, child-birth, and child-life are represented by a sufficient number of hymns: they are in close touch with the corresponding saṃskāras of the Gṛhya-sūtras, which reproduce with more or less variation a considerable number of the stanzas of these hymns. The four lunar divinities Anumati, Rākā, Sinīvālī, and Kuhū are invoked with great predilection; Prajāpati, Tvaṣṭar, Dhātar figure frequently. The *garbhādhāna* is represented by the robust epithalamium 5. 25, and by the more peculiarly Atharvanic charm 6. 81, in which a bracelet, 'a holder', called *parihasta*, is invoked to secure conception: 'The bracelet that Aditi wore, when she desired a son, god Tvaṣṭar shall fasten upon this woman, intending that she shall bear a son'. To obviate sterility Kauś. 34. 1 ff. prescribes a practice centering about AV. 1. 32, an original cosmic hymn in praise of heaven, earth, and especially the atmosphere (*antarikṣa*): the relation of the hymn to the practice is obscure. The protection of the embryo in the womb, i. e., the prevention of miscarriage, is secured by the recital of 6. 17, along with 5. 1. 1, and the hymn contained in Kauś. 98. 2[11]. The elaborate conjuration of evil demons with the greatest variety of unheard-of names, 8. 6, is used, Kauś. 35. 20, in a rite which Keśava describes as the *sīmanta-karma*[12]. Charms to secure the birth of a son (*puṁsavana*) are 3. 23; 6. 11; 7. 17; and 7. 19. A clap-trap god Sūṣan, made from the root *sū* 'beget' after the pattern of Pūṣan, is invoked in the lively hymn 1. 11 to secure safe delivery: it belongs to the sphere of the *sosyantī-karma*, as it is called in the Gṛhya-sūtras and elsewhere[13]. If the child is born under an unlucky star the expiatory charm 6. 110 is recited: »Him that hath been born under (the constellation) *jyeṣṭhaghnī* ('she that slays the oldest'), or under the *vicṛtau* ('they that uproot'), save thou (O Agni) from being torn up by the root by Yama . . . On a tiger-like day the hero was born . . . Let him not slay, when he grows up, his father, let him not injure the mother that hath begotten him«. Finally the appearance, perhaps the irregular appearance, of the first pair of teeth 'the two tigers' calls for the expiatory hymn, 6. 140.

1 WEBER, IS. V. 177—266; ZIMMER, p. 305 ff.; SBE. XLII, p. 94—110, and the notes on the hymns there treated. — 2 See below, § 61. — 3 WEBER, IS. V. 78, note; XVII. 215. — 4 See MEYER's Introduction, p. XIV, XXXIII. Pāṇini's statement above is probably based directly on Rig-vidhāna 3. 15. 3: the '*ṛṣi*' referred to is RV. 10. 83 and 84 = AV. 4. 31 and 32. — 5 WEBER, Verz. I. 270 ff.; II. 318, 1184; IS. III. 156. — 6 WEINHOLD, Die deutschen Frauen, p. 148; WEBER,

IS. V. 243. — 7 SBE. XLII. 359. — 8 They are employed ApG. 3. 9. 6 and 9. — 9 See, Seven Hymns, AJPh. VII. 473—6; SBE. XLII. 252 ff. — 10 AG. 1. 5; SG. 1. 5. 5 ff.; Kauś. 37. 7 ff.; GG. 2. 1. 1 ff.; ApG. 1. 3. 11; HG. 1. 19. 4 ff.; Gṛhya-saṃgraha 2. 21—23 (*dārālakṣaṇa*); Manu 3. 4 ff.; Yājñav. 1. 52. Cp. HAAS, IS. V. 288; BLOOMFIELD, ZDMG. XXXV. 573; WINTERNITZ, AWAW., 1892, vol. XL. 33 ff.; HILLEBRANDT, Ritual-Litteratur, p. 64. — 11 These hymns are called *garbhadṛṃhaṇāni*, Kauś. 35. 12; the one whose pratīka is *acyutā* (Kauś. 98. 2) is said by Dārila to be from another *śākhā* (*śākhāntarīyasūktam*): we may expect it in AVP. Cp. ŚG. 1. 21; AG. 1. 13. 1. — 12 WEBER, IS. 5. 251 ff.; LUDWIG, Der Rig-Veda, III, 523 ff.; HENRY, Les Livres VIII et IX, p. 17, 54 ff. — 13 See SBE. XLII. 99, 242 ff.

§ 54. Class 5). Charms to secure harmony, influence in the assembly, and the like (sāṃmanasyāni, etc.). — The present class of hymns[1] exhibits many points of contact with the preceding, differing from it most conspicuously by the absence of the element of romantic, sexual love. The boundary between the two classes is hard to set: a conciliatory charm like 1. 34 may be, and is employed to secure the love of a person of the opposite sex (Kauś. 76. 8, 9; 79. 10), or it may be recited by one who wishes to gain the ear of the *sabhā*, the village assembly (Kauś. 38. 17). Or, the hymn 6.42 aims to appease anger without specifying the enraged person (cp. HG. 1. 15. 3); it may however have been constructed originally to end the conflict between a woman and her husband or paramour (Kauś. 36. 28—31). The later tradition harbors both classes of charms and practices within the terms *hṛdya*, *saṃvanana*, and *vaśīkaraṇa* (see above, § 53), blending the two in its literary presentations[2]. The Śrauta-texts are also acquainted with practices of this sort which figure among the *kāmyā iṣṭayaḥ*; e. g. ŚS. 3. 6. 1, and the so-called *mitravindā*, ŚS. 3. 7; AŚ. 2. 11; KŚ. 5. 12. 13. The key-note of the present class is harmony (*saṃmanas*, *sāṃmanasya*, *saumanasa*, *saṃjñāna*); harmony, of course, from the point of view of the person practising the charm; harmony that agrees with his personal views and desires, and leaves him in the position of arbiter and superior. The Brāhmaṇa-story of Cyavana the Bhārgava, or Āṅgirasa, vividly portrays family dissensions as a curse: 'Father fought with son, and brother with brother'. 'Then neither did mother know son, nor son mother'[3]. Quarrels in the family (*kule kalahini*; *yatraitat kulaṃ kalahi bhavati*) are regarded as portentous, the family has been attacked by Nirṛti: they require elaborate expiation[4]. This, then, is the theme of one group of hymns in this class: the stilling of wrath and discord, and the establishment of harmony between contending persons or parties. The other group, more subjectively, aims at success, prominence, or superiority in social and political life: favor among men, influence in the assembly, success in debate, and subordination to one's will. None of these themes are entirely unknown in Vedic literature in general, but nowhere are they treated as prominently or distinctly as in the Atharvan. The RV. has two hymns of this sort, 10. 166 and 191 (cp. RV. Khila 10. 191); similar stanzas occur MS. 2. 6. 6; TB. 2. 4. 4. 4. ff.; cp. also VS. 7. 25; ŚB. 4. 2. 4. 23. Practices bearing upon such hymns are described Kauś. 12. 5 ff.; 38. 12 ff.; 97. 1 ff.; HG. 1. 13. 19 ff.; 15. 2 ff.; ApG. 8. 22. 19 ff.; Svidh. 2. 5; Rvidh. 4. 20. 3; 24. 4.

Two hymns, 6.42 and 43, are constructed to appease anger; the latter charm is reinforced by the use of *darbha*-grass which for the nonce wears the title 'appeaser of wrath' (*manyuśamana*). They are the converse of the two hymns 4. 31 and 32 (= RV. 10. 84 and 83) in which Wrath personified is conjured to destroy enemies[5]. Four hymns, 6. 64; 73; 74; 7. 52, allay disord, suspend strife and bloodshed. Especially fervent and picturesque is the appeal for harmony in the family, 3. 30: 'Unity of heart, and unity of mind, freedom from hatred do I procure for you. Do ye take delight in one another, as a cow in her new-born calf! The son shall be devoted to his father, be of the same mind with his mother; the wife shall speak honied, sweet, words to her husband! The brother shall not hate the brother, and the sister not the sister! Harmonious, devoted to the same purpose, speak ye words in kindly spirit!' Another charm, 3. 8, is employed specifically at the *upanayana*, Kauś. 55. 17, 18, to ensure harmony between teacher and pupil[6]; the stanza 7. 44 (= RV. 6. 69. 8) is adapted deftly, Kauś. 42. 6, as a charm for the reconciliation of two enemies. Of the charms to secure influence in the assembly 2. 27 and 7. 12 are the most significant. The former undertakes with the aid of a talisman of the *pāṭā*-plant to overcome the debate (*prāś*) of a hostile disputant (*pratiprāś*)[7]; the latter addresses 'assembly and meeting, the two daughters of Prajāpati': they shall aid him to capture the power and understanding of those that are sitting in council. Very similar to the last is the tenor of 6. 94 whose key-note is the technical word *saṃnam* 'to bend to one's will'. This word and its derivative *saṃnati* (*-homāḥ*) is used elsewhere to bend the heavenly powers to one's will[8]. More or less connected with these themes are also the hymns 1. 34 (see above); 5. 15; 6. 15; 7. 94, and the sts. 5. 1. 5; 19. 62. 1.

[1] SBE. XLII, p. 134—139; cp. Kauś. 12. 5; Ludwig, Der Rig-Veda, III. 253 ff., 344; Zimmer, p. 172; Weber, IS. XVII. 212, 307. — [2] ApG. 8. 22. 19—23. 6; HG. 1. 14. 6—15. 8; Svidh. 2. 5 and 6. — [3] ŚB. 4. 1. 5. 3 ff.; cp. the version of the JB., as rendered by Whitney, JAOS. XI, p. cxlv. — [4] Kauś. 97; ṢB. 5. 3 = Adbhuta-Br. 1. 3; Adbhutaśānti, Ath. Pariś. 67. 4 (Weber, Omina und Portenta, p. 317, 320); cp. also ŚŚ. 3. 6. — [5] Used as battle-charms, below, § 55, end. — [6] Weber, IS. XVII. 212. — [7] Seven Hymns, AJPh. VII. 479 ff.; SBE. XLII. 137, 304 ff. — [8] Cp. AV. 4. 39; Kauś. 5. 8; 59. 16; 68. 37; 72. 37; TS. 3. 4. 4. 1; 7. 5. 23. 1; MS. 1. 4. 14; TB. 3. 8. 18. 5; ApŚ. 20. 12. 8; PG. 1. 5. 10; cp. IS. XVII. 214; SBE. XLII. 508.

§ 55. Class 6). Charms pertaining to royalty (rājakarmāṇi).— The Atharvan moves in social extremes. On the one hand the practitioners of this Veda catered largely to the wants and fears of the poor villagers of India; hence later the scornful epithets *grāmayājin* and *pūgayajñiya*[1]. On the other hand the most practical interests of the higher classes, the kings and priests, were also largely dependent upon Atharvanic priests and rites. The interests of the priests are expounded in the hymns of the next class; the spiritual specialties of their religion (*brahma*) figure also, to be sure in a peculiarly exaggerated and confused form, in the theosophic hymns (class 10): it is not to be doubted that the presence of these elements contributed to the claim of the Atharvanic ritualists that their Veda was the Brahma-Veda[2]. With scarcely less show of justice the Atharvan might have assumed the designation *kṣatra-veda*, had it been advantageous to name it so. Indeed Prof. Weber and the writer have pointed out certain circumstances and literary statements, not altogether unambiguous, which make it seem that the Atharvan was in certain moods regarded as the Veda of the Kṣatriyas[3]. Such it was without doubt to a considerable extent, but other phases of the same Veda succeeded in impressing themselves still more vigorously. In this matter the attitude of the Atharvan schools may be said to be significant for the development of Hindu religion, after the Vedic (*śrauta*) ritual had passed its halcyon days. But for the overwhelming interest in theosophic speculations of the Upaniṣad variety the later Atharvans would not have found it to their advantage to spin out treatises on the *brahma* and the *om* (Atharvan Upaniṣads), but would have confined themselves more to the worldly advantages derivable from their profession. In practice their aspirations found during all this period, down to the times of the Daśakumāracarita, their most profitable field in the service of kings as Purohitas and chaplains on the field of battle[4]. The basis for these functions are the hymns of the present class: they deal with the assumption of royalty (consecration and election); with the development and aggrandisement of its strength and lustre; with the defence of king and country against enemies from outside; in a measure also they aim to bestow upon the Purohita the spiritual force necessary for his effectiveness as the prime coadjutor of the king[5]. All these subjects are alluded to scatteringly in the RV. and the other Saṃhitās (cp. especially RV. 10. 103; 152; 173; 174, and 6. 47. 26 ff; 6. 75), but the AV. manifests itself here, as elsewhere, in closer touch with real popular life in presenting the largest number of hymns of this sort. They are supported by a long section of so-called *rājakarmāṇi* ('royal rites') in the Kauśika (14—17)[6]. The inherent importance of these subjects accounts for the presence in the Śrauta-ritual of a very large number of practices intimately connected with the welfare of the Kṣatriyas, such as *rājasūya*, *vājapeya*, *sautrāmaṇī*, and *aśvamedha*, all of which were elaborated by the priests out of existing popular practices. Also the *kāmyeṣṭayaḥ*, the sacrifices designed to secure the fulfilment of special desires, incidentally and trustworthily reflect the frequency and familiarity of royal practices: e. g. in the offering to Indra and Bṛhaspati, the heavenly king and his Purohita, designed to remedy the decadence of sovereignty (*śaktistambhananivāraka*), TS. 2. 4. 13; MS. 2. 1. 12; or in the sacrifices of him that desires conquest (*jayakāma*), TS. 2. 1. 13; MS. 2. 5. 3, 8, 9. The Gṛhya-sūtras have little, if anything, of this sort (e. g. the battle-charms, AG. 3. 12), whereas the Vidhāna-literature and the AV. Pariśiṣṭas abound in *rājakarmāṇi*: Rvidh. 2. 22. 1; 24. 3—5; 4. 2. 3; 8. 1, 2; 14. 5; 21. 1 ff.; Svidh. 3. 5 and 6; Yvidh., Agni-Purāṇa, adhyāya 259, sts. 66—73; Ath. Pariś. 2 ff. That the existence of similar practices is presupposed by the Dharma-texts, the Epic, and thence through classical times, has been shown above[7]. Throughout these hymns Indra, the king, is the heavenly prototype of the earthly king, admitting complete identification or merging of the two (3. 3. 2; 4. 6); King Varuṇa figures similarly, suggesting occasionally, with a pun on the name, the electoral power (*var* 'choose': 3. 4. 5, 6). Bṛhaspati or Brahmaṇaspati, of course, represents the Purohita (11. 10. 10 ff.).

The consecration of a king has elicited the hymn 4. 8, composed with true appreciation of the dignity of royalty, and reflecting genuine popular institutions. In perfect accord with the descriptions of the *rājasūya* in the Śrauta-texts two prominent acts are indicated: the king is sprinkled with holy water mixed with the essence of auspicious plants; and he steps upon a tiger-skin[8]. Conceived in a similar high spirit is 3. 4, a prayer at the election of a king: the god Varuṇa, himself a heavenly king, figures as the divine elector, his name being for the nonce derived from the root *var* 'choose'[9]. The restoration of an exiled king is accomplished with 3. 3, reinforced by Kauśika with significant symbolic practices. Quite a number of hymns are designed to ensure to a king superiority over other kings, sole rulership, and royal power generally: 4. 22; 6. 54; 86—88; 7. 84. An amulet of *parṇa*-wood is praised as the strengthener of sovereignty in 3. 5. Quite a number of hymns are engaged in securing to a monarch specific qualities befitting such a personage: 'the strength (*varcas*) that is in the lion, the tiger, the serpent; in Agni, the Brāhmaṇa, and Sūrya . . .; the strength that is in the elephant, panther, and in gold; in the waters, cattle, and in men' (6. 38; cp. 1. 9; 19. 37). To the acquisition of the strength of an elephant (*hastivarcas*) a special hymn, 3. 22, is devoted. Glory (*yaśas*) is another quality ardently bespoken for a king, 6. 39, as also for the Brahmans themselves (6. 58; 69). And 6. 61 seems to be a piece of self glorification on the part of a king (or Brahman): it sounds as though it were adapted from, or patterned after a hymn representing Indra engaged in self-praise; but it does not occur elsewhere. The hymns to Rohita and Rohiṇī (book 13) are at least related to the present class; they represent this pair of divinities allegorically as king and queen (see below, § 61), and the terms in which they are exalted reflect the praise and adulation of terrestrial monarchs. The ritual connected with the royal hymns, as also the *rājasūya* in the Śrauta-texts, represents the king and his Purohita in mutual interdependence[10]: without successful *purohiti* there can be no sound *kṣatra*. With pardonable self-consciousness, considering the temper of the times, the Purohita assumes responsibility for the king's success in 3. 19: 'Keen (sharpened) is this prayer of mine, keen my manly force and strength; keen therefore shall be the rule, and imperishable, of him whose victorious Purohita I am'. Similarly the stanza 7. 16. In humbler spirit the prose litany 5. 24 contains prayers addressed to the pantheon for success in the function of Purohita; and 19. 63 (RV. 1. 40. 1) is adapted as an exhortation addressed to a Purohita (Brahmaṇaspati), to captivate the gods and make powerful the king (*yajamāna*).

In their extent and vigor, and in their eager exploitation of details elsewhere unknown, the war and battle charms of the Atharvan constitute also a decided peculiarity of that Veda[11]. The armament of weapons, snares, traps, nets[12], and the stench produced by a rotten rope burned in the fire, in order to bewilder and bring to fall the enemy (8. 8), bear the earmarks of the Veda of the *ghoram*. The battle-charms appear generally in pairs, or groups of three: 1. 19 is a charm against arrow-wounds, followed by 1. 20 and 21, battle-charms in general. The group 6. 65—67 is of similar import; in the first two the words *nirhasta* and *nairhasta* figure prominently: handless the scheming enemy shall be, his arms shall be broken. Still other groups are 3. 1, 2, battle songs addressed to Agni to confuse the enemy; 4. 31, 32 (RV. 10. 84, 83) addressed to Manyu, 'Wrath', as the victorious spirit of battle (cp. 6. 65); 6. 97—99, prayers of the king to Agni, Indra, &c. upon the eve of battle; 6. 103—104 charms to paralyse the enemy (*saṃdāna, ādāna*). Especially fierce and prolongued is the attack upon the foe undertaken with 11. 9 and 10, addressed to the battle-demons Arbudi, Nyarbudi, and Triṣaṃdhi, who are regarded as allies of Indra. The god Triṣaṃdhi, 'Three-joints', is evidently a personification of the three-pointed bolt of Indra (11. 10.3); Arbudi and Nyarbudi are pretty certainly derived from the myth of the demon Arbuda, the cloud-serpent, whom Indra slays: Nyarbudi seems to owe its intrinsically meaningless prefix *ni* to verbal juxtapositions such as, *ny arbudaṃ vāvṛdhāno astaḥ*, RV. 2. 11. 20[13]. HENRY regards Arbuda as originally a mythic double of Indra; we may preferably suppose that the friendly relation of Indra and these secondary precipitates from Arbuda are due to a later view of Arbudi and Nyarbudi as serpent-gods who are by these very terms auspicious. The earlier import of the myth has passed out of sight[14]. Another pair of hymns, 5. 20 and 21, representing the better grade of Atharvanic literary endeavor, are addressed to the battle-drum, the terror of the enemy: 'When the wife of the enemy hears the voice of the drum that speaks to a far distance, may she, starting up at the sound, distressed, snatch her child to her arms and run, frightened at the clash of arms'. Cp. also 6. 126 (RV. 6. 47. 29—31). Still other specialties are dealt with in 19. 20, the prayer of a king while putting on his armor (cp. the st. 7. 118 = RV. 6. 75. 18); in 6. 125 (RV. 6. 47. 26—28) and 7. 3, prayers of a king as he mounts his war-chariot. Finally there belong to this class the Atharvan version of the famous *apratiratha-sūkta*, 19. 13 (RV. 10. 103), and the hymns more vaguely redolent of war, 6. 13; 7. 86; 91; 92; 93; 108; and 110.

1 See above, § 26; SBE. XLII, p. XL note, LI. — 2 Above, § 33; SBE. XLII, p. XXVII, LXII ff. — 3 Weber, SPAW., 1891, p. 785—7; APAW., 1893, p. 4, 23 note, 143; Bloomfield, SBE. XLII, p. XXV ff.; above, p. 10. — 4 SBE. XLII, p. LV, LXII ff.; above, § 26—28. — 5 SBE. XLII, p. 111—133; cp. Weber, IS. X. 26 ff.; Ludwig, Der Rig-Veda, III, 248 ff.; Zimmer, p. 158 ff. Cp. the *rāṣtrasaṃvarga*-hymns, Kauś., p. 299, note 7. — 6 Cp. also the Pariśiṣṭa-like *indramahotsava*, Kauś. 140; Ath. Pariś. 19 (Kauśika, Introd. p. XXVI). — 7 See § 26 ff.; SBE. XLII, p. XLVIII, LI. — 8 Weber, Rājasūya (APAW., 1893), Index, under 'salbūng', and 'tiger-fell'. — 9 See RV. 10. 173, and cp. Ludwig, ibid., p. 250; Zimmer, 162 ff.; SBE. XLII. 331. — 10 Kauś. 17. 6, 7; Weber, Rājasūya (APAW., 1893), p. 4, 140—143. — 11 The Kauśika designates the battle-charms as *sāmgrāmikāṇi* (14. 7); special varieties are known as *apanodanāni* (14. 14), and *mohanāni* (14. 17). The Gaṇamālā, Ath. Pariś. 34. 13, presents in the *aparājitā-gaṇa* a similar collection. Cp. Svidh. 3. 6, and the terms *mohana* and *senāstambhana* in Tantric texts: Weber, Verz. I, 270; II. 1184. — 12 Cp. the *indrajāla-vidhāna*, Weber, Verz. I. 270, with AV. 8. 8. 5—8. — 13 Cp. also RV. 1. 51. 6; 2. 14. 4; 8. 32. 3. — 14 SBE. XLII. 631 ff.; Henry, Les Livres X, XI, et XII, p. 164 ff.

§ 56. Class 7). **Prayers and imprecations in the interest of Brahmans.** — The claims and prerogatives of the Brahmans[1] have reached in the AV. their highest pitch, excepting that the hyperbolic amounts of live stock and other property, reputed to have been given them as *dakṣiṇā* in the *dānastutis*, *nārāśaṃsyaḥ*, and the incidental reports of the Śrauta-literature, is restricted within more reasonable bounds in the numerous *dakṣiṇā*-hymns of the AV. The Brahmans bestow upon themselves freely the epithet *deva* 'god'[2], which is after all perhaps, at least in the beginning, nothing more than a bit of awkward logic, derived from the perception that the sacrifice and the priestly reward (*iṣṭā-pūrtam*) are both sanctified acts which therefore must each address themselves to a divine being. They are further fully conscious of being in charge by virtue of their function as Purohitas of the sovereignty of kings and the safety of countries; in addition, all blessings of the private folk flow from the Brahmans as the middle-men between the human race and the gods. The social and economic conditions of the Brāhmaṇas in the AV. are very much the same as those elicited from statements in the Śrauta-literature such as have been gathered by Weber in his 'Collectanea on the Castes', IS. X. 1—160. Especially pronounced is their claim of 'inviolability' (*ajyeyatā*, *abadhyatā*[3]) and the still exorbitant demand of *dakṣiṇā*, moderate as it seems compared with the lies of the *dānastuti*[4]. The Atharvanic element appears in the former class in the shape of imprecations, fierce beyond anything known elsewhere in the literature: oppression and murder of Brahmans is the sin against the holy ghost. The hymns describing the bestowal of *dakṣiṇā* are quite unique: the performances are treated, sometimes at great length, as independent sacrificial acts delineated with the most pains-taking detail; they are correlated with all that is holy or mystic in nature and theosophic speculation (*brahma*). This is one of the marked specialties of these hymns: when a goat (*aja*) is the *pièce de résistance* of a *dakṣiṇā* it is both goat and the divine Aja Ekapād; when a steer, it is both sacrificial animal and divine steer (*anaḍvān*)[5]. Thus it is difficult in individual cases to decide whether a theosophic chain — often a jumble — of statements has been adapted to the *dakṣiṇā*, or whether the *dakṣiṇā* is the original theme, being merely decked out with the familiar mock-profundities of the *brahma*.

The inviolability of Brahmans and their belongings is the subject of four of the most graphic hymns of the AV. (5. 17—19; 12. 5). The first of these occurs fragmentarily in RV. 10. 109, which presents only 7 stanzas, but occurs in a position in the RV. redaction pointing to a fuller version of 11 sts., perhaps identical with the first 11 sts. of AV. The last 7 sts. of AV. may therefore, as also for intrinsic reasons, be regarded as later than the first 11[6]. The entire hymn is an imprecation against the violator of the wife of a Brahman: kings or arrogant nobles (sts. 3, 10) seem to be the culprits in the mind of the poet. Even king Soma ceded his mythical prerogative as the first husband of every woman in favor of the Brahmans, the gods themselves conducted the wedding ceremonies. Woe betide the king and country where a Brahman's spouse is injured. Prosperity vanishes, children are not born, portentous occurrences terrify the people. The other three hymns[7] are directed against the oppressors of Brahmans, especially against those that rob (withhold) their cattle[8]: 'That kingdom verily she (the cow) swamps, as water a leaking ship; misfortune smites that kingdom in which they injure a Brāhmaṇa. The trees chase away with the words: "do not come within our shade", him that covets the wealth that belongs to a Brāhmaṇa, O Nārada' (5. 19. 8, 9). The vials of the Brahman's wrath are not thus emptied; fiercely they consign their oppressor to death, accentuating their theme by suggestive references to the harrowing details of the funeral-practices: 'The *kūdī*-plant that wipes away the track (of death)[9], which they fasten to the dead, that very one, O oppressor of Brahmans, the gods did declare thy couch' . . . 'The water with which they bathe the dead, with which they moisten his beard, that very water, O oppressor of Brahmans, the gods did assign to thee as thy share of water' (5. 19. 12, 14).

On the positive side the Brahmans assert the importance and power of the *purohiti* (3. 19; 5. 24; 7. 16; 19. 63, above, p. 75). But above all the AV., as almost every other phase of Vedic literature[10], pleads not at all shame-facedly but with the wholesome courage of its convictions for the perquisites of the Brahmans. The *dānastuti* which narrates fabulous feats of giving, doubtless by way of stimulus to future givers, is to be sure almost entirely absent[11]. In this matter the attitude of the Atharvan is rather prescriptive or didactic than quasi-historical. Or, the witchery of magic formula and prayer is applied, to exorcise avarice and conjure liberality. The pretty hymn 5. 7, addressed to the demon 'Grudge' (*arāti*) cajoles her, though she be 'golden-complexioned, lovely, resting upon golden cushions', quite an Apsaras or 'schoene Teufelinne' in her fascinations, to go away. Instead, 'him whom I implore with Vāc Sarasvatī (holy speech), the yoke-fellow of thought, Śraddhā (faith that expresses itself in works, sc. in *dakṣiṇā*) shall find to-day, bestowed by the brown Soma' (st. 5)[12]. The same result is craved in the following rather plaintive ejaculation, showing that even a Brahman might be χρησμοσύνῃ τ' εἴκων καὶ στυγερῇ πενίῃ: 'What king, desirous of more possessions, will get us out of this wretched misery? Who is desirous of sacrifice, and who of (getting the heavenly reward of) presents (to the Brahmans)? Who seeks for long life from the gods?' (7. 103; cp. 7. 104)[13]. Within this sphere belongs also 5. 11, a conversation between Varuṇa and Atharvan (the typical priest) about a wonderful cow bestowed by the former upon the latter. Varuṇa tries to take it back, but is induced by Atharvan to desist[14]. Aside from the regular *dakṣiṇā* the thrifty Brahmans stood ready to gather in all sorts of odds and ends. Thus the birth of twin-calves (3. 28), contrary to modern superstition which regards animals born in pairs as auspicious, is made to appear as a portentuous occurrence requiring expiation, part of which consists in making over 'the growling and cross cow that injureth the cattle' to the Brahmans[15]. A cow which after a certain time is discovered to be sterile (*vaśā*) is viewed in a similar light: the long anuṣṭubh-hymn 12. 4 recounts in picturesque language, accompanied by fierce threats, urgent reasons for passing her on to the Brahmans whom nothing hurts. But the brunt of the Atharvan's activity in this line is directed towards the composition of elaborate hymns which are obviously intended to accompany the bestowal of substantial *dakṣiṇās*, and, what is more singular, to elevate the ceremonies connected therewith to the position of independent sacral acts of great formality and dignity. These *dakṣiṇās* are designated by Kauśika as *sava* (*savān dā* 'to give *savas*') — the word *sava* in this sense does not occur in the text of the Saṃhitā; see, however, RV. 1. 126. 1. The Śrauta-texts are acquainted with *savas* which are accounted as forms of the *ekāha*; they are solemn consecrations (*abhiṣeka*) for special ceremonies of considerable variety[16]. TB. 2. 7 recounts seven of these, one being styled *odanasava* (2. 7. 7), performed by an *annādyakāma*: Kauśika specializes this idea altogether in the direction of the bestowal of *dakṣiṇā*, devoting to his *savas* the entire eighth adhyāya. Two versions of the *savas* are there presented, one 60—66, the other in the nature of a Pariśiṣṭa, 67—68. Both the sacrificer and his wife (*patnī*) participate in the ceremonious details of these performances as *kartārau*; special utensils (*sāvikāḥ saṃbhārāḥ*, 67. 1) are employed. Keśava, p. 364, summarizes these *savas*, stating their number as 22. The most pronounced type of these appears in the two hymns 11. 1 and 12.3 which Keś. designates respectively as *brahmaudana* and *svargaudana*. They represent the stanzas chanted at a solemn combination of a soma-sacrifice with the preparation of porridge for the Brahmans' *dakṣiṇā*. Presents of gold and clothes 11. 1. 28; 12. 3. 51) are also hinted at; nevertheless there is something real and homely about these performances in which the wife takes part, and which are spoken of (11.1.19) as a practice of long standing in the family: 'Grandfathers, fathers, children, grandchildren — I am the fifteenth that did cook thee (O porridge)'! They are far removed from the suspicious bluster of the *dānastuti*. Allied to these is 11. 3, an allegoric liturgic exaltation of the *odana*, in Brāhmaṇa-prose: in sts. 50 ff. the porridge is assimilated to the sun. A goat (*aja*, assimilated, as a matter of course, to Aja Ekapād), garnished with five *odanas* (*aja pañcaudana*) is the subject of 9. 5 (cp. 4. 14); a cow, accompanied by a hundred *odanas* (*śataudanā*), similarly correlated with the pantheistic heavenly cow, is bestowed in 10. 9. An *odana* whose main motive is escape from death (*ati tarāṇi mṛtyum*)[17] is dealt with in 4. 35; another, prepared with succulent sauces and called *viṣṭārin* 'spreader', is described in mystic cosmogonic language as conducive to happiness in the other world. And 6.123 also represents explicitly the doctrine that presents to the Brahmans are a treasure laid up in heaven. Many of these *savas* centre around an animal: 10. 10 a *vaśā*; 9. 4 an *ṛṣabha*, assimilated to the various celestial bulls (Rohita, Indra, Tvaṣṭar, etc.); 4. 11 (adapted secondarily) an *anaḍvān*; 7. 22, corrupt and unintelligible formulas occurring elsewhere[18], a *go-sava*; 6. 31, a hymn to the rising sun (*gauḥ pṛśniḥ*), a *pṛśni-sava*; 3. 29. 1—6 an *avi-sava*, followed in sts. 7, 8 by a *prāyaścitta* to expiate for its acceptance (IS. 10. 55); 6. 30. 1, in praise of grain (*yava*) mixed with honey, is called *paunaḥśila madhumantha* (Kauś. 66. 15). Keśava's list of 22 *savas* exhibits yet other hymns and stanzas recited, at times quite secondarily, in connection with *dakṣiṇā*: e. g. 1. 31, a prayer to the regions of space (*āśāḥ*) for health and prosperity, at a *catuḥśarāva-sava* (Kauś. 64. 1). Decidedly the most interesting of all these dakṣiṇās is depicted in 9. 3 (*śālāsava*): a house is gradually taken apart; like a living thing it is handled very gingerly during the process; then it is made over to the Brahman who receives it with solemn prayers for his own future well-being in it, and finally takes it to his own place of residence[19]. Of importance also is the distinct presence of the notion, more or less like those of the Dharmaśāstras etc., that the gift of water to Brahmans, either independently, or as part of a more substantial *dakṣiṇā*, is a holy act: 6. 122 (10. 9. 27; 11. 1. 17, 27)[20]. The occasional squeamishness of the Brahmans which arises from the feeling that they are too much 'on the make', or are receiving improper gifts, gains expression in the expiatory prayer 6. 71, or in the formulas 3. 29. 7, 8; cp. WEBER's collections, IS. 10. 55 ff.

The chapter of the greed and self-assertion of the Brahmans is relieved considerably here, as throughout Brahmanical literature, by opposite currents of thought and feeling. The redemptory note of their character is their consciousness of *noblesse oblige*. A Brahman must be well-regarded among men and therefore well-qualified for his holy office. Two prayers (6. 58 and 69) signalize their craving for the esteem of men[21]. To gain this end they must be wise, illumined, spiritually pure, firmly rooted in holy learning. Very properly then the famous hymn *ahaṃ rudrebhir*, in praise of Vāc, 4. 30 (RV. 10. 125), even in modern times one of the mainstays of the *saṃnyāsin*, is employed in a rite to beget wisdom, or at the study of the Vedas[22]. More directly 6. 108 (cp. RVKh. 10. 151) is an explicit prayer for *medhā*, 'wisdom'; 19. 4 for *ākūti* 'perception'; 19. 41—43 are prayers for *brahma* 'spiritual elevation', and *dīkṣā* 'consecration'; and 19. 64 is a prayer for wisdom and other more worldly advantages on the part of a Brahmacārin as he builds the fire. Related with these, though of a more general character, are three prayers for purification, 6. 19; 51; and 62. Devotion to Vedic learning[23] is at the base of such compositions as 7. 105 and 19. 68, stanzas introductory to the teaching of the Veda; 7. 54 and 7. 61, prayers for success in the study of the Veda; 7. 66 and 67, prayers for regaining holy learning; and 19. 71, the praise of the *gāyatrī*[24]. Cp. also the very late matter 19. 21—23 (§ 37, note 14). The opening hymn of the Saṃhitā (1. 1) is a prayer to Vācaspati, the 'lord of speech', for comprehension and retention of the *śruta*, the holy learning following in the Saṃhitā: 'the thrice seven (sounds or syllables) wearing all forms, their powers the lord of speech shall make mine to-day'[25]. A similar stanza at the end of book 19 (72) contains a blessing at the conclusion of this Veda, confirming the theory of the late and secondary character of book 20 (§ 35).

[1] SBE. XLII. 169—198, and the notes thereto; cp. WEBER, IS. X. 1 ff.; LUDWIG, Der Rig-Veda, III. 268 ff.; ZIMMER, 168 ff., 195 ff. — [2] AV. 3. 3. 26; 6. 13. 1; 58. 2; 11. 1. 23; 12. 3. 38: cp. WEBER, IS. 10. 35 ff.; above, p. 3. — [3] WEBER, l. c., p. 60 ff.; ZIMMER, 197 ff. — [4] WEBER, ib., p. 53; SPAW., 1891, p. 771; below § 63, end. — [5] AV. 4. 11; cp. JACOB, Concordance to the Upanishads, s. v. *anaḍuh*. — [6] OLDENBERG, Die Hymnen des Rig-Veda, p. 240 ff. — [7] St. 1 of 5. 19 occurs with variants JB. 1. 152; the hymn 12. 5 is mixed prose and quasi-poetry. Cp. Svidh. 1. 6. — [8] Hence 5. 18 and 19 are designated as *brahmagavī*, Kauś. 48. 13 ff. — [9] ROTH, Festgruss an Böhtlingk, p. 98—99, quotes a similar Hellenic custom from Antoninus Liberalis 23; cp. SBE. XLII. 436. — [10] Cp. RV. 1. 125. 4—7; and 8. 31. — [11] Excepting the *nārāśaṃsī*-stanzas of the *kuntāpa*-hymn 20. 127. 1—3. — [12] SBE. XLII. 172, 423 ff.; BLOOMFIELD, AJPh. XVII. 411; OLDENBERG, ZDMG. L. 423 ff. The little hymn 7. 57 seems also a charm to secure *dakṣiṇā* (cp. *pṛṇad ghṛtena*), but it appears to have been adapted secondarily from another sphere. — [13] BLOOMFIELD, AJPh. XVII. 408 ff. — [14] ROTH, Abhandlung, p. 1; MUIR, OST. I². 395; cp. AV. 7. 104. — [15] Kauś. 109—111. — [16] Pet. Lex., s. v. *sava*; ŚŚ., Index, s. v. *sava*; HILLEBRANDT, Ritual-Litteratur, p. 140. — [17] Kauś., *atimṛtyu*; Keś. and Sāy. *atimṛtyusava*. — [18] SV. 1. 458; ĀpŚ. 21. 9. 15; PB. 4. 9. 1; Svidh. 1. 6. 2; 3. 1. 4; Kauś. 66. 14; Vait. 13. 8. — [19] SBE. XLII. 193 ff., 593 ff. — [20] Cp. Manu 3. 244; 4. 229; 6. 7; 9. 168, 186; Nārada 5. 41; Śakuntalā, śloka 155 (ed. BÖHTLINGK). — [21] This is the domain of *yaśas* and *brahmavarcasa*, IS. X.

105 ff.; Svidh. 2. 7. — [22] Kauś. 10. 16; 139. 15 — [23] Cp. IS. X. 111 ff. — [24] The MSS. read *vedamātā* for which the vulgate substitutes *vandamānā*. Sāyaṇa, *gāyatrī*. Cp. GB. 1. 1. 38, end. — [25] WHITNEY, Festgruss an Roth, p. 94. Cp. Kauś. Index B, p. 385, under *viśvakarma*.

§ 57. Class 8). Charms to secure prosperity and freedom from danger (pauṣṭikāni). — In a sense the entire Veda is a long-drawn cry for prosperity, beginning with the word *ratnadhātama*, RV. 1. 1. 1, and running through almost every hymn and ceremony. The province of the Atharvan is to provide for individual desires and special exigencies, very mueh in the manner of the *kāmyeṣṭi* of the Śrauta-literature, and in a measure also of the Gṛhya-literature[1], but to an extent and with a degree of thoroughness elsewhere unknown. Nowhere does the exceeding practicality of Vedic literature appear in a stronger light. In the later systematization this type of activity receives the name *puṣṭikarma* (*pauṣṭikāni karmāṇi*)[2], a pendant to *bheṣaja* and *abhicāra*, terms that are also in the main precipitates from the Atharvan literature. House and home, field and river, grain and rain, cattle and horses, trading and gambling, journeying and returning, serpents and vermin, furnish the special themes for these prayers and charms. And over it all is the still more persistent outcry after wealth and progeny; exemption and protection from calamity and danger[3]. Such is the impression gained from this class which, barring the 20th book, forms rather more than one fifth of the hymns of the Saṃhitā. We may follow conveniently the order indicated above in the brief characterization of the materials herein concerned.

The rite of house-building is represented by 3. 12, stanzas of which occur in almost all the Gṛhya-sūtras in connection with the same practice[4]. A certain accessory ceremony called *śyenayāga* or *śyenejyā*, unearthed by the present writer[5], takes place in connection with 7. 41. The hymn is addressed to the divine eagle (lightning): according to the commentators at Kauś. 43. 3 the ceremony is performed on the ground upon which a new house is to be built, or within the new house after its completion, its purpose being to forefend untoward circumstances. Apparently the house shall not be struck by lightning: 'the eagle looking for a resting-place shall come hither kindly (*śiva*) together with his friend Indra'. Other charms to conciliate the 'goddess lightning' and to cause her to spare the stores of grain, are 1. 13 and 7. 11. Protection from conflagrations is secured by means of 6. 106, accompanied by significant practices with water-plants and a frog[6], whereas 3. 21 more broadly aims to quiet the destructive force of all sorts of fires, especially the funeral-fire. A charm for conducting a river into a new channel, 3. 13, is built up upon six stanzas of a general character, in praise of the waters; the seventh stanza points in the direction of the underlying practices: Kauś. 40. 1—6 adds exceedingly interesting details[7]. The field is ploughed while reciting the very composite hymn 3. 17, which is supported by further mantras and significant practices in Kauś. 20. (cp. RV. 4. 57). The little hymn to Indra 6. 33 (ŚS. 18. 3. 2 with variants) is also prescribed, Kauś. 23. 17, at a ploughing ceremony; it is followed by a blessing over the seed as it is being sowed, 6. 142. Charms to procure abundance or increase of grain are 3. 24 and 6. 79, the latter with notable variants, TS. 3. 3. 8. 2—3; the very original hymn 6. 50 exorcises the vermin which infests the grain in the field. Of charms to secure rain, that greatest desideratum of the Hindu agrarian, there are three: 4. 15; 6. 22; and 7. 18; of these the first contains original materials, and is partly in close touch with the frog-hymn, RV. 7. 103, also a rain-charm[8]. Quite common are charms connected with cattle: 2. 26; 3. 14; 4. 21; and 7. 75, to secure prosperity of cattle; 6. 59, a prayer to the plant *arundhatī* for the protection of cattle. The three sts. 4. 38. 5—7, designated, Kauś. 21. 11, as *karkīpravādāḥ* (sc. *ṛcaḥ*), according to the scholiast ensure the prosperity of cattle: we have interpreted them more particularly as a prayer to secure the return of calves that have strayed to a distance[9]. Of special interest are 6. 70, a charm to secure the attachment of a cow to her calf; 6. 141, a prayer pronounced while marking the ears of cattle (cp. 12. 4. 6)[10]; and 4. 3, a very forceful shepherds, charm against wild beasts and robbers (tiger, man, wolf, and serpent). The time-honored love for racing gains expression in 6. 92, a charm to endow a horse with fleetness: the stanzas seem to have originated in connection with the *vājapeya*-ceremony[11]; similarly perhaps 19. 25. Trading and travelling are closely allied: 3. 15 is a lively merchants prayer to 'Indra the merchant' for a safe journey and abundant gain; 6. 55; 7. 8; and 7. 55 are stanzas adapted as prayers for a safe journey; and the rather indefinable mixtum compositum 5. 6 seems to be an oracle to find out whether one will survive a journey[12]. On returning from a journey there is the prayer, 7. 60, to the house, to remove from it fear of the owner, and to make it prosperous[13]. Of especial interest is 6. 128, the propitiation of the weather-prophet who predicts the weather for a person about to start on a journey (Kauś. 50. 15, 16): 'When the stars made Śakadhūma (he who predicts the weather from the smoke of burning dung) their king, they bestowed good weather upon him: "This shall be his dominion", they said'. Whether Śakadhūma is really originally the human weather-prophet or some mythical conception is not to be made out with certainty[14]. The special danger besetting both traveller and householder in India are serpents: 6. 56 seems to be an exorcism of serpents from the premises; whereas the so-called *dig-yukte* (sc. *sūkte*), 3. 26 and 27, seem to have in mind the danger from serpents when abroad, as they mention all directions of the compass[15]. Especially noteworthy is 10. 4, a long charm against serpents, invoking the white horse of Pedu, probably the horse of the sun[16]; in practice an insect that has come by the name of Paidva is substituted for the unattainable horse (Kauś. 32. 20 ff.). The hymn 7. 9, mixed stanzas addressed to Pūṣan[17], makes up a charm for finding lost property; and there are finally three or four prayers for success in gambling at dice, 4. 38. 1—4; 7. 50; 7. 109; and perhaps also 2. 2, addressed especially to Apsarā (Apsaras) who otherwise also bears an unsavory reputation: the passion for gambling is quite as fierce as it is depicted in the classical complaint of the gambler who would reform, RV. 10. 34.

The remaining hymns of this class are more general in character, divisible into two classes: one designed to procure health, wealth, and prosperity; the other to ward off danger and calamity. Three hymns, 1. 15; 2. 26; and 19. 1, centre about the so-called *sāṃsrāvya havis*, an oblation which secures the 'flowing together' of all possible wealth[18] (see § 60, end); the hymns 4. 13; 7. 69; 19. 9—11 are prayers for *śam* 'prosperity'; the prose formulas 4. 39, known as *saṃnati*[19], are designed to bend the heavenly powers to one's desire for all the good things of life; the st. 7. 24 is a prayer to the gods to engage personally in procuring prosperity; 1. 31 is a prayer to the regions of space for health and prosperity; 1. 32 and 6. 10 are cosmic stanzas or formulas similarly designed; 3. 16 (RV. 7. 41) and 3. 20 (RV. 10. 141), addressed to Agni, are morning prayers for prosperity; similar is the purpose of 19. 55. The *udumbara*-tree furnishes an amulet to secure prosperity, 19. 31. The members of the Vedic pantheon are called upon individually to furnish prosperity, the stanzas frequently coinciding with those of other texts, with the presumption in favor of their origin outside of the AV.: Indra in 19. 5

(RV. 7. 27. 3); Agni in 7. 82 and 19. 3 (TB. 1. 2. 1. 21 ff.); Agni Vaiśvānara in 6. 35 and 36 (AŚ. 8. 11. 4; ŚŚ. 10. 9. 17; SV. 2. 1058—60); Savitar in 6. 1 (AŚ. 8. 1. 18), 7. 14 (SV. 1. 464 ff.), and 7. 15 (MS. 2. 10. 6); Uṣas in 19. 12 (RV. 10. 172. 4, and 6. 17. 15); Sarasvatī in 7. 68 (MS. 4. 12. 6); Sarasvant in 7. 40 (TS. 3. 1. 11. 3); the divine eagle in 7.39 (RV. 1.164. 52); Tārkṣya Ariṣṭanemi in 7. 85 (RV. 10. 178. 1); the *devapatnyaḥ* in 7. 49 (RV. 5. 46. 7, 8). Especially the personified phases of the moon, *amāvāsyā*, *paurṇamāsī*, *darśa* (7. 79—81), and the female genii of these phases, Anumati (7. 20), Sinīvālī (7. 46), Kuhū (7. 47), Rākā (7. 48)[20], are implored for wealth and, especially, offspring; the very late hymns 19. 7, 8 engage the favor of the constellations (*nakṣatra*)[21]; finally the hymn 3. 10 to Ekāṣṭakā, a personified lunar day near the beginning of the year[22], viewed as the wife, or epitomized equivalent of the year, is implored to make the year prosperous.

The hymns designed to ward off calamity and danger exhibit many points of contact with the charms against witchcraft, as well as with the battle-charms, sorcery and war being conspicuous sources of danger. Of these the most notable are the group 4. 23—29, known as the *mṛgārāṇi*, or *mṛgārasūktāni*[23]. They were obviously compiled by the Atharvanist for purification and against misfortune: the refrain contains throughout the expression *muc aṁhasaḥ* 'release from misfortune'. The hymns are a curious expansion of the so-called *mṛgāreṣṭi* of the Yajus-texts[24], to which they are unquestionably secondary (see § 45). The first and the last stanzas of most of these hymns are derived from the Yajus; the intervening stanzas are padding. Only 4. 28 does not seem to occur in the Yajus at all; the theme, prayer to Bhava and Śarva, marks it as Atharvanic by distinction (cp. 11. 2): these gods were not to be omitted from such an appeal to the pantheon. Note also the contents: *kṛtyākṛt* and *mūlakṛt* in st. 6; *kimīdin* in st. 7. Very similar to the *mṛgarāṇi*, and having the same refrain, is 11. 6, a prayer for deliverance from calamity, addressed to the pantheon: the clear and fairly complete list of divinities, very much on the plain of the Yajus-texts, imparts to the hymn its chief interest; cp. also 1. 26; 6. 3, 4, 7; 7. 112. The divinity to whom this class of prayers is addressed most frequently is Rudra (Śiva-Agni), under the large variety of names of embodiments (*mūrti*) customary with that divinity[25]. In addition to 4. 28 the long prayer 11. 2, to Bhava and Śarva, two of the embodiments of Rudra, is conspicuous for its intensity; cp. also 6. 93 and 7. 87. Other divinities and personifications are occasionally appealed to individually: Agni Sāṃtapana in 6. 76; personified Death by weapons wielded by Brahmans (*deva*), Kṣatriyas, Vaiśyas, etc. in 6. 13[26]; Soma, the slayer of demons, in 6. 7; Aditi, the universe, and therefore the universal protector, in 7. 6 (cp. 7. 7); Night, the protector against the robbers, wild animals, and demons that infest her, in the late hymns 19. 47—49 (cp. RV. 10. 127); and the shallow though characteristic personifications Viśvajit, Trāyamāṇa, Kalyāṇī, and Sarvavid in the prose-formulas 6. 107. In the manner of the *mṛgāra*-hymns, which accentuate the idea of release from calamity (*muc aṁhasaḥ*)[27], other hymns employ other catch-words to gain similar results: the word *abhaya* 'freedom from danger'[28] is the keynote of 6. 40; 19. 14 and 15 (followed by similar trashy matter in 19. 17—19); the hymn 4. 33 (RV. 1. 97, et al.) with its refrain, *apa naḥ śośucad agham*, the so-called *apāgha*-hymn[29], figures as a matter of course; the prose-formulas 5. 10 harp upon the word *aśmavarma* 'protection firm as stone', being exploited practically in that sense Kauś. 5. 14[30]. Finally there is to be mentioned the singular charm 1. 27 in which danger is warded off by an amulet made from the skin of a moulting serpent, the serpents in this condition symbolizing the powerless enemy. The amulet is homœopathic, as it were[31]. The hymns to the waters (see § 50, end), though very general in character, are also in close touch with this class.

[1] See the list of the *kāmyā iṣṭayaḥ* in WEBER's edition of the TS., vol. II, p. 343; OLDENBERG, SBE. XXX, p. 303 ff., 306. Cp. MEYER, Rig-vidhāna, Introd., p. XII; Svidh. 3. 1 ff. — [2] Cp. HILLEBRANDT, Ritual-Litteratur, p. 169. — [3] SBE. XLII, p. 140—162, and the notes on these hymns. — [4] See OLDENBERG's citations, SBE. XXX, p. 303, bottom; cp. HILLEBRANDT, l. c., p. 80. — [5] JAOS. XVI. 12 ff.; cp. COLEBROOKE, Essays I. 319. — [6] Contributions. Second Series, AJPh. XI. 342 ff.; SBE. XLII, p. 147, 514 ff. — [7] SBE. XLII, p. 146, 348 ff. — [8] HILLEBRANDT, GGA., 1889, p. 406; BLOOMFIELD, JAOS. XVII. 173 ff. Cp. RV. 7. 101—105; 10. 98, and the hymns to Parjanya in general. — [9] SBE. XLII, p. 150, 413. — [10] DELBRÜCK, Gurupūjākaumudī, p. 48. — [11] WEBER, SPAW., 1892, p. 788; BLOOMFIELD, SBE. XLII, p. 508. — [12] Cp. Kauś. 15. 12; 18. 27: the hymn is especially related to ApŚ. 16. 18. 7 ff. — [13] A number of these stanzas occur in the Gṛhya-sūtras and elsewhere; cp. in general Kauś. 89. 12. — [14] Seven Hymns, AJPh. VII. 484 ff.; SBE. XLII, p. 160, 532 ff. — [15] Cp. the so-called *sarpāhuti*, TS. 5. 5. 10. 1—5; MS. 2. 13. 21; ApMB. 2. 17; WEBER, IS. XVII. 291 ff. — [16] WEBER, IS. I. 292; BERGAIGNE, La Religion Védique, II. 451—2, 498; SBE. XLII. 152, 605 ff. — [17] RV. 10. 17. 6, 5, and 6. 54. 9, 10. — [18] LUDWIG, Der Rig-Veda, III. 371; HILLEBRANDT, Ritual-Litteratur, p. 114. — [19] See § 54, note 8. — [20] Cp. Kauś. 1. 29, 30; GB. 2. 1. 10. — [21] Nakṣatrakalpa 10 presents them in full, not by pratīka, showing that these pieces did not figure in the Śaunakīya-Saṃhitā at the time of the compilation of the Nakṣatrakalpa. — [22] WEBER, IS. XVII. 218 ff.; HILLEBRANDT, Ritual-Litteratur, p. 94. — [23] Kauś. 9. 1; 27. 34; cp. also 32. 27, note. The word *mṛgāra* seems to be from *marj* 'purify', but that is not certain. Cp. the *mṛgāra-vrata*, Keś. to Kauś. 42. 12 ff.; Ath. Paddh. to Kauś. 57. 32. — [24] TS. 4. 7. 15; MS. 3. 16. 5; cp. IS. III. 395. — [25] Most of the others appear in the hymn incidentally; cp. SBE. XLII. 618. — [26] Closely related, of course, to the battle-charms, and employed in that function, Kauś. 14. 25; 15. 6. — [27] See Kauśika, Index B, under, *aṁholiṅgāḥ* (p. 383). — [28] See ibid. — [29] See ibid. — [30] Read, *sraktiṣū 'pary* with Bū. for *sraktiṣu pary* in Kauś.; cp. the parallel formulas Kauś. 49. 7 ff. — [31] WEBER, IS. IV. 421; cp. SBE. XLII, Index, under 'homœopathy'.

§ 58. Class 9). Charms in expiation of sin and defilement (prāyaścittāni). — The Hindu conceptions of sin are very complex. Not only is sin an individual, conscious act in violation of the laws of the gods and the universe, but it exists as an independent morbid substance or entity which may fasten itself upon man without his conscious participation, or at least without his choice or sanction. In this sense sin or evil, *enas*, *pāpman*, etc., assume the character of an almost physical deficiency or disease. Sin, too, is transferable from man to man, from father to son, yea from gods to men; the sin of the gods plays no mean part in endangering the peace of men[1]: e. g. in 6. 111. 3 mania is produced by sins of the gods. He who is seized by sin (*pāpmagṛhīta*) is deprived of his strength by Indra and held captive in Varuṇa's toils (TS. 2. 3. 13). Personal defects and mishaps, evil dreams, aspersion of one's character, ominous and portentous occurrences in the sphere within which one lives, or in nature about one, and, *a fortiore*, irregularities and mishaps in the course of religious ceremonies are conceived as closely allied, and confluent with sin and personal offences; they all require expiation, correction, or cure: *prāyaścitti* or *prāyaścitta*[2]. Neither of these words occur in the RV., the former only once in AV. 14. 1. 30, but expiatory stanzas are common throughout the mantra-literature[3]. They are supported moreover by countless practices in the Śrauta-texts in connection with faults in the sacrifice[4], or in the *kāmyā iṣṭayaḥ* of persons attacked by sin, calumny, and misfortune[5]; in the extensive sections on *prāyaścitta* in the *dharma*-texts; in the Gṛhya-sūtras, where they are not very common[6]; and in the Vidhāna-texts[7]. A special variety of *prāyaścitta*, namely those connected with omens and portents (*adbhuta*), has passed through a somewhat independent development, so as to assume the character of a special and extensive class of literature; the most notable compositions of this sort are the 13th book of the Kauśika and the so-called Adbhuta-Brāhmaṇa (ṢB. 5)[8].

More than 40 hymns of the AV. are devoted to this class of subjects[9], quite a considerable part of them covering a single tract, 6. 110—121. It is worthy of note that these hymns, with the exception of 6. 114 and perhaps also 19. 59, do not expressly deal with *prāyaścittas* for defects in the sacrifice. The late Gopatha-Brāhmaṇa in whose view the fourth priest at a Vedic sacrifice, the so-called Brahman, must be an Atharvavedin, repeatedly assigns to him *ex officio* the correction of blunders in the ritual, the *saṃdhāna* of what is *viriṣṭa*[10]. Nevertheless *prāyaścitta*-mantras that pertain directly to the events of the ritual, such as those of Vait. 12. 8, 9; GB. 1. 2. 7, are presented by these texts in *sakalapāṭha,* and do not occur in the Saṃhitā, which in this as in all other respects touches but lightly upon the sphere of the *śrauta*-practices, although it does not fail entirely to take cognizance of them (see below § 60). That ritualistic *prāyaścitta* became later very prominent in the Atharvan schools we may gather from the existence of the unpublished six *prāyaścitta*-chapters of the Vaitāna[11]. The largest number of these hymns address themselves in general terms to the expiation and consequent release from sin, frequently cataloguing a variety of misdemeanors, but not specifying what particular one it is that burdens the conscience; identical or similar stanzas frequently recur in the other Saṃhitās, most especially in TA. 2. 3—6. Thus 6. 45 (cp. RV. 10. 164) is in expiation of mental delinquency (*manas-pāpa*); 6. 26 is directed against *pāpman*, 'evil', personified as a 'thousand-eyed immortal'; 6. 115 against sin, this time called *enas*; 6. 119 and 120 are prayers to Agni Vaiśvānara for remission of sins and ultimate paradise; 6. 121 aims at release from Varuṇa's fetters of sin. Three of these hymns 6. 117—119 harp upon the word *ṛṇa* 'debt', carrying with it the notion of debts incurred, but not paid; especially 6. 118, addressed to the two Apsaras suggests gambling-debts. Another, 6. 116, exhibits a conscience afflicted by the sin of sorcery-practice, *yady āmaṃ cakrur nikhanantaḥ*[12]. The boundary-line between sin and misfortune (*nirṛti*) is evanescent: hymns like 6. 63 and 84 do not differ much in spirit and diction from the preceding. Similarly curses from the outside and sin are correlated in 7. 65 and 112, and the rather obscure stanza 7. 43, rubricated Kauś. 46. 1 in a practice to avert calumnious accusation, may also be of this sort. Also the general purificatory charms, 6. 19; 51; and 62 (above § 56, end), contain certain touches of expression which ally them to this sphere. Frequently, on the other hand, the fault requiring *prāyaścitta* is stated more or less clearly: 6. 114 seems to be an expiatory formula to correct imperfections in the sacrifice (cp. 19. 59); 7. 106 is a prayer to Agni to forgive sins due to forgetfulness (in religious matters); 19. 40 seems to be the *prāyaścitta* of one consecrated for the soma-sacrifice (*dīkṣita*) who has committed a disturbing fault (anger); 7. 66 and 67 seem to be prayers for regaining one's holy learning (*brāhmaṇam*), perhaps after it has been lost through some sin; 7. 102 is a *prāyaścitta* for urinating while standing erect, addressed to the offended deities (μηδ' ἀντ' ἠελίου τετραμμένος ὀρθὸς ὀμιχεῖν, Hes. Erga, v. 727); cp. 13. 1. 56. The obscure mixtum compositum, 6. 49, is recited Kauś. 46. 14 by a Brahmacārin at the death of his teacher, whereas ApŚ. 14. 29. 3 puts the first two stanzas in the mouth of a *dīkṣita* who has fallen from grace (*yadi dīkṣito 'vakiret*)[13]. That the receipt of gifts by the Brahmans is occasionally looked upon as an act requiring penance (3. 29. 7, 8; 6. 71; 7. 57) has been shown above (§ 56). Related with these last is 2. 35 (TS. 3. 2. 8. 3; MS. 2. 3. 8), an expiatory hymn recited to atone for the sin of depriving them that are justly entitled to it of their share of food. Thus in TS. at the *sattra*, when all participants are entitled to *dakṣiṇā*, but do not receive it[14]. See the stanza about the *kevalādin* whose food is in vain (*mogham annam*, TB. 2. 8. 8. 3), or sinful (*agha*, Manu 3. 118). In Kauś. 38. 22 the hymn is recited by one who eats alone in company, in defence against the evil eye of those that do not participate. The slaughter of cattle is constantly looked at askant by the Hindus; hence every bloody sacrifice is overlaid with the fiction that the proper execution of the animal can be performed without injury to it, and even with its consent[15]. The hymn 2. 34 is in the nature of an atonement for a sacrifice in which the victim is conceived as in reality ransomed from death, and following the sinless sacrificer to heaven[16]. One of the greatest crimes of ancient India, affecting both injurer and injured, is the precedence of the younger brother before the older on various solemn occasions in life, especially in the matter of marriage (*pari vid*). Two hymns, 6. 112 and 113, atone for this sort of sin, which, like sundry others, is looked upon as having originated with the gods who 'wiped it off' on their scape-goat, the god Trita, by whom it was in turn passed on to men[17].

But, as stated before, the notion of expiation extends also to circumstances inherent or accidental which cannot and do not involve personal responsibility. Here expiation assumes the character of cure or correction of inauspicious conditions and accidents, naturally broaching upon the domain of *bheṣaja* 'cure'[18]. The conception of the goddess Nirṛti 'misfortune' (6. 63 and 84) is founded largely upon these ideas[19]. Thus 7. 115 is a charm for the removal of evil characteristics (*pāpī lakṣmī*) and the acquisition of auspicious ones (*puṇyā lakṣmī*); cp. 1. 18. The puzzling composite stanzas 6. 30. 2, 3 are prescribed, Kauś. 31. 1, for one whose hair has been cut by a *śamī* and one who has evil characteristics (*śamīlūnapāpalakṣaṇayoḥ*). St. 2 seems to allude to drunkenness which might cover the ground of *pāpalakṣaṇa*; the *śamī* would then appear in some way responsible for drunkenness, or perhaps merely the drunken dishevelled appearance of him whose hair has been cut with an instrument of *śamī*: st. 3 seems to be addressed to such an instrument, used for hair-cutting. It is implored not to harm the hair, in the manner in which the razor (*kṣura*) is elsewhere addressed (8. 2. 17). The juxtaposition of the two sts. may be merely redactorial, due to the occurrence of *śamī* and *keśa* in each: their metres are different[20]. Atonement for personal mishaps is the motive also of 6. 110, a *prāyaścitta* for a child born under an unlucky star; and 6. 140 for the irregular appearance of the first pair of teeth (see § 53, end). Again the birth of twins or the appearance of a sterile cow in the herd (3. 28; 12. 4) require their own peculiar atonements (§ 56): they belong to the domain of *adbhuta* (omens and portents). Of this sort also are the so-called *śākuna*, charms against pigeons, owls, and other black birds whose appearance or contact forebodes evil, or defiles: 6. 27—29 (RV. 10. 165), and 7. 64[21]; and similarly 6. 124, recited by one who has been struck ominously from above (water from heaven, or fruit from a tree); cp. TS. 3. 1. 1. 2. Finally there belong here the charms against evil dreams, or nightmares, 6. 46; 7. 23; 100; 101; 16. 5 ff.; 19. 56; 57, as also sundry stanzas (e. g. 10. 3. 3) scattered throughout the Saṃhitā[22].

1 SBE. XLII. 59, 82, 293, 520, 521, 581, 604. — 2 STENZLER, On the Hindu doctrine of expiation, Proc. Second International Congress of Orientalists, p. 22 f.; BURNELL, Sāmavidhānabrāhmaṇa, p. XX; HARDY, Vedisch-Brahmanische Periode, p. 189; OLDENBERG, Religion des Veda, p. 287 ff., 317 ff.; KONOW, Sāmavidhānabrāhmaṇa, p. 4; JOLLY, Recht und Sitte, p. 115 ff.; HILLEBRANDT, Ritual-Litteratur, p. 166. — 3 E. g. RV. 7. 89. 5; 10. 164. 3; VS. 20. 14—16; TS. 3. 3. 8. 1; MS. 4. 14. 17; TB. 2. 4. 4. 8; and especially the mantras connected with the so-called

kūṣmāṇḍahoma, TA. 2. 3—6. These *kūṣmāṇḍa* are used later to an enormous extent, especially in the *dharma*-texts; e. g. Vās. Dh. 22. 9; Viṣ. Dh. 86. 22; Gaut. Dh. 19. 12; Baudh. Dh. 3. 10. 10; Manu 8. 106; Yājñav. 3. 304; Laghu-Atri Dh. 2. 4; Vṛddha-Atri Dh. 3. 11; Vṛddha-Hārīta Dh. 8. 270, etc., cp. MG. 2. 14. 27. — 4 See the references, HILLEBRANDT, l. c. — 5 Cp., e. g., the *pāpmanā gṛhītasyeṣṭi*, TS. 2. 3. 13; the *abhiśastīṣṭi*, TS. 2. 2. 5. 1; the *yajñavibhraṣṭeṣṭi*, TS. 2. 3. 3. 1—2. — 6 See OLDENBERG, SBE. XXX. 307, for the citations. — 7 Rig-vidhāna, MEYER's Introduction, p. XIII; under *śāntiḥ*; Svidh. 1. 2 ff. — 8 WEBER, Omina und Portenta, APAW., 1859; HATFIELD, The Auśanasādbhutāni, JAOS. XV. 207 ff. (with bibliographical notices in the foot-note on p. 208, and parallels from classical sources on p. 220); HILLEBRANDT, ibid. p. 182. — 9 SBE. XLII. 163—168, and the notes on these hymns; LUDWIG, Der Rig-Veda, III. 442 ff. — 10 1. 1. 14, 15, 22, etc. Cp. M. MÜLLER, HASL. p. 450; BLOOMFIELD, SBE. XLII, p. LXXI; cp. below, § 67 end, and ff. — 11 See GARBE, in the preface to the edition of the text, p. 5; WEBER, Verz. II. 83; Kauśika, Introduction, p. XXXIII. These chapters are probably identical with the Yajñaprāyaścittasūtra, called Vaitāyana, EGGELING, Catalogue, nr. 367; cp. HILLEBRANDT, Ritual-Litteratur, p. 36, note, 1; and above, p. 16. — 12 The padapāṭha erroneously, *yád yāmám* etc. (there is no oxytone *yāmá*); the passage means, 'if they have made a spell of an unburned (vessel) digging it down'. See 5. 31. 1, and cp. SBE. XLII. 457. — 13 Cp. PG. 3. 12. — 14 *yāvanto vai sadasyās te sarve dakṣiṇyās, tebhyo yo dakṣiṇāṃ na nayed aibhyo vṛścyeta, yad vaiśvakarmaṇāni juhoti sadasyān eva tat prīṇāti* (cp. LUDWIG, Der Rig-Veda, V. 601). — 15 Contributions. Sixth Series, ZDMG. XLVIII. 556. — 16 ROTH, Abhandlung, p. 14; WEBER, IS. XIII. 207; LUDWIG, ibid. III. 433. Cp. the similar hymn AVP. = Vait. 10. 17 (GB. 1. 1. 12). — 17 Contributions. Seventh Series, AJPh. XVII. 430 ff.; SBE. XLII. 164, 521 ff. — 18 Cp. Dārila to Kauś. 31. 1 (note 8). — 19 Cp. the *nirṛtikarmāṇi*, Kauś. 18. — 20 LUDWIG, ibid. III 512; ZIMMER, 60, 274; and FLORENZ, BB. XII. 288, do not throw light upon the situation. — 21 Adbhuta-Brāhmaṇa 6 and 8 (ṢB. 5. 6, 8); cp. HULTZCH, Prolegomena zu des Vasantarāja Śākuna; SBE. XLII. 474. — 22 See Kauś., Index B, p. 384., s. v. *duḥsvapnanāśanāni*; SBE. XLII. 484, and, Index, p. 697, under 'dreams'; Rig-vidhāna, Introduction, p. XIII (*infausta somnia*).

§ 59. Class 10). Cosmogonic and theosophic hymns.—The presence in the AV. of a considerable number of cosmogonic-theosophic hymns[1], marking in a way the extreme distance from the ordinary witchcraft-formula, is not readily explained. The common village-practitioner is not likely to have had much use for them, and even the Purohita in his ordinary offices in the *rājakarmāṇi* might well have dispensed with them. Though they occur for the most part, barring the opening-hymns of several of the first books (2. 1; 4. 1, 2; 5. 1, 2; 7. 1, 2)[2], in the books 8—19, yet there is no reason to regard them as late on the whole. Their greater length excluded them from the first seven books, in accordance with the requirements of the redactors. But it is not saying too much that some of them at least, say the Dīrghatamas *brahmodya*, 9. 9 and 10 (RV. 1. 164), were adopted at a time when the adherents of the *atharvāṇaḥ* and *aṅgirasaḥ* had coquetted for some time with the notion that their true place in the Vedic economy was the *brahma* as a whole, in distinction from the individual Vedic types of the *trayī* within which there was for them no place. In other words, that consciousness which later led to the name Brahma-Veda for the Atharvan is likely to have been to a certain extent a stimulus productive of just such compositions as would tend to strengthen this consciousness still further[3]. But it would be a mistake to suppose that theosophic speculation is foreign to the Atharvan, and inorganic; or, that all hymns of this sort are loosely attached to the main body of its compositions. On the contrary, there is evidence that theosophic ideas and formulas had to some extent worked their way into the very tissue of its composition. The charm 4. 19 with the *apāmārga*-plant has for its sixth stanza: 'Non-being (*asat*) arose from the earth; that goes to heaven, (as) a great expansion. Thence, verily, that, spreading vapours, shall turn against the performer (of spells)!' The hymn 9. 2 presents in an ordinary witchcraft charm a personalized god Kāma as a destroyer of enemies, not very different from Agni; yet this Kāma is not to be separated entirely from that *kāma* which is the 'first seed (product) of the mind' that came from 'the one', after it had sprung into existence through creative fervor (*tapas*): RV. 10.129.4 (cp. AV. 19. 52)[4]. Even more intricate is the blend of theosophic conceptions and material purposes in the hymns to Rohita (book 13): in the third hymn of this book the sun-principle is exalted in the best theosophic diction, often in the very formulas characteristic of this style, but the refrain exhibits the hymn in the service of the doctrine of the inviolability (*ajyeyatā*) of the Brahmans: Rohita is here the wrathful god who punishes the persecutors of Brahmans (*yo brahmāṇaṃ jināti*); they are the theme and object of his displeasure and wrath (*āgas*, ἀνάθεμα)[5]. Or, the first part of the first hymn (13. 1. 1—35) correlates consciously with obvious puns the terrestrial Rohita, i. e., the king, with the divine Rohita; the king and his queen (*mahiṣī*) are exalted allegorically to the position of Rohita and his female Rohiṇī: the fusion of the two is so thorough-going that it is at times difficult to decide which, the king or the god, is in the mind of the versifex[6]. The attentive reader of the Atharvan will frequently encounter this transition from philosophy to sophistry: philosophical ideas gone to seed, half decomposed, mixed and coagulated, bandied about and transferred in the relentless desire to produce some magic effect, or to exalt some divinity or ritualistic object far beyond its proper sphere (e. g. 7. 20. 6; 18. 4. 5; 19. 32. 9). The most notable medium for the culture of these false and excessive philosophemata are, as has been hinted above (§ 56), the numerous *dakṣiṇā* or *sava*-hymns. Every animal offered as *dakṣiṇā* is both itself and a cosmic power of the first rank: the gift of a goat, *aja* (4. 14; 9. 5) introduces Aja Ekapād with his mystic punning attributes; in 9. 4 a bull (*ṛṣabha*) is exalted beyond bounds, 'he carries all forms in his body', 'he was at the beginning of things the counterpart of the waters' (sts. 1, 2); but after all it is naught but an ordinary sacrificial bull. Similarly the devoted *vaśā*, 10. 10, provokes metaphysical disquisitions so fleeting, disjointed, and unsteady, that it is a relief to reassure one's self with the aid of st. 1 that, it is after all a cow with hoofs and a tail. Here and there, as e. g., in hymn 4. 11, to the steer (*anaḍvān*), doubt remains as to whether we are facing a theosophical hymn, or a *sava* (Kauś. 66. 12). Similarly, but even more boldly naive, because unsupported by any kind of prior naturalistic conceptions, the *brahmaudana*, the porridge cooked for the Brahmans, is made the vehicle of theosophy (4. 34 and 35; cp. 11. 3. 21); the *brahmaudana* is pertly identified with the 'Ding an sich', or the supreme creative and sustaining principle (4. 35. 3, 5). Within this sphere of conceptions arose the famous hymn 11. 7, to the *ucchiṣṭa*, the leavings of the *brahmaudana*[7], with its momentary symbolic transfer of the highest divine or pantheistic attributes to an intrinsically most trivial ritualistic circumstance. It is well to remember that another high sphere of thought, the ethical, has similarly been pressed into the service of ordinary concerns: the noble hymn to Varuṇa, 4. 16, apparently quite original in the AV., is in reality a witchcraft charm, betraying its purpose in the gross curse at the end — *in cauda venenum.*

In general this class of hymns in the AV. is not devoid of a certain kind of originality and independence which isolates them to a considerable extent from the theosophic mantras of the RV. and the other Saṃhitās, as well as from the speculations of the Upaniṣads. It is not saying too much that the Atharvan hymns are characterized by an even greater degree of garishness, unsteadiness, and gaucherie; of mock-profundity, and impotent reaching out after the inexpressible, than the corresponding hymns of the RV. To this is to be added a growing mechanicalness in the handling of these ideas: the important theosophic attributes are taken out of pigeon-holes, as it were, and applied to the particular subject in hand, not without syncretism and awkward muddling. Occasionally the whole trick is to substitute one name for another: one and the same pāda and stanza is predicated in effect to different subjects of speculation. Cp. e. g. the Rohita-stanzas, AV. 13. 1. 45—55 with the Puruṣa-hymn, RV. 10. 90 = AV. 19. 6; or the even more literal equation, AV. 4. 11. 1 = 10. 7. 35. And these subjects have increased in number and variety. The AV. shares with the RV. the *brahmodya*-stanzas of Dīrghatamas, 9. 9, 10 (RV. 1. 164), which present in the form of theological charades the doctrine of the essential oneness of the universe, of its laws, and also of the nature of the sacrifice; the division of the stanzas into two hymns corresponds in general with the division of the subject matter: the second part (AV. 9. 10 = RV. 1. 164. 23 ff.) deals more directly with the relation of the sacrifice and its attributes (metres, priests, holy speech) to the universal order, whereas the first part deals with the manifestations of the universal one in the universe. The *puruṣa*-hymn, RV. 10. 90, reappears here, AV. 19. 6 (as also in other texts), with some variations that ease the sense, and point to later handling[8]. Two independent Atharvan-hymns (10. 2; 11. 8) owe their origin at least in part to suggestions derived from the *puruṣa-sūkta*: 10. 2 is a mystic meditation, in the form of question (*ka*), of the origin, form, parts of the body, and biological character of the *puruṣa*, the primeval cosmic man, who is, of course, described in the terms of the natural man. The questions introducing the stem *ka* allude to Prajāpati-Brahman, and assimilate the hymn furthermore to the famous *hiraṇyagarbha-sūkta*, RV. 10. 121, of which the AV. also presents a poor version, 4. 2. Another even more mystic derivation of *puruṣa* in his double cosmic and human aspect is contained in 11. 8; the *puruṣa* is derived from a cosmic marriage in the manner of the wedding-hymn (*sūryā-sūkta*, AV. 14 = RV. 10. 85), but all the parties concerned are psychological and religious forces: Manyu ('Will') leads Ākūti ('Intellect') from the house of Saṃkalpa ('Determination'); Tapas and Karman are the woers, Brahman the woer-in-chief. It is a kind of a soul-marriage: Manyu is identified further on with ten psycho-physical forces, *prāṇa*, *apāna*, *cakṣuḥ*, *śrotram*, etc., and it is they that produce the *puruṣa*. Thus in reality Brahman and the psychic and religious forces connected with him express themselves in the soul-life of the *puruṣa*. On the other hand the Vedic gods, Indra, Agni, and even Bṛhaspati, occupy a very subordinate position, being regarded (st. 10) as 'children', each born out of himself, Indra from Indra, Agni from Agni, etc., Devas from Devas; to them the world is made over. The hymn seems to postulate distinctly enough the identity of soul (*ātman*) with *brahma*, clearly expressed in the Upaniṣads, though the word *ātman* does not occur in it[9]. The conception of the *ātman* appears also in the hymn to Prāṇa (11. 4), life or breath personified as the supreme spirit; and the two peculiarly abstract and involved hymns to Skambha 'Support' (10. 7 and 8), which seem to reach out after an even more subtle formulation of the last cause of things than that contained in Puruṣa or Brahma, wind up after all in sts. 10. 8. 43, 44 with a statement that presents the knowledge of Brahma and Ātman as the highest goal[10]. Related with this hymn is the *brahmodya* 5. 1. The *brahma*, prayer (Veda), as supreme principle, is modulated in the greatest variety of keys: in 4. 1 it appears in its own neuter character as 'the first born *brahma* begotten of yore', but passes over quickly (st. 2) into the related conception of Vāc 'speech', i. e. holy speech embodied in the Veda, and in this form it is represented especially by the hymn to Vāc, 4. 30 (RV. 10. 125), and in the *brahmodya*-stanzas 7. 1. The enigmatic *brahmodya*-

hymn 8. 9, addressed to Virāj, has also in mind Vāc Virāj (9. 2. 5); in startling language st. 7 asserts the paradox, 'they call Virāj (female) the father of Brahma'. She in turn acts as the creative principle, her two calves (sun and moon) came forth from the waters (st. 1). The following piece, 8. 10, recites in Brāhmaṇa-prose the curious migrations and metamorphoses of Virāj, posited as the first principle (*virāḍ vā idam agra āsīt*); the pervasive quality of Virāj (holy speech) culminates in the truly Atharvanic anti-climax at the end of the hymn, 30—33, which betrays the bathos and specious mysticism of both hymns (9 and 10): they are an intellectual exercise preparatory to counter-witchcraft; if one merely says, 'in my mind do I repel sorcery', he does (by that mere statement) repel it. The conception of prayer or holy knowledge as the spiritual light that causes and reveals the world gradually roots itself within more concrete individual facts and entities of the universe. Thus st. 7 of the above-mentioned hymn 4. 1, from its Atharvanic point of view, passes the *brahma* on to its typical priest, the Atharvan (Bṛhaspati), who henceforth takes the place, or is intimately associated with Brahma, Prajāpati, and the creative principle: AV. 7. 2[11]. This is in reality the Atharvanic version of the change of *bráhma* to *brahmá*. But especially the dominant power of the visible world, the sun, is blended so inextricably with the conception of the *brahma*, beginning with the famous gāyatrī-stanza, RV. 3. 62. 10[12], as to justify the statement that there is scarcely any theosophic hymn which does not more or less distinctly, primarily or secondarily, have in mind the great heavenly body.

Thus the hymn to Vena 'the lovely', 2. 1, is founded upon the epithet *vena*, attributed to the sun, RV. 1. 83. 5, and more particularly to the Gandharva, the child of the sun (the rainbow?), RV. 10. 123 and 139. This Vena appears as the first cause of things in AV. 2. 1, but no longer simply as the sun, or the Gandharva, but as a seer of the divine revelation, i. e. as a personification of the *brahma*, the spiritual light that reveals the world[13]. Less subtly, but defaced by all sorts of secondary, often grossly practical lucubrations, the red ('ascending') sun, Rohita, figures as creator and preserver of the world in the Rohita-book, AV. 13 (TB. 2. 5. 2. 1—8)[14]. Rohita, or any other solar or creative principle, measures and pervades time (AV. 13. 2. 39); cp. the familiar chain *brahma-prajāpati-saṃvatsara* in the Brāhmaṇas (e. g. ŚB. 1. 5. 1. 16; 11. 1. 6. 13). Hence in 19. 53 and 54 Kāla 'Time', 'Father Time' (53. 8), the first of the gods, creates heaven and earth and all they contain; even the otherwise primordial principles, *tapas, jyeṣṭham* (the highest), *brahma* are fixed in time. A little to one side of this chain of developments, yet clearly within the sphere of conceptions that correlate the *brahma* with the sun, is 11. 5; here a Brahman disciple (*brahmacārin*) in the full glory of his holy functions and monastic habits is treated as an incarnation of the *brahma*: from him the *brahma* springs, and in his holy life (*brāhmaṇam*) the *brahma* is glorified. Yet at the same time it is the shining *brahma* (*brahma bhrājat*, st. 24); or, the *brahmacārin* 'that moves inciting both hemispheres of the world' (st. 1), who 'within the day passes from the eastern to the northern sea' (st. 6); cp. also sts. 11, 23, 26, and GB. 1. 2. 1. Similarly RV. 10. 136 glorifies the sun as a solitary ascetic[15]. Underneath and along with the conception of the *brahma* there is always the more concrete and monotheistic personification of the personal creator, Prajāpati 'the lord of creatures'. This more direct and popular conception also allies itself familiarly with the solar divinities as the lusty creative principle of the world: hence the familiar identification in the Brāhmaṇas of Prajāpati with Savitar and Tvaṣṭar. As a whole this propagative force is symbolized still more tangibly as a bull, steer, or cow; the bestowal of such animals as *dakṣiṇā* (*sava*) especially elicits this animal-symbolism; to such an extent is this true, that the victim is animal and pantheistic-monotheistic divinity at the same time. Thus the bull, *ṛṣabha,* in 9. 4 is assimilated in turn to the various celestial bulls, Rohita, Indra, Tvaṣṭar etc.; or 9. 7, a pantheistic meditation in Brāhmaṇa-prose, compares each limb or part of the bull senselessly with a divinity or cosmic force. The *sava* of a steer (*anaḍvān*, 4. 11) furnishes occasion with equal facility to make the steer the exponent of the same sublime conditions as the very much more abstract Skambha; cp. 4. 11. 1 with 10. 7. 35 (see above). The gift of a goat, *aja* (4. 14; 9. 5), finds in the divine Aja Ekapād a convenient peg to fasten theosophic disquisitions upon. And finally when occasion arises for the bestowal of the female *vaśā* (p. 87) it requires but little more sophistry and oddity to make her the wife of Parjanya, the guardian of heaven and earth (12. 4. 4, 6). We have seen above that the purely ritualistic *brahmaudana* and especially its leavings (*ucchiṣṭa*) also appear in the light of the universal pantheistic force: we may suspect this to be an extension of the treatment of the animal-*savas*. To the same sphere of conceptions, but more liturgic in tone, is 9. 6, in praise of the mystic merits of hospitality (*arghya*); the details of its acts are compared with a sacrifice in which the host (*atithipati*) as sacrificer (*yajamāna*) virtually accomplishes a sacrifice, providing he understands the mystic purport of his own acts.

In striking contrast with the vigorous though peculiar development of theosophic speculations in the AV. is its barrenness on the side of purely mythological fancy. The RV. deals with the gods of nature as the theme of its poetry: the Atharvan cultivates the more homely genii like Aryaman, Anumati, etc., or substitutes demonology. The character of the leading divinities of the RV., Agni, Indra, Sūrya, is scarcely developed at all, barring the undoubtedly popular advance of that fusion of Agni with Rudra in the direction which finally produces the god Śiva[16]. The hymns and stanzas addressed to the mythological gods are in the main borrowed from outside sources; thus when we encounter the long Indra-hymn, 5. 2, it is in reality RV. 10. 120 (employed as a battle-charm, Kauś. 15. 1), or the still longer hymn to Agni, 8. 3 (RV. 10. 87), is addressed to Agni in the character of Rakṣas-killer. Like a fresh breath of wind upon the sultry atmosphere of both demonology and theosophy comes the singular and exceptional hymn 12. 1, addressed to Goddess Earth. This is one of the most attractive compositions of the AV., rising at times to poetic conception of no mean merit, and comparatively free from the stock-artificialities of the Vedic poets. The relation of the real visible earth to man, animals, and plants preponderates wholesomely over the remoter mythological and mystic conceptions[17]. Somewhat in the same vein, though decidedly inferior, is 9. 1, the so-called *madhusūkta*, a hymn to the 'honey-lash' of the Aśvins (*madhukaśā*). The mythic or realistic back-ground of the honey-lash may possibly be 'the honey (the heavenly water) that lashes', or the lightning which whips the clouds and produces rain. The hymn symbolizes prosperity in its widest aspect (*varcasya*)[18]. The cosmic hymn 1. 32, dealing in praise of the physical atmosphere (*antarikṣa*), also deserves mention in this connection.

[1] Cp. the interesting repertory of the theosophic hymns of the AV. in the Cūlikā Up. 11 ff.; and see, MÜLLER, HASL. p. 556 ff.; MUIR, OST., V. 350 ff.; LUDWIG, Der Rig-Veda, III. 393 ff.; SCHERMAN, Philosophische Hymnen, p. 44—88; v. SCHROEDER, Indien's Litteratur, p. 79 ff.; HARDY, Vedisch-Brahmanische Periode, p. 207 ff.; DEUSSEN, Allgemeine Geschichte der Philosophie, vol. I, part 1, p. 209 ff.; BLOOMFIELD, SBE. XLII, p. 199—232, and the notes to these hymns. See also the translations of nearly all these hymns in HENRY, Les Livres VIII et IX de l'AV.;

Les Livres IX, X, et XI de l'AV.; and Les Hymnes Rohitas (livre XIII). — 2 See on this point § 37. — 3 Cp. above § 33. — 4 SBE. XLII. 591. — 5 See above, § 56; cp. DEUSSEN, p. 216. — 6 BLOOMFIELD, Contributions. Fourth Series, AJPh. XII. 430 ff. — 7 Cp. TB. 1. 1. 9. 1; MS. 2. 1. 12. — 8 Cp. DEUSSEN, p. 150. — 9 The hymn is unquestionably very late and paradoxical, but it is not therefore necessary to assume with DEUSSEN (p. 270) that its author deals disrespectfully with earlier traditions, except in the sense in which all theosophic speculations attach inferior importance to all divinities and religious acts, except the search after and knowledge of the fundamental cause, the one being. — 10 Cp. DEUSSEN, p. 310 ff. — 11 Cp. GB. 1. 1. 4 ff.; Muṇḍaka Up. 1. 1. 2; Nyāsa Up. 1. — 12 'The light of Savitar which impels our holy thought'. Cp. RĀJENDRALĀLA MITRA in the introduction to the GB., p. 24. — 13 See WEBER, IS. XIII. 129; LUDWIG, l. c. III. 393; SCHERMAN, p. 82; DEUSSEN, p. 252 ff. HILLEBRANDT, Soma, p. 322 ff., regards *vena* as the moon. — 14 MUIR, OST. V. 395; HENRY, Les Hymnes Rohitas; BLOOMFIELD, AJPh. XII. 429 ff.; DEUSSEN, p. 212 ff. — 15 SBE. XLII. 214, 626 ff.; HENRY, Les Livres X, XI, et XII, p. 114, 150 ff.; DEUSSEN, p. 277. The *vrātya*-sections, book 15, exalt an outcast, or vagabond, who has however entered into the Brahmanical life, as the supreme being (Brahma); see § 61. — 16 See especially AV. 4. 28 and 11. 2; cp. SBE. XLII. 406, 618. — 17 LUDWIG, l. c. III. 544 ff.; SBE. XLII. 199, 639; HENRY, l. c. 179, 215 ff. — 18 HENRY, Les Livres VIII et IX, p. 81, 115 ff.; SBE. XLII, p. 229, 587 ff.

§ 60. Class 11). Ritualistic and general hymns. — The question arises whether the AV. contains hymns which owe their presence in the collection from the start to the existence of Atharvanic Śrauta-rites. Since the Śrauta-manual of the AV., the Vaitāna-sūtra, is late[1], the appearance in it of many hymns of the Śaunakīya-śākhā is non-significant and otiose. The Vait. rubricates practically the entire 20th book of the AV., but this is itself a late Śrauta-supplement to the collection, proving nothing for its original scope and intention[2]. In addition the Vait. employs many scattered hymns and stanzas, especially of the sixth and seventh books, in a manner more or less befitting its own subject matter, and frequently coincident with the employment of the same kind of stanzas in other Śrauta-works. But, as it happens, the same stanzas are as a rule worked up in the Kauśika as well; they may therefore owe their presence in the AV. originally to circumstances and practices such as the Kauśika has in mind; the Vait. may have later taken them up anew in a sense suitable to its own sphere of activity. The inner content of a hymn or stanza is under these circumstances not calculated to decide as to the original intention of the diaskeuasis: a secondary employment of a hymn in Kauś. may be chronologically anterior to the more primary in Vait., providing we trust, as we well may, the author of the Vait. with a sufficient knowledge of the habits of the Śrauta-practices to recognize the obvious and correct applicability of such hymns to Śrauta-practices. Thus the hymn 6. 1, a seemingly inferior version of AŚ. 8. 1. 18, is an evening-song to Savitar, rubricated three times, Kauś. 23. 2; 50. 13; 59. 25: its employment in all three places is secondary and very general. Notwithstanding this, and granting its intrinsic Śrauta-character in more or less close correspondence with its employment at Vait. 17. 2, there is no proof that it was originally incorporated into the AV. in its capacity as a Śrauta-hymn: some such use as is manifested in one or the other of its occurrences in Kauśika may have been the original one with the Atharvavedins, or its employment both in Kauś. and Vait. may be different from and secondary to the original intention.

Recognizing these cautionary circumstances we may nevertheless say outright that the AV. is acquainted with pretty much the entire sphere of Śrauta-rites[3], and, what is more important, that some of its hymns cannot be imagined have been composed or absorbed from other Vedic sources without direct reference to practices which are ordinarily treated in the Śrauta-manuals. Thus the rudiments at least of the *agniṣṭoma*, possibly in some simpler form than that exhibited by the *kalpa*-works of the *trayī*, are represented by 6. 47 and 48. The first of these is not mentioned in Kauś. at all, but appears altogether suitably in connection with the three *savanas*, Vait. 21. 7. These stanzas, probably not original with the AV., can hardly have been absorbed in the redaction except for the reason that they were at that time in vogue at the three *savanas*, as practiced by adherents of the AV. The second of these hymns (6. 48) consists of Yajus-formulas differing more or less from the corresponding formulas of the Śrauta-texts[4]; it is quoted in Kauś. 56. 4; 59. 26, 27 under circumstances that betray unmistakably its secondary employment. Here also by the very force of their contents it seems unlikely that they owe their Atharvanic composition to anything else than the *savanas*. The Vait. employs them accordingly, 17. 10; 21. 7, and that too in the order of the three sts. demanded by their context and the parallel formulas: in this instance the ritualistic tradition surpasses that of the Saṃhitā, either reaching behind it, or correcting it by superior information[5]. Again, the loosely attached st. 7. 76. 6 (RV. 6. 47. 6), addressed to Indra at the *mādhyaṃdina-savana*, is not mentioned in Kauś., whereas it appears in a proper place, Vait. 16. 14. Add to this the familiarity with the *savanas* betrayed by incidental allusions, such as in 9. 1. 11—13 (cp. also 7. 72. 3), or the elaborate invitations to Indra to partake of soma, 2. 5; 6 (cp. also 7. 58 and 117), and it is not too much to say that the Atharvans knew and practised soma-rites prior to the redaction of the Saṃhitā. Whether this was carried on in the spirit and with the equipment of the Vedic schools of the *trayī*, or in some more elementary form that did, above all, not require a variety of priests, can hardly be discerned[6] The same kind of enquiry is suggested by the two *āprī*-hymns, 5. 12 (RV. 10. 110, et al.), and 5. 27 (VS. 27. 11 ff.; MS. 2. 12. 6; TS. 4. 1. 8). The Vait., 10. 11 ff., exhibits them in accordance with the original intention of *āprī*-hymns at the *paśubandha*, a Śrauta-performance; Kauś. 45. 8 at the sacrifice of the *vaśā* as *dakṣiṇā* (cp. AV. 10. 10; 12. 4), a kind of practice which the AV. at any rate has elaborated independently of Śrauta-types as a sacrifice with one priest and one fire. It is impossible to judge from this whether the *paśubandha* represents the original Atharvanic intention of these hymns, or whether the Vait. has merely revamped them according to other Śrauta-models. Similar questions may be asked in connection with a considerable list of ritualistic hymns: the hymn 2. 6 (VS. 27. 1 ff.; MS. 2. 12. 5; TS. 4. 1. 7) is employed Vait. 28. 4, 10 in accordance with its original intention, at the *agnicayana*, whereas Kauś. 59. 15; 102. 4 presents it under obviously secondary aspects (cp. also 7. 62; 63; and 78); the hymn 7. 73 is a prayer to the Aśvins while offering hot milk (cp. the *gharma*-hymn from the AVP. in Vait. 14. 1); the hymn 7.97 consists of Yajus-stanzas and formulas (VS. 8. 15 ff.; MS. 1. 3. 38; TS. 1. 4. 44), addressed to Agni, Indra, and other gods. Of marked ritualistic character are further 7. 27, a stanza to Iḍā (Vait. 3. 15; cp. ŚB. 1. 8. 1. 7 ff.); 7. 28, addressed to certain sacrificial instruments (Vait. 4. 12; 13. 2; cp. TS. 3. 2. 4. 1); 7. 30, a st. pronounced while annointing; 7. 98, while annointing the *barhis*; 7. 99 while preparing the *vedi* (cp. TB. 3. 7. 6. 1); 7. 33 while sprinkling (TA. 2. 18. 1); 7. 71, *paryagnikaraṇa* (RV. 10. 87. 22, et al.); 7. 74. 4, to Agni, lord of vows; 6. 10, prayer to the cosmic triad[7]; 7. 89, sts. to the waters and Yajus-formulas to the fagots (repeated in almost all Vedic collections)[8]. Cp. also such hymns as 7. 25; 26; 29, and many others, especially in books 6 and 7, that are addressed to members of the pantheon, regarding which it is impossible to say whether their originally ritualistic function, or some secondary use (*pauṣṭika*) secured them a place in the Saṃhitā. The same doubt is suggested by the numerous hymns to the waters,

1. 4—6; 33; 6. 23; 7. 89; 16. 1; 19. 2; 69; and especially the long composite rigmarole, 10. 5. Cp. the *apāṃ sūktāni,* Kauśika, Index B, p. 383; the *salilāni,* ib. 385; and the *gaṇa,* Kauś. 41. 14.

A special ritualistic flavor attaches to a considerable number of hymns of varying import all of which state distinctly that they are accompanied by an oblation, or *havis.* This *havis* is preceded by an adjective or noun which expresses tersely the purpose of the hymn. Thus 1. 15; 2. 26; and 19. 1 are accompanied by *sāṃsrāvya havis* 'that causes the flowing together of wealth'; 6.39 by *yaśo havis* 'that confers glory'; 6.40 by *saptarṣīṇāṃ havis* 'oblation to the Seven Rishis (that frees from danger)'; 6. 64 by *samāna havis* 'that makes harmonious'; 6.65 (and 66) by *nairhasta havis* 'that makes (the enemy) handless'; 6.75 by *nairbādhya havis* 'that suppresses (the enemy); 6. 78 by *bhūta havis* 'that produces power'; 6. 80 by *śuno divyasya mahas havis* 'that contains the majesty of the heavenly dog'; 6. 87 (and 88); 7. 94 by *dhruva havis* 'that makes stable'; cp. also the less clearly defined *havis* in 1. 31; 6. 41; 7. 70; 77; the *guhya ghṛta* in 7. 29, and the *pratrāsa ājya* in 5. 21. 2. Once, in 1. 29. 1, the AV. substitutes characteristically *abhīvarta maṇi* for *abhīvarta havis,* RV. 10. 174. 1. The RV. mentions such special *havis* in hymns of Atharvanic character: *rathavāhana havis* in 6.75.8; *dhruva havis* in 10. 173. 6 (AV. 7. 94). LUDWIG, who first invited attention to this feature and its peculiar development in the AV.[9], fitly describes it as a 'teilcærimonie' for a special purpose: it may be defined further by describing it as the hymnal correspondent of the *kāmyā iṣṭayaḥ* of the Śrauta-literature. In the course of other practices a special libation for a purpose, aside perhaps from the main action, might be naturally introduced. Since this action bore upon matters of ordinary life it insinuated itself more particularly into the prayers and performances of the Atharvans, assuming there a more independent and technical form.

[1] GARBE, Vaitāna Sūtra, Preface, p. VII; BLOOMFIELD, JAOS. XI. 375 ff.; HILLEBRANDT, Ritual-Litteratur, p. 35. — [2] See below, § 62. — [3] The *sautrāmaṇī* is mentioned in 3. 3. 2; an almost exhaustive catalogue of sacrifices and liturgical terms is presented in 11. 5. 5 ff. — [4] JAOS. XV. 3, 4. — [5] Ibid. p. 5, note. — [6] The *triṣavaṇa-vrata* mentioned in the late Atharvanic manual, Ath. Paddh. to Kauś. 57. 32, is not likely to bear directly upon this sacrifice; cp. BRW. s. v., and HILLEBRANDT, Ritual-Litteratur, p. 58. — [7] The GB. regularly substitutes an Atharvanic tetrad or pentad in such cases: 1. 1. 17—20, 29; 2. 16, 24; 3. 24, etc.; AV. 2. 19—23; Kauś. 119. 2, 3. — [8] RV. 1. 23. 22—24, et al. — [9] Der Rig-Veda, III. 371 ff.; cp. SBE. XLII, in the notes on these hymns, especially p. 479, 498, and 500.

§ 61. Class 12). The books dealing with individual themes (books 13—18). — The six books 13—18 are devoted to special themes. Book 13[1] contains four long hymns addressed to a form of the sun-god called Rohita 'The Red', with constant puns on the root *ruh,* as though, 'he that has been led up (to the sky)'; his female Rohiṇī (Sūryā, Uṣas)[2] figures also. Rohita is not merely the heavenly body or its divinity, but he is swelled out by means of theosophic notions, so as to appear as the creator and preserver of the universe, a form of Prajāpati. A considerable part of the book, however, is either not connected with the main theme at all, or exhibits the main theme in secondary application[3]. The first 35 sts. of the first hymn, apparently the main stock of the entire book, correlate Rohita with an earthly king whose kingdom is given him, and whose kingdom is preserved by Rohita. Sts. 36—44 are a mystic presentation of the wonders connected with the appearance and disappearance of the sun; sts. 45—55 present Rohita (sun, fire) as a Rishi who kindles with his prayers the two sacrificial fires, winter and summer, upon which the life of nature is founded. The remaining sts. of this hymn are even more extraneous. The second hymn is addressed to the sun in his more general aspects; only sts. 25—26 and 39—41 deal directly with Rohita. The third hymn presents Rohita as the avenger of the oppressors of Brahmans; the fourth hymn, partly prose, engages in praise of the god in hackneyed terms.

Book 14 contains the wedding-stanzas of the Atharvans[4]. They coincide largely, though by no means entirely, with the *sūryā-sūkta*, RV. 10. 85. Other stanzas of the RV., notably 10. 40. 10 ff., and scatteringly still others, reappear; yet a considerable number are not found in the RV. In the Gṛhya-sūtras most of these stanzas recur with many variants. The chronology and inter-relation of the wedding-stanzas in all these texts is a subject for special investigation: none of the existing collections of these stanzas present them in anything like their primary aspect.

Book 15 in Brāhmaṇa-prose is devoted to the mystic exaltation of the *vrātya*[5]. In the list of theosophic subjects which the Cūlikā Up. 11 ascribes to the AV. the *vrātya* figures between the Brahmacārin (AV. 11. 5) and Skambha (AV. 10. 7, 8)[6]. There can be no doubt that the theme is in reality Brahma, but section 5 which introduces the *mūrtis* of Rudra shows it to be under Śivaitic influence. The *vrātya* (*vrātīna*) seems to be a kind of a Brahmacārin, or at any rate one who has entered the Brahmanical community after having been converted from an Aryan, but non-Brahmanical tribe. This is the theme of the so-called *vrātyastomāḥ*, described especially in the Śrauta-books of the SV. (PB. 17. 1; LŚ. 8. 6)[7]; these rites make it possible for an unholy, half-savage, community (*na hi brahmacaryaṃ caranti na kṛṣiṃ na vaṇijyām*, PB. 17. 1. 2) to become Brahmans. The connection between the *vrātya*-book and the *vrātyastoma* is not to be questioned: in 15. 2 the statement that 'faith has become his paramour, holy words (*mantra*) his Māgadha (outcaste associate)' clearly refers to the conversion of the *vrātya*; the occurrence of such words as *uṣṇīṣa*, *pratoda*, and *vipatha* in AV. 15. 2, as well as in PB. 17. 1. 14, clinches the connection still further[8]. The *vrātya*, having become holy through his acquired *brahmacaryam* is emphatically the representative of *brahma*; like the Brahmacārin (11. 5) he is apotheosized. The mention of a large number of Sāmans in the book seems to point to some sort of a connection with the schools of the Sāma-Veda. The contents are too abstruse and too absurd for analysis. The book is wanting in AVP.

The sixteenth book contains two distinct parts not related in any way. AV. 19. 23. 26 seems to refer to them in the expression *prājāpatyābhyāṃ svāhā*. The first four pieces (first anuvāka) consist of prose-formulas, running into metre occasionally (4. 2); they are designated, Ath. Pariś. 10, as *abhiṣekamantrāḥ*. They clearly consist of ritualistic formulas dealing to some extent with the praise of the waters[9]. Their purpose however is not quite clear, even in the light of Kauśika's employment of them. Section 2 recurs ĀpŚ. 6. 20. 2 with interesting variations. The rest of the book, 5—9 (second anuvāka) is an elaborate conjuration against nightmare which is driven out from one's self and imposed upon enemies. Why these two sections have been gathered up in a separate book does not appear.

Nor is it possible to point out the reason why the single hymn, book 17, should have reached the distinction of a separate book for itself. The hymn, known as the *viṣāsahi* (AV. 19. 23. 27), is one of the most prominent of the *āyuṣyāṇi* (class 2) and figures especially in the rites connected with the life of the young Ārya[10]. Keśava to Kauś. 42. 12 ff., and Ath. Paddh. to

Kauś. 57. 32 mention a *viṣāsahi-vrata*[11] from the same sphere of practices; doubtless this hymn figured prominently in it.

Book 18 in four hymns (each an anuvāka) contains the funeral-stanzas, being pretty certainly a later version of the corresponding materials in RV. X. This is evident especially from the incorporation into the AV. of RV. X. 10—12; sts. 1—39 of AV. 18. 1 contain these three hymns in the same order as the RV., omitting only six stanzas. The reappearance of RV. 10. 10 in the AV. is natural, because the hymn contains the famous dialogue between Yama and Yamī, whereas RV. 10. 11 and 12 which have no direct relation to Yama or the funeral-practices, are incorporated in the AV. in deference to the redaction of the RV. All 39 sts. are ignored by Kauśika. The remaining sts. of hymn 1 and the whole of hymn 2 repeat in totally changed order sts. from RV. 10. 14—17, introducing occasionally other RV. sts., or such as do not appear in RV. at all. Of the 73 sts. of the third hymn only 32 are found in RV.; the rest are peculiar to the AV. and the Yajus (TA. 6). Still more original is hymn 4: only 12 of its 89 sts. are recruited from various books of the RV., and only 7 others coincide with the funeral stanzas of TA. 6[12]. The Atharvan version of this subject is to some extent original, and is not in complete accord with the practices of Kauśika which in turn present many individual traits elsewhere unknown. A single original funeral stanza, 7. 21, is stranded outside of the main collection, being seemingly employed, Kauś. 86. 16, in a connection which does not bear upon its contents. Very valuable side-lights upon the funeral-practices are afforded by numerous Atharvan conjurations which allude to details freer and more convincing than many that are codified either in the funeral-stanzas or in the Sūtras; thus the practices of mourning-women which are alluded to in many passages[13]. For other suggestions of this kind see SBE. XLII, Index, under 'funeral practices'. ALBERUNI, India (SACHAU'S translation), vol. I, p. 129, remarks that the AV. contains injunctions regarding the dead, and what is to be done with them.

[1] MUIR, OST. V. 395; HENRY, Les Hymnes Rohitas; BLOOMFIELD, AJPh. XII. 429 ff.; REGNAUD, Le Rig-Véda et les origines de la mythologie indo-européenne, p. 311 ff.; DEUSSEN, Allgemeine Geschichte der Philosophie, vol. I, part 1, p. 209 ff. — [2] JAOS. XV. 186; AJPh. XII. 430. — [3] Cp. above, § 59. — [4] Translated by WEBER, IS. V. 195 ff. — [5] A tentative translation by AUFRECHT, IS. I. 130 ff. — [6] Cp. also Praśna Up. 2. 11. — [7] Cp. AŚ. 9. 8. 25; KŚ. 12. 1. 2; 22. 4. 1, 27; Yājñav. 1. 34. — [8] AUFRECHT, IS. I. 138; WEBER, IS. I. 33, 52, 445 note; WL². 73, 85 ff., 122—4, 163, 196; HILLEBRANDT, Ritual-Litteratur, p. 140, 168, 179. The term *vrātya* is probably derived from compounds like *anyavrata*, *apavrata*, etc. 'having different customs'. — [9] See Kauś. 9. 9; 2. 18, and the Index of Citations, p. 410. — [10] See Kauśika, Index of Citations, p. 410. — [11] Cp. HILLEBRANDT, Ritual-Litteratur, p. 58. — [12] Book 18 has been translated, explained, and analysed by WEBER, SPAW., 1895, p. 815 ff; 1896, p. 253 ff.; cp. also his remark, SPAW., 1891, p. 786. For the literature and criticism of the funeral-ceremonies see CALAND, Die Altindischen Todten- und Bestattungsgebräuche, in the Transactions of the Amsterdam Academy, 1896, especially the introduction and p. 163 ff.; HILLEBRANDT, Ritual-Litteratur, p. 87 ff. — [13] BLOOMFIELD, Contributions. Second Series, AJPh. XI. 336 ff.

§ 62. Class 13). The twentieth book.. — Of the 143 hymns of book 20 only 13 are in any way peculiar to the AV., namely 2, 48, 49, 127—136; in addition the sts. 34. 12, 16, 17, and 107. 13 = 13. 2. 34[1]. Of these the so-called *kuntāpa-sūktāni*, 127—136, in their Atharvanic form and extent are original, and no pada-text of them appears to exist; they are wanting in AVP. The other hymns and stanzas, just catalogued, are borrowed from AVP.[2] The remaining hymns of the book, mostly addressed to Indra, are derived bodily, without a single variant, from the RV., largely the eighth maṇḍala. Thus, e. g., RV. 10. 163 is repeated verbatim AV. 20. 96. 17—22, although its Atharvan version with the usual variations has occurred previously, 2. 33. Compare similarly AV. 5. 2 with RV. 10. 120 = AV. 20. 107. 4—12. The book is known as the *śastrakāṇḍa*, being largely rubricated in Vait., beginning with 19. 6 (in the course of the *agniṣṭoma*), and extending through to the end of that text. It was compiled for use of the Brahman-priest, or more particularly his Atharvanic assistent, the Brāhmaṇācchaṁsin, at the *śastras* and *stotras* of the soma-sacrifices[3], at a time when the Atharvans had adopted systematic and extensive Śrauta-rites in imitation of the other Vedic schools; its ritualistic character may be observed especially in connection with the *kuntāpa*-hymns which are preceded and followed by the RV. hymns in the order in which they are called for by the ritual as described in the Brāhmaṇas and Sūtras[4]. The AV. Prātiśākhya does not take it into account (any more than book 19)[5]; it would seem therefore that these books did not at that time form part of the Śaunakīya-Saṃhitā, although, of course, this may be due to conscious neglect, induced on the one hand by the exceeding corruption of the Atharvanic parts of these books; on the other by the knowledge that the Rig-Vedic parts of book 20 belong to another śākhā, were therefore not *prātiśākhya*. Of the Atharvanic materials hymn 2 consists of Yajus-formulas recited in connection with the *ṛtu-grahas* at the *agniṣṭoma*, Vait. 19. 23[6]; the three Indra-stanzas 34. 12, 16, 17 are original; hymns 48 and 49 are not even rubricated in Vait. All these are from AVP. The single st. 107. 13 = 13. 2. 34 is a later modification of 13. 2. 35 (= RV. 1. 115. 1, et al.). The *kuntāpa*-hymns call for a separate and more searching statement of their contents, purpose, and relation to the ritual, since their Atharvan version seems to be the fullest and most original in existence.

1 WHITNEY, Index Verborum, p. 2; OLDENBERG, Die Hymnen des RV., 348 ff. — 2 ROTH, AV. in Kaschmir, p. 23. — 3 ROTH, Abhandlung, p. 21; AV. in Kaschmir, l. c.; WL.[2] 162, note; GARBE, Vaitāna-Sūtra, Preface, p. 8, and the notes on the translation of Vait. 25. 11; 26. 10; 27. 28, 29; WEBER, SPAW., 1891, p. 787, note; APAW., 1893, p. 5; OLDENBERG, ibid. p. 346. — 4 See below, § 63, near the end. 5 WHITNEY, JAOS. VII. 334, 581; cp. WL.[2], p. 168, note. — 6 Similar formulas, KŚ. 9. 8. 9 ff.; ApŚ. 11. 9. 8 (cp. ŚB. 4. 6. 6. 5).

§ 63. Class 14). **The kuntāpa-hymns.** — AV. 20. 127—136 are designated in the mss. as *kuntāpasūktāni*[1], being introduced and concluded by the expressions, *atha kuntāpasūktāni*, and, *iti kuntāpasūktāni samāptāni*. The exact scope of the designation *kuntāpa* is not certain. Sāyaṇa at AB. 6. 32. 1; 33. 1 defines as the *kuntāpa*-hymn the thirty stanzas, equal to the first two hymns of the *kuntāpa-saṃhitā*, as given in the AV. (20. 127 and 128), but the whole collection also figures in his view as a supplementary book (*khila*) with the name *kuntāpa*[2]. This seems also to be the view of the Vait. 32. 19, which assigns the name to the first two hymns, and employs the designations *aitaśapralāpa*, etc. for the following hymns (32. 20 ff.). In ŚŚ. 12. 13. 7 (cp. 12. 6. 13) the term *kuntāpa* seems to be restricted to a part of the collection, as given in that Sūtra (12. 14—16 = AV. 20. 127. 1—6, 11—13; 128. 12, 13, 15; 135. 13, 11, 12). But inasmuch as all parts of the collection, including those just mentioned, have specific names in addition to the generic *kuntāpa* (see below), the latter word may after all have been used by Śāṅkhāyana (as also by Vait.) at the beginning of his presentation of the *kuntāpa*-materials as a name for the whole to the neglect of the specific names (*nārāśaṁsyaḥ*, *raibhyaḥ*, etc.)[3], until he arrived (12. 17) at the *pārikṣityāḥ*. This view is born out by KB. 30. 5. Similarly AŚ. 8. 3. 7 the word *kuntāpa* is used by way of introduction to these materials, none of the subsidiary designations appearing until the *bhūtechadaḥ*-stanzas (AV. 20. 135. 11 ff.) are reached, sūtra 27. Again, GB. 2. 6. 12 begins with, *atha kuntāpaṃ śaṁsati*, neglecting the subsidiary name *nārāśaṁsyaḥ* for the opening passage, *idaṃ janā upa śruta* (AV. 20. 127. 1—3), but introducing the following subdivisions with their proper designations, *atha raibhīḥ śaṁsati*, *vyacasva* etc. (AV. 20. 127. 4—6). On the whole it seems quite clear that the name *kuntāpa* is understood to belong to the whole collection which varies somewhat in extent and arrangement in each of the texts that employ it, but that the name was sometimes employed for one or two of the initial hymns; in the latter case the specific designations of the opening hymns were more or less suppressed, although they were probably well known in each of the schools.

In addition to AV. only ŚŚ. gives the *kuntāpa*-materials in full: the other texts (AB. GB. AŚ. Vait.) give only the pratīkas, with an occasional stanza in full; the KB. does not even cite the pratīkas but mentions the subdivisions under their specific designations (*nārāśaṁsyaḥ*, etc.). The *kuntāpa*-texts in the ŚŚ. (12. 14 ff.) read like an extract from the AV. in an arrangement markedly different; this version also underlies the statements of KB. 30. 5 ff.[4], being therefore the traditional material in vogue in the school of the Śāṅkhāyanas or Kauṣītakins. All the stanzas, riddles, and answers of the ŚŚ. appear also in the much larger collection of the AV., excepting the bracketed st. 7 in ŚŚ. 12. 21. 1, which occurs on the margin of some mss., being omitted by others altogether[5]. In many cases the readings of the ŚŚ. mss. agree with those at the basis of the vulgata: HILLEBRANDT has frequently adopted the corrections proposed by the editors of the vulgata[6]. The remaining texts, AB. GB. AŚ. Vait., presuppose a version nearly if not quite identical with the AV.: the few differences are almost entirely in the nature of variant readings whose substantiality however is often rendered suspicious by the exceeding corruption of the text of the *kuntāpa*[7]. In some respects the AŚ. handles its materials, as might be expected, rather in accordance with ŚŚ. than AV., e. g., in its treatment of the *aitaśapralāpa*, AŚ. 8. 3. 14—17 (see below).

The liturgic tradition of the *kuntāpa-śastra* corresponds obviously to the natural subdivisions according to subject-matter in the *kuntāpa*-hymns themselves: their treatment therefore from the combined points of view of hymns and ritual is imperative. The following division of the hymns as reported in the AV. appears to be founded upon their intrinsic contents as well as their use in the śastras:

I. AV. 20. 127. 1—3 = ŚŚ. 12. 14. 1—3. St. 1 in AŚ. 8. 3. 10; its pratīka, GB. 2. 6. 12; Vait. 32. 19. The AB. 6. 32; 3 ff. (cp. also 1), KB. 30. 5, as also the commentators generally (e. g. at ŚŚ. 12. 16. 1), designate these stanzas as *nārāśaṁsyaḥ* (sc. *ṛcaḥ*). The subject is a fabulous *dānastuti* in praise of Kaurama, a prince of the Ruśamas[8]. See SBE. XLII. 197, 690.

II. AV. 20. 127. 4—6 = ŚŚ. 12. 14. 4—15. 1 (in different order). The pratīka in GB. 2. 6. 12. The GB., AB. 6. 32. 7 ff. (cp. also 1), KB. 30. 5, and the comms. designate them as *raibhyaḥ*. The theme is the praise of Rebha (Agni) who bestows cattle and wealth, or an exhortation to a human chanter (poet) to perform his functions. A comparison of the chanter with Agni is involved in any case. See SBE. XLII. 197, 690 ff.

III. AV. 20. 127. 7—10 = ŚŚ. 12. 17. 1. 1—4. The pratīka in GB. 2. 6. 12. The GB., AB. 6. 32. 10 ff. (cp. also 1), ŚŚ., KB. 30. 5, and the comms. designate them as *pārikṣityāḥ*. Praise of Agni Parikṣit, the typical god of Brahmanical piety[9]. See SBE. XLII. 197, 691 ff.

IV. AV. 20. 127. 11—14 = ŚŚ. 12. 15. 2—4[10]. The pratīka in GB. 2. 6. 12. The GB., AB. 6. 32. 16 ff. (cp. also 1), KB. 30. 5, and the comms. designate them as *kāravyāḥ*. Exhortation of the poet by Indra who, as reward for a song of praise, grants wealth and destroys enemies. See SBE. XLII. 198, 692.

V. AV. 20. 128. 1—5 = ŚŚ. 12. 20. 1. 1—5. The pratīka in GB. 2. 6. 12. The GB., AB. 6. 32. 19 ff., KB. 30. 7, ŚŚ., and the comms. designate them as *diśāṃ kḷptayaḥ*, 'arrangement of the directions of space, orientation'. The paragraph consists of didactic stanzas (*nīti*), in which certain kinds of conduct are correlated with the five directions of space, *prāk*, *adharāk*, *udak*, *apāk*, and, apparently, *ūrdhvam* as the fifth, implied in the words, *divam iva gatvāya*, in st. 5. Proper conduct seems to be associated in 1, 3, 5 with *prāk*, *udak*, and *ūrdhvam*; improper conduct in 2, 4 with *adharāk*, and *apāk*. The possible pejorative sense of the last two in contrast to the good sense of the other three seems to be the main point of these wise saws, but the untrustworthiness of the text (cp. ŚŚ.) renders this entire construction problematic. St. 1: 'The man of good house, of rich establishment, who presses (the soma) and brings sacrifices, as well as yonder sun, the illustrious gods fixed as east'[11]. The opposite kind of a man (a stingy one) is correlated in st. 4 with 'west' (*apāk*).

VI. AV. 20. 128. 6—11 = ŚŚ. 12. 21. 2. 1—6. The pratīka in GB. 2. 6. 12. The GB., AB. 6. 32. 23 ff., KB. 30. 7, ŚŚ., and the comms. designate them as *janakalpāḥ*, 'containing the classification of folk', or the like. The subject is didactic and related to the preceding: desirable and undesirable folks are compared in classes. E. g. sts. 8, 9: 'A lake without watering-place, a rich man who is stingy, and an unseductive, ugly maid are of like character; of like character (on the other hand are also) a lake with a good watering-place, a liberal rich man, and a seductive, beautiful maid'. The classification in sts. 10, 11 of the *parivṛktā mahiṣī* and the *vāvātā mahiṣī*, of a slow and a swift horse, and the obscenity which appears here, as also frequently in the sequel, suggest conditions similar to the notorious practices at the *aśvamedha* and *puruṣamedha*. Indeed the three abusive stanzas (*aślīlabhāṣaṇam*) 10, 8, 6 (inverse order), are employed ŚŚ. 16. 13. 10 in the course of the *puruṣamedha*; cp. Vait. 38. 2.

VII. AV. 20. 128. 12—16 = ŚŚ. 12. 15. 1. 5—12. 16. 1. 2 (sts. 14, 16 of AV. wanting in ŚŚ.). The pratīka in GB. 2. 6. 12. The GB., AB. 6. 32. 25 ff., KB. 30. 5, and the comms. designate them as *indragāthāḥ*. The theme is praise of Indra, the conqueror of demons and enemies.

VIII. AV. 20. 129—132. ŚŚ. has only a limited number of these pādas: AV. 20. 129. 1—10 = ŚŚ. 12. 18. 1. 1—9; AV. 20. 132. 2—7, 9, 11, 12 = ŚŚ. 12. 18. 1. 10—18; AV. 20. 131. 10, 11 = ŚŚ. 12. 18. 1. 19, 20. The AŚ. 8. 3. 14—17 presents the same three groups of stanzas as appear in ŚŚ., giving as pratīkas ŚŚ. 12. 18. 1. 1 and 10, followed by 19 and 20 in full[12]. In AB. 6. 33. 2; GB. 2. 6. 13; Vait. 32. 20 the pratīka appears; AB., GB., ŚŚ., KB. 30. 5, and the comms. designate it as *aitaśapralāpa* (or *etaśa°*) 'the chatter of Aitaśa'[13]. The Brāhmaṇa-texts present mystic, apologetic legends in explanation of this chatter of the sage Aitaśa, designed to show its great liturgic power. But there is certainly no basis in the text itself for a sage Aitaśa. Either the name was abstracted verbally from the initial words *etā aśvā*, or the variegated horse of the sun, *etaśa*, is supposed to underlie the enigmatic (*brahmodya*) nonsense of the text[14]. The first part has been rendered tentatively and without explanation by Zimmer, p. 131.

IX. AV. 20. 133 = ŚŚ. 12. 22, where an additional riddle without answer is added by some mss. (st. 7). The pratīka, GB. 2. 6. 13; AŚ. 8. 3. 18; Vait. 32. 21. The answers to these riddles are inserted in AV., are stated separately AŚ. 8. 3. 19; Vait. 32. 25, but are altogether absent from ŚŚ. The GB., AB. 6. 33. 16, KB. 30. 7, ŚŚ., and the comms. designate them as *pravalhikāḥ*[15], 'riddles'; by propounding them the gods (*à la* Sphinx) got the better of the Asuras. In the AV. the riddle is given first, then the answer, and finally a curious refrain, addressed apparently to an (innocent) girl who is thus instructed in these *jeux d'esprit*. In the śastra the riddles seem to be chanted by the Hotar, the answers figuring as *pratigaras* in the mouth of the Adhvaryu who addresses the Hotar as *jaritar*. These riddles are either obscene or naive folk productions. Of the latter sort are 3 and 4: 'By drawing two little ears to oneself they are gotten out in the middle (: what is it?)'. Answer: 'The tying of a knot in a rope'. 'In what lies stretched out there is hidden that which stands (: what is it?)'. Answer: 'The foot in the shoe'.

X. AV. 20. 134 = ŚS. 12. 23. 1, where only four of these riddles are given (1—3, 6 of AV.[16]): the answers in ŚS. 12. 23. 3. AŚ. 8. 3. 20 has the pratīka of the hymn: the answers to the same four as appear in ŚS. are given as *pratigaras* in 8. 3. 21. Vait. 32. 22 has the pratīka: the answers to all six in the order 1—3, 6, 5, 4 in 32. 25. The pratīka also in GB. 2. 6. 13. The GB., AB. 6. 33. 18 ff. (omitted in KB. 30. 7), and the comms. designate them as *ājijñāsenyāḥ* 'puzzles'. They are riddles derived from the vegetable and mineral kingdoms. Riddle 4: 'Well, here it is, east, west, north, and south; as soon as you touch it it melts (or vanishes: what is it?)'. Answer: 'A drop'.

XI. AV. 20. 135, 1—3 = ŚS. 12. 23. 2 with the answers (*pratigaras*) in 3. The pratīka, AŚ. 8. 3. 22: the answers in 23; the pratīka, Vait. 32. 23: the answers in 25; the pratīka also, GB. 2. 6. 13. The GB., AB. 6. 33. 19, KB. 30. 7, ŚS., and the comms. designate them as *pratirādha* 'hindrance, handicap'. They are three riddles from the animal and vegetable kingdoms, typifying the actions of quick arrival, swift disappearance, and firm standing. Riddle 1: 'Bounce, he has come (: what is it?). Answer: 'The dog'. 2. 'Whist, it is gone (: what is it?)'. Answer: 'The fall of the leaf'. 3. 'Bang, it has trodden (: what is it?)'. Answer: 'The hoof of an ox'.

XII. AV. 20. 135. 4, 5 = ŚS. 12. 23. 4, 5. The pratīka, AŚ. 8. 3. 23: the *pratigaras* in 24. The pratīka, Vait. 32. 26: the *pratigaras* in 27. The pratīka also, GB. 2. 6. 13. The GB., AB. 6. 33. 20, KB. 30. 7, and the comms. designate it as *ativāda* 'outtalking'. Seems also to be a riddle or two with obscene answers (cp. AV. 20. 136. 4, et al.).

XIII. AV. 20. 135. 6—10 = ŚS. 12. 19. 1—5 = AB. 6. 35. 5 ff. = GB. 2. 6. 14[17]. The pratīka, AŚ. 8. 3. 25[18]; Vait. 32. 28. The AB., GB. designate it as *devanītha*; the ŚS., KB. 30. 6, as *ādityāṅgirasyaḥ*[19]. The subject seems to be an interesting *ākhyāna*, indicated fragmentarily in the stanzas, but fitting well in to the story as told in the Brāhmaṇas. According to this the Aṅgiras, ordinarily inferior and hostile to the Ādityas[20], once helped them at a soma-sacrifice. For this the Ādityas gave to the Aṅgiras the white horse of the sun as sacrificial reward. The *devanītha* is therefore a heavenly *dānastuti*.

XIV. AV. 20. 135. 11—13 = ŚS. 12. 16. 1. 3—5 in changed order (st. 13 of AV. also AG. 2. 9. 4). The pratīka, GB. 2. 6. 14; AŚ. 8. 3. 27; Vait. 32. 30. The GB., AB. 6. 36. 1 ff., KB. 30. 5, and the comms. designate them as *bhūtechadaḥ* (AB., *asurāṇāṃ bhūtaṃ chādayitvā*). The passage is in praise of Indra.

XV. AV. 20. 136 = ŚS. 12. 24. 2 (sts. 4, 1, 2, 11, 10, 9, 6, 15 of AV., to which are added AV. 20. 137, 2 and 1). The pratīka, GB. 2. 6. 15; AŚ. 8. 3. 28; Vait. 32. 1. The GB., AB. 6. 36. 4 ff., KB. 30. 5, ŚS., and the comms. designate them as *āhanasyāḥ* (10 in number according to AB., ŚS.; cp. schol. AŚ. 8. 3. 31). Sts. 1 and 4 occur also VS. 23. 28, 29; LŚ. 9. 10. 5, 6, in the course of the *aśvamedha*, and the theme of the *āhanasyāh*, 'lechery' (*āhanasyād vai retaḥ sicyate*, AB. 6. 36. 5), is an even more outspoken variety of *aślīlabhāṣaṇam* than that familiar at the *aśvamedha*[21]. In

7*

Rig-vidhāna 3. 24. 4 the *āhanasyāḥ* are recited over a woman who runs about with other men; cp. MEYER'S introduction, p. XV, XVII.

The *kuntāpa*-hymns are preceded in the AV. by the *vṛṣākapi*-hymn (126) and followed by the *dādhikra*-stanzas (137. 3 ff.), exactly as in the Brāhmaṇas and Sūtras. Their preservation is therefore due to the presence in the śastra-kāṇḍa (book 20) of the hymnal material recited primarily in the RV. schools on the sixth day of the *pṛṣṭhyaṣaḍaha*, a sacrificial week of six days belonging to the so-called *ahīna*-sacrifices, lasting from 2 to 12 days. The *pṛṣṭhyaṣaḍaha* is a part of the *dvādaśāha*[22]. The entire series of hymns in question, the so-called *śilpas* 'works of art' (AB. 6. 27 ff.) bear a popular character. As regards the *kuntāpa*-pieces, their presence in the ritual is taken with the utmost seriousness by the ritualists, though not without apologies for their disgusting, foolish, and obscene character. Thus GB. 2. 6. 12 etymologizes upon *kuntāpa* as *kutsitam ... yat tapati* 'loathsome and offensive', and the nonsense of the *aitaśapralāpa* is whitewashed by liturgic legends (see above). The entire material bears the impress of a fossil in the midst of an honest serious performance: it is something which must have stood outside in a prehistoric period of the sacrifice, being connected with it at first by looser, more accidental ties, until the rigid formalism of which the existing texts are the final expression had placed everything upon the same footing of sanctity. The nursery-charade and the song of the brothel cannot reasonably be supposed to have found its way into the Śrauta-ritual in any other way. Traces of such extra-Brahmanical doings occur in connection with many other Śrauta-sacrifices, notably the *rājasūya*, *aśvamedha*, and *puruṣamedha*[23]: they, as indeed most other sacrifices, mark the presence of popular customs and festivities encrusted within Brahmanical solemnities. One source of the more natural human element in the sacrifice was unquestionably the *dakṣiṇā*, the priests' reward. The *dānastutis* even in the RV. betray the exhilarated frame of mind of those that received the *dakṣiṇā*. The exaggerated statements of gifts received were not only intended to stimulate future givers, but mark the note of festivity. Closely related to the *dānastutis* are the *gāthā nārāśaṁsyaḥ*, or *gāthāḥ* and *nārāśaṁsyaḥ*, 'stanzas which sing the praises of generous men', in the Brāhmaṇas and Sūtras[24]. They sing them so loudly that the texts in their soberer moments decry them as *anṛtam* 'lies' (KS. 14. 15), and *śamalam* 'pollution' (TB. 1. 3. 2. 6)[25]. In the last-mentioned place the reciter of the *gāthā nārāśaṁsī*, and the man drunk with *surā* are placed on the same level: they are polluted, their gifts must not be accepted. Now the merry and unsavory literature of the *kuntāpa*-variety is likely to have been associated with *dānastuti*, *nārāśaṁsī*, and *ākhyāna* (see already RV. 1. 126, and 8. 1. 30 ff.), just as the obscene practices — in part to be sure symbolic — of the *aśvamedha* follow upon the great and festive slaughter of cattle customary on that occasion. And it is noteworthy that both *aśvamedha* and *puruṣamedha* are the special repositories of *nārāśaṁsa*-literature[26].

The *dānastutis* and *nārāśaṁsīs* are therefore one of the more hilarious elements which tended to bridge over from the solemn acts of the sacrifice to what for lack of a better term we might call a kind of liturgic 'saukneipe'. Plainly speaking, the bestowal of the *dakṣiṇā* in many instances must have lead to gormandizing and drunkenness, and these were probably in turn followed — the practice is not entirely unknown in our days — by shallow witticisms, by obscene talk, and worse. This we must not imagine to have taken place uninterruptedly without sporadic recollection of the religious character of the event (cp. the theosophic and cosmogonic *brahmodya* at the *aśvamedha*)[27]; in the main however social jollification was the motive, until, in the course of the ossification of the ritual, even the most trivial moments marched past in the procession of the sacrifice, misunderstood and suspected, but now as sacred and ineradicable as the most thoughtful prayer to the gods.

[1] ROTH, Abhandlung, p. 7, 21, 32; AV. in Kaschmir, p. 6, 8, 23; HAUG, Aitareya-Brāhmaṇa, Translation, p. 430, note; WI.[2], p. 162, note. The *kuntāpasūktāni* are wanting in the AVP., and are the only hymns of which a pada-version does not exist. — [2] *kuntāpākhyaṃ sūktaṃ khile kuntāpanāmake granthe samāmnātaṃ triṁśadṛcam* (AB. 6. 32. 1); *kuntāpanāmakaṃ triṁśadṛcaṃ sūktam* (AB. 6. 33. 1). — [3] The commentary at ŚŚ. 12. 16 is however well acquainted with the terms *nārāśaṁsyaḥ*, etc., as is also KB. 30. 5 which defines them explicitly as subdivisions of the *kuntāpa*. — [4] The order *nārāśaṁsī, raibhī, kāravyā, indragāthā, bhūtechadaḥ*, etc., KB. 30. 5, is precisely that of the *saṃhitā*-version, ŚŚ. 12. 14 ff. — [5] See HILLEBRANDT's edition, vol. I, p. 261; vol. III, p. 165. — [6] See ibid. I, p. 259; cp. ROTH, Abhandlung, p. 7. — [7] Thus AB. 6. 35. 15 ff. omits the pāda, *idaṃ rādho vibhu prabhu*, which appears AV. 20. 135. 9c; GB. 2. 6. 14c. The first of the two *pratigaras* to the so-called *ativāda*-stanza, AV. 20. 135. 4; ŚŚ. 12. 23. 4; GB. 2. 6. 13; AŚ. 8. 3. 23; Vait. 32. 26, are given in the forms, *patnī yīyapsyamānā*, ŚŚ. 12. 23. 5; *patnī yīyapsyate*, AŚ. 8. 3. 24; *patnī yad dṛśyate*, Vait. 32. 27: the formulas are omitted by the editors, AV. 20. 135. 5. — [8] Cp. ZIMMER, p. 129, 259. — [9] Possibly only a human king: ZIMMER, p. 131; OLDENBERG, DLZ, 1897, col. 370. — [10] St. 14 of AV. is wanting there, but it is alluded to AŚ. 8. 3. 8 and 12 (the commentary quotes it corruptly as, *upa vo nara enamasi!*). Stanza 12 is common: AB. 8. 11. 5; LŚ. 3. 3. 2; ĀpŚ. 9. 17. 1; SMB. 1. 3. 13; GG. 2. 4. 6; ApMB. 1. 9. 1 (ApG. 2. 6. 10); cp. also PG. 1. 8. 10; HG. 1. 22. 9. — [11] PISCHEL, Ved. Stud. I. 302; BLOOMFIELD, JAOS. XIX. 18. — [12] According to AŚ. and Sāy. to AB. 6. 33. 1 this passage (the *aitaśapralāpa*) consists of 70 pādas, *śākhāntare*. AŚ. 8. 3. 15 reports as an alternative 18 pādas (doubtless = ŚŚ. 12. 3. 18. 1—18), or even the first 9 (doubtless = ŚŚ. 12. 3. 18. 1—9). The AB. 6. 33. 6 is also acquainted with *aitaśapralāpas* of different extent; cp. the schol. ibid. — [13] KB. 30. 5; ŚŚ. 12. 7. 3 write *etaśa*. — [14] Cp. the *pāriplavam ākhyānam* of the *aśvamedha*, ŚB. 13. 4. 3. 2—15; AŚ. 10. 6. 10 ff.; ŚŚ. 16. 1. 22 ff.; LŚ. 9. 9. 10 ff, which, however, is not nonsense. — [15] Cp. the *saṃvatsarapravalha* in the course of the *aśvamedha*, AŚ. 10. 5. 7; ŚŚ. 16. 26. 4, and the riddle-hymn RV. 8. 29, known as *manupravalha*. — [16] In the Atharvan mss. sts. 4, 5 of the vulgata seem to have formed part of hymn 135: see the note in the edition. — [17] These stanzas occur also JB. 2. 116 ff. — [18] AŚ. estimates the passage as consisting of 17 pādas which corresponds with the subdivision of the *devanītha*, as given in AUFRECHT's edition of the AB. — [19] So I would emend the unintelligible expression *ādityā aṅgirasya* (*evāha*) in HILLEBRANDT's edition, ŚŚ. 12. 19. 5. — [20] See WEBER, IS. I. 176, 292; IStr. II. 470; III. 80; SPAW. 1891, p. 811 ff. — [21] Cp. WEBER, IS. IX. 307; GELDNER, Ved. Stud. I. 280. — [22] See HILLEBRANDT, Ritual-Litteratur, p. 148, 155. — [23] See WEBER, Rājasūya, APAW., 1893, p. 4, 67 of the reprint; HILLEBRANDT, Festgruss an Otto von Böhtlingk, p. 40 ff.; Ritual-Litteratur, p. 149 ff. — [24] Cp. Bṛhaddevatā 3. 154, where *dānastuti* and *nārāśaṁsī* are correlated. Both *nārāśaṁsī* and *gāthā* as early as RV. 10. 85. 6, et al. Elsewhere, e. g. TS. 7. 5. 11. 2; ŚB. 11. 5. 6. 8; PB. 10. 6. 6; AG. 3. 3. 1 ff.; Yājñav. 1. 45; cp. SBE. XLII, p. 688—9. — [25] WEBER, Episches etc., ibid. p. 771 (5 of the reprint). — [26] WEBER, ibid. p. 772 ff., 776 ff. (p. 6, 10 of the reprint). — [27] Cp. OLDENBERG, Religion des Veda, p. 248, 475.

PART IV. THE GOPATHA-BRĀHMAṆA.

A. RELATION OF THE TEXT TO THE ATHARVA-VEDA AND ITS POSITION IN VEDIC LITERATURE.

§ 64. General remarks[1].—The GB. like the Vaitāna-Sūtra does not favor us with a report of the name of its author or authors. It is divided into two parts, the *pūrva-brāhmaṇa* in five prapāṭhakas, and the *uttara-brāhmaṇa* in six prapāṭhakas[2]. The pūrva shows considerable originality, especially when it is engaged in the glorification of the Atharvan and its priests; this is indeed its main purpose. Its materials are by no means all of the usual Brāhmaṇa-character; they broach frequently upon the domain of

Upaniṣad; indeed one passage, GB. 1. 1. 16—30, is practically identical with the Pranou (Praṇava) Upaniṣad in ANQUETIL-DUPERRON'S Latin translation of the Persian Oupnekhat; another, GB. 1. 1. 31—38, itself claims the title of Upaniṣad (1. 1. 38, end); see §§ 18 and 68 ff. Nor are they presented in accord with and in the order of the sacrifice (*yajñakrama*) either in Vait. or any other Śrauta-text. The uttara, on the other hand, follows in the main the order of Vait. by compiling from various sources a fairly connected Brāhmaṇa to accompany the action of Vait. This is attended inevitably by Atharvanic adaptations, sporadic, hap-hazard, and imperfect, both as regards subject-matter and mantras: the scrappy character of the product is evident on the surface. In a general way the uttara in its relation to Vait. may be compared with the relation of the first nine books of ŚB. to the original nucleus of the VS. (books 1—18); the pūrva being comparable with (as it is to some extent dependent upon) the remaining five books of ŚB.[3] Both parts, however, are very late productions, one cannot say from how recent a century; both parts were composed after Vait., resting upon a most slender basis of ancient Atharvanic tradition: the uttara, moreover, leaves the impression of a date still later than the pūrva. Thus the usual chronological relations in the redaction of Brāhmaṇa, Śrauta-sūtra, and Gṛhya-sūtra are turned about in the Atharvan: the Kauśika (Gṛhya-sūtra) was composed before the Vaitāna (Śrauta-sūtra)[4], the Vaitāna before the GB., — the cone is inverted and balances upon a mere point of genuine Atharvanic tradition as far as both Vait. and GB. are concerned.

§ 65. The Uttara-Brāhmaṇa. — The history of this production is well illustrated by its treatment of the *cāturmāsyāni*, or seasonal offerings, sections 2. 1. 19—26 of GB. These are purloined with slight modifications from KB., being its fifth book in toto. The Vait. treats this subject in 8. 8—9. 27, and there are, of course, correspondences between it and GB., due to the sameness of the subject. Thus Vait. 8. 8 is literally identical with the opening of GB. 2. 1. 19. The GB. does not mention the mantras of Vait., except that it works in the two formulas, *oṃ svadhā*, and, *astu svadhā* (Vait. 9. 11), in 2. 1. 24. The adaptation is most superficial; at any rate there can be no question that this part of GB. was composed subsequently to both Vait. and KB. Even more characteristic is the treatment of the *atirātra* (soma-sacrifice), GB. 2. 5. 1—5. This is compiled from two sources, AB. 4. 5 and 6, and KB. 17. 7—9, baldly put down, one after another, without any attempt to harmonize. Thus the three *paryayas* (periods) of the *atirātra* are explained twice as typifying the successive expulsion of the Asuras from the three periods of the night, once in the words of AB. 4. 5, the second time in the words of KB. 17. 8. Very striking, too, is GB. 2. 3. 11, illustrating in the course of the *agniṣṭoma* the passage Vait. 21. 3. 4: the Brāhmaṇa is copied with slight alterations from KB. 11. 4 and 5; the compiler is not even at pains to expunge the expression, *iti ha smāha kauṣītakiḥ*, which of itself betrays its origin. Indeed throughout the text the Atharvavedin borrows the Rishis along with the passages in which they figure. Again, cases of undisguised pilfering are the three *kāmyeṣṭayaḥ*, GB. 2. 1. 13—15, which reproduce almost verbatim MS. 2. 1. 10, and the statement about the *anvāhārya*, GB. 2. 1. 6, taken from MS. 1. 4. 6 (p. 54, l. 3 ff.). These are specimen cases: the uttara exploits especially AB. and KB., but other Brāhmaṇas, ŚB., TS., MS., and even PB., are not exempt from depredation.

Stated numerically, about 80 of the 123 sections of the uttara owe their materials either entirely or largely to older texts, as far as is known now. Doubtless future search will reveal still other instances of the dependence of GB., since there are at present no regular channels for investigations of this kind. The correspondences stated in the order of the uttara are: 2. 1. 1: KB. 6. 13; — 2. 1. 3 (latter half): KB. 6. 14 (beginning); — 2. 1. 4: TS. 2. 6. 9; — 2. 1. 6: MS. 1. 4. 6 (p. 54, l. 3 ff.); — 2. 1. 9, very similar to TS. 2. 5. 5. 1 ff.; — 2. 1. 10 (beginning): Kauś. 1. 29, 30; — 2. 1. 11: TS. 2. 5. 5. 2 ff.; — 2. 1. 13—15: MS. 2. 1. 10; — 2. 1. 18: MS. 3. 3. 7 (p. 40, l. 2 ff.); — 2. 1. 19—26: KB. 5 (entire); — 2. 2. 2—4: TS. 6. 2. 2. 1 ff.; — 2. 2. 6: AB. 1. 18; — 2. 2. 13: TS. 3. 5. 2. 1; — 2. 2. 20—22: AB. 6. 10 (complete), 6. 11. 6 ff., and 6. 12. 6 ff.; — 2. 3. 1—6: AB. 3. 5—8; — 2. 3. 6 (latter half): AB. 7. 33. 5 ff.; — 2. 3. 7, 8: AB. 2. 29, and 6. 14. 5; — 2. 3. 10: AB. 3. 12; — 2. 3. 11: KB. 11. 4, 5; — 2. 3. 12: AB. 3. 14; — 2. 3. 17—19: MS. 4. 8. 3; — 2. 3. 20, 21: AB. 3. 23; — 2. 3. 22: AB. 3. 24; — 2. 4. 5: AB. 6. 3. 8—11; — 2. 4. 6: KB. 18. 7, 8; — 2. 4. 8: TS. 3. 3. 8. 2 ff.; — 2. 4. 9: TS. 3. 3. 8. 4 ff.; — 2. 4. 10: AB. 3. 44; — 2. 4. 19: AB. 4. 1. 5—8; — 2. 5. 1—3: AB. 4. 5, 6; — 2. 5. 4—5: KB. 17. 7—9; — 2. 5. 6: ŚB. 12. 8. 3. 1, 2; — 2. 5. 7: ŚB. 12. 8. 3. 23—28; — 2. 5. 8: PB. 18. 7; — 2. 5. 11: AB. 6. 17. 1, 2, and 6. 5; — 2. 5. 12: AB. 6. 6; — 2. 5. 13: AB. 6. 7; — 2. 5. 14: AB. 6. 8; — 2. 5. 15: AB. 6. 18. 4 ff., introduced by a sentence from AB. 6. 17. 2, and ending in a passage from AB. 6. 17. 3, 4; — finally of the 16 sections of the sixth prapāṭhaka all except one and a half (2. 6. 6, and the first half of 2. 6. 7) are entirely or largely dependent upon the fifth and especially the sixth book of AB. These 80 sections do not mark the limit of the materials in the uttara that can lay no claim to originality. Thus GB. 2. 1. 16; 2. 9; and 2. 12 are apparently nothing but Brāhmaṇized extracts from Vait. itself, respectively, 11. 1; 15. 3; and 16. 15—17; there are also other verbal correspondences between Vait. and GB. which suggest the superficial creation of Brāhmaṇa-matter directly out of the sūtras of Vait. Again, quite a considerable number of sections, dealing with the *śastras* of the three daily *savanas* (2. 3. 13—15; 2. 4. 1—3; and 2. 4. 11—8) seem to be little more than the statements of the RV.-sūtras worked over slightly into Brāhmaṇa form; cp., e. g., GB. 2. 4. 1—3 with ŚS. 7. 22—24; AŚ. 7. 4. 1 ff. Future investigations on the part of a second editor of GB. will doubtless narrow down the limits of the original matter of the uttara to a minimum.

Just as the uttara presupposes the older Brāhmaṇas, so it is no less certainly based upon the existing text of the Vaitāna. One may say, in accordance with the paradoxical inter-relation of these secondary Atharvan texts, that to some extent the Vait. figures, as it were, as the Saṃhitā of GB. Thus original mantras of Vait., or, at any rate, mantras stated in full, are frequently cited in the uttara by their pratīka. The Brāhmaṇa is not consistent in these matters: the long yajus, Vait. 3. 20, is repeated in full GB. 2. 1. 7, but the formulas, Vait. 3. 14; 4. 16, are cited by pratīka, GB. 2. 1. 3 and 4. Similarly the *gharma-sūkta* from AVP. is given in full Vait. 14. 1, but its pratīka only appears GB. 2. 1. 6. Note especially GB. 2. 2. 12 and 18 where the mantras of Vait. 16. 17 and 18. 11 are cited fragmentarily, with explanations in the manner of ŚB. when engaged in expounding mantras of VS. Very characteristic, too, for the priority of Vait. is GB. 2. 1. 16 which treats its theme out of order and connection, whereas in Vait. 11. 1 it properly introduces the *agniṣṭoma*.

Nevertheless the uttara has certainly some, though probably very few original sections. Thus the *prāśitra*-legend, GB. 2. 1. 2, though based upon materials from older texts, betrays itself as an Atharvanic fabrication by the introduction of the clap-trap Rishis, Idhma Āṅgirasa, and Barhi Āṅgirasa, leading up to Bṛhaspati Āṅgirasa who, of course, represents the Atharvanic (fourth) priest. Section 2. 2. 5 starts with an explanation of the word *makha* in Nirukta-manner, leading up to one of those disquisitions on the defects of the sacrifice (common in the pūrva) which can be corrected only by the glorified Bhṛgvaṅgirovid. Cp. also certain touches in 2. 1. 17; 2. 6, 14, 15; 3. 9, etc. In addition the originality of the uttara consists in a certain freedom in transfusing the diction of the Brāhmaṇas which it has borrowed; in assimilating some — though by no means all — of their sayings to Atharvanic conditions; and, above all, in changing in no small measure the mantras cited in these Brāhmaṇas to those in vogue with the Atharvans. Thus in 2. 1. 1, a passage borrowed from KB. 6. 13, the formula, *idam aham arvāvasoḥ*, is changed to, *idam aham arvāgvasoḥ* (Kauś. 3. 7; 137. 39); in the *stomabhāga*-legend, TS. 3. 5. 2. 1, the GB. 2. 3. 13 omits, *tasmād vāsiṣtho brahmā kāryaḥ*, because its ideal of a Brahman-priest is a Bhṛgvaṅgirovid. Other adaptations of this sort, at times quite clever, more often superficial and bungling, will appear in the analysis of the text that is to follow.

§ 66. The Pūrva-Brāhmaṇa. — The most conspicuous feature of the first part of the GB. is that it does not follow at all the order (*yajñakrama*) of the Vait., nor is its object in the main the illustration of the normal kinds of Śrauta-sacrifices. It is, to begin with, also a large borrower, but the source drawn upon is almost exclusively the Śatapatha-Brāhmaṇa (books 11 and 12). From the beginning of the fourth prapāṭhaka through to 1. 5. 22 the text seems to be nothing but a secondary mouthing over of a considerable part of the 12th book of ŚB. The subject is a mystic, theosophic treatment of the *sattra* of the year and other forms of the soma-sacrifice. Though there is some degree of independence on the part of GB., both in the wording, and in an occasional mantra, there can be in this part no question of independent Atharvan school-tradition; nor can the subject as treated by both texts be referred to a common earlier source. The GB. purloins the materials of the ŚB. quite undisguisedly; occasionally only it infuses into them those special Atharvanic traits which that text affects: the praise of the fourth Veda, the mention of Atharvan, Aṅgiras, Bhṛgu, etc.; see, e. g., GB. 1. 4. 24; 5. 10, 11, 15, 19. The dependence in general of the Vait. upon the school of the white YV. ensures a certain correspondence with the treatment of the *sattra* in Vait. 31—34; but this is no more in the nature of close companionship than is the case in the relation of ŚB. 12 to its Saṃhitā (VS.). Aside from this, only the eleventh book of ŚB. and a section or two of the AB. have been exploited by GB.: 1. 3. 2: AB. 5. 32. 3 ff.; — 1. 3. 3: AB. 5. 32. 5—33. 4; — 1. 3. 4: AB. 5. 31. 1 ff.; — 1. 3. 6—10: ŚB. 11. 4. 1; — 1. 3. 11, 12: ŚB. 11. 5. 3. 1—7; — 1. 3. 13, 14: ŚB. 11. 5. 3. 8 ff.; — 1. 3. 18: AB. 7. 1. 1[5].

The last three sections of the pūrva are metrical, and not far removed from the type of Pariśiṣṭa; they are, apparently, not from one and the same hand. They do not bear upon the individual acts of the ritual, but seem to be a statement of the position and beliefs of the Atharvans in regard to the general aspects of Vedic lore and sacrifice, with the special purpose of defining and glorifying the AV. This, indeed, is the leading theme of the pūrva as a whole; to this it adheres throughout the considerable variety of subjects which are handled in the first three prapāṭhakas, whether they are cosmogonies, speculations in Upaniṣad style, comments on sacrificial details, grammatical disquisitions (1. 1. 24—28), or even statements in the manner of the Caraṇavyūha (1. 1. 29). To carry to the front the AV. and the fourth priest (the so-called Brahman), who must be an Atharvāṅgirovid, and to point to failure and discomfiture in all holy concerns managed without the fourth Veda, is beyond question the original motive underlying the production of the Atharvan Brāhmaṇa. Every tetrad is a veritable god-send to the author or authors. Whether it be the four-footed animal (1. 2. 24); four metres (often); the sacred syllable *oṃ*, divided artificially into four moras (1. 1. 16); the cosmic tetrads, earth and fire; atmosphere and wind; heaven and sun; moon and waters (1. 1. 29, et al.); or psycho-physical tetrads like speech, breath, sight, and mind (1. 2. 11; 3. 14): they are all pressed into service to show the inherent need and primordiality of the *catur-veda*, as stated most formally 1. 1. 16. Occasionally, yet quite familiarly (1. 2. 21, 24; 5. 10; cf. also 1. 1. 7 and 1. 3. 3), the fourfold Veda is expanded into the Atharvanic pentad by dividing the AV. into two, *śānta* = *atharvan*, and *ghora* = *aṅgiras* (see p. 8). These two assume such reality in the mind of the author as to be furnished each with an independent *vyāhṛti*, *oṃ* for the Atharvan, *janat* for the Aṅgiras: between these two the *vyāhṛtis* of the *trayī* (*bhūḥ*, *bhuvaḥ*, *svaḥ*) are placed for protection (*gup*)[6]. Very neat manipulations are carried on to this end, as when GB. 1. 4. 24 substitutes *catvāro vedāḥ* for *catuṣpādaḥ paśavaḥ* in ŚB. 12. 2. 2. 20, or when GB. 1. 5. 10 assumes the above-mentioned five Vedas for three in ŚB. 12. 3. 3. 2. That the GB. clearly associates the AV. and its functionaries with *bráhma* in the sense of universal religion (*sarvavidyā*), and *brahmá* in the sense of universal theologian (*sarvavid*) may be gathered from 1. 2. 18; 5. 11, 15, 19: see SBE. XLII, p. LII ff.; above, § 33.

Though the pūrva, in distinction from the uttara, impresses one with a certain elemental, energetic independence in style and subject-matter; though it does not borrow as much and as bare-facedly as the uttara; though it does not make it its business to follow and illustrate any other Atharvan text; yet it is without question an exceedingly late production, and also presupposes Kauś. and Vait., as well as the Śaunakīya-saṃhitā in 20 books[7]. Nor are its materials at all from the same hand, as may be seen on comparing, e. g., the opening cosmogony, 1. 1. 1—15, with the second part, 1. 1. 16—30, the so-called Praṇava-Upaniṣad. Section 1. 2. 8 mentions the god Śiva and is Paurānic. Section 1. 1. 28 mentions an evil divinity Doṣapati, who figured as a Rishi at the beginning of the *dvāpara*-age, reminding us of Dūṣin, a name of the Buddhist devil Māra[8]. Sections 1. 1. 25—27 contain grammatical matters of an advanced type; 1. 1. 29 is in the nature of a Caraṇavyūha, certainly very late. The proof that the pūrva came after Vait., just as Vait. is later than Kauś., can be stated definitely and technically. In Vait. 5. 10 two classes of plants, one Atharvanic (blessed, holy), the other Aṅgirasic (terrible, sorcery-plants), are mentioned; the latter, unknown to Kauś., is catalogued in full; the former, having been stated, Kauś. 8. 16, is merely alluded to with the words, *cityādibhir ātharvaṇībhiḥ*[9]. GB. 1. 2. 18, in its turn, having both Kauś. and Vait. behind it, is content to allude to both classes with the vague words *ātharvaṇībhiś cāṅgirasībhiś ca*: they would be unintelligible but for their reference to the preceding texts. Again, as in the case of the uttara, the pūrva at times treats Vait. as its Saṃhitā, as far as the mantras are concerned. Thus GB. 1. 1. 12 quotes the pāda, *agnir yajñaṃ trivṛtaṃ saptatantum*, from the Paippalāda-hymn given in full, Vait. 10. 17; and GB. 1. 2. 18 (end) quotes by pratīka the five stanzas, Vait. 6. 1. Finally, aside from the general correspondence of subject-matter and terminology, as when, e. g., GB. 1. 3. 11, 12 shares with Vait. important words unknown elsewhere[10], the GB. occasionally presents Brāhmaṇas which read like late notes on Vait. Thus GB. 1. 3. 17, describing the variety of *agniṣṭoma* called *ekagu*, is scarcely more than an afterthought to Vait. 24. 20; or GB. 1. 2. 18 (second half) contains an Atharvanic legend clearly built upon Vait. 5. 10, and, more remotely, upon Kauś. 8 and 9.

Yet the pūrva is not devoid of a certain originality. The cosmogony, 1. 1. 1—15; the Praṇava-Upaniṣad, 1. 1. 16—30; the Gāyatrī-Upaniṣad, 1. 1. 31—38; the sections on the duties of the Brahmacārin (rubricating AV. 11. 5) in 1. 2. 1—9; the Brāhmaṇa of the 'fire-footed horse' at the *agnyādhāna* in 1. 2. 18—21, with quite a number of original words at the end of 1. 2. 21; and other sections seem to represent a form of scholastic activity unknown elsewhere in this precise form. The list of subsidiary writings in 1. 2. 10 (1. 2. 9 of the edition), though again late in character, does not occur elsewhere in this arrangement and extent[11]. A somewhat independent statement of the *yajñakrama* is presented in 1. 5. 7. No Vedic text is wanting in independent mantras and formulas, or fails to introduce independent variants into such as are paralleled by other texts. In this regard the pūrva is much like other Brāhmaṇas: 1. 1. 9 contains a mantra of Upaniṣad-character (*śreṣṭho ha vedas*), repeated with variants by Sāyaṇa in his introduction to the AV., p. 5, but otherwise unknown. In 1. 1. 39 the pratīka, *āpo garbhaṃ janayantīḥ*, seems to be a version (Paippalāda?) of AV. 4. 2. 8. In 1. 2. 7 an expiatory mantra, recited by Brahmacārins in case they happen to step upon a burial-ground, is added to other *prāyaścitta*-stanzas which GB. shares with Vait. 12. 8, 9. At the end of the same section (1. 2. 7) AV. 11. 5. 23 in its Paippalāda form is presented in *sakalapāṭha*; similarly the mantra, *catvāri śṛṅgās* (for *śṛṅgā*, RV. 4. 58. 3, et al.), in 1. 2. 17[12]. In 1. 2. 9 the mantra, *antarikṣe pathibhir* etc., shows marked variants as compared with its parallel, RV. 10. 168. 3; the formulas in 1. 3. 13 do not occur in Vait., and differ from those in the corresponding passage, ŚB. 11. 5. 3. 8 ff.; the two stanzas at the end of 1. 5. 5 also present variants as compared with ŚB. 12. 3. 2. 7—8, occurring nowhere else. Above all, the typical mantras at the three daily soma-offerings (*śyeno 'si* etc.) in 1. 5. 12 differ not only from those of the corresponding passage, ŚB. 12. 3. 4. 3—5, but also from those of the Śaunakīya-saṃhitā (AV. 6. 48), and, as far as known, from all other versions of these formulas[13]. And throughout the text, aside from the three metrical chapters 1. 5. 23—25, there are ślokas and other metrical passages so clearly Atharvanic in character that they may not be expected to turn up in older texts (e. g. 1. 1. 32, end; cp. 2. 2. 5): their Pariśiṣṭa-character and their originality are equally obvious.

The following brief account of the contents of the GB. follows the text section by section. The more or less original themes of the text are dealt with at greater length; the parts which are extracted with or without modifications and adaptations from other Brāhmaṇas are dealt with very lightly: frequently a mere reference to the source from which the GB. has derived its material was found sufficient.

The Gopatha-Brāhmaṇa of the Atharva-Veda. Edited by RĀJENDRALĀLA MITRA and HARACANDRA VIDYĀBHŪṢAṆA, Calcutta 1872. Critical remarks on the text of this edition: OTTO V. BÖHTLINGK, BKSGW., April, 1896, p. 12 ff. of the reprint; BLOOMFIELD, JAOS. XIX, p. 1 ff. The first account of the contents and character of the GB. appeared in MAX MÜLLER, HASL., p. 445—455; cp. COLEBROOKE, Essays, I². 82; WL.², p. 167.

1 This and the following two paragraphs are based on the author's article on the GB., JAOS. XIX, p. 3—11. — 2 *tatra gopathaḥ śataprapāṭhakam* (!) *brāhmaṇam āsīt, tasyāvaśiṣṭe dve brāhmaṇe pūrvam uttaraṃ ca*: Caraṇavyūha, Ath. Pariś. 49. The existing text contains a total of only 11 prapāṭhakas. — 3 Cp. WL.², p. 118 and 130 ff. — 4 BLOOMFIELD, JAOS. XI, p. 375 ff.; HILLEBRANDT, Ritual-Litteratur, p. 35 ff. — 5 Note also the passage beginning with, *tad yathā lavaṇena*, GB. 1. 1. 14, which seems borrowed from Chānd. Up. 4. 17. 7; and GB. 1. 5. 11

end = Kauś. 94. 3, 4. — [6] See the remark on *janat*, below, § 67, note 9. For the Atharvans as *goptāraḥ*, see GB. 1. 1. 13. — [7] Cp. GB. 1. 1. 4, 5, 8, which allude in a cloudy way to the finished diaskeuasis in 20 books (see § 35). Note the contrast between *ṛcām maṇḍalaiḥ* (RV.) and *ṛcām kāṇḍaiḥ* (AV.) in 1. 2. 9. That the late Caraṇavyūha-passage, 1. 1. 29, presents *śaṃ no devīḥ* (AV. 1. 1. 6) as the initial stanza of the AV. does not militate against the view that the GB. belongs to the school of Śaunaka, rather than to the Paippalāda; see p. 14. The GB. is, however, not unacquainted with the Paippalāda; see below. — [8] WINDISCH, Buddha und Māra, p. 151. Cp. also the *āsura pāpman*, as a personification of the evil principle, in Nṛsiṁhottaropaniṣad 6. — [9] BLOOMFIELD, JAOS. XI. 387. — [10] Cp. for other cases of this kind, JAOS. XIX. 10, note 3. — [11] Cp. similar lists in 1. 1. 10, 21, 23, 24; 3. 3. Cp. also 2. 2. 6. — [12] Cp. ROTH, Der AV. in Kaschmir p. 23, and see note 6 on p. 113. — [13] See BLOOMFIELD, JAOS. XVI. 1 ff.

B. CONTENTS OF THE PŪRVA-BRĀHMAṆA.

§ 67. First Prapāṭhaka: 1. 1. 1—15. An Atharvanic cosmogony in Upaniṣad manner[1]. — The lonely Brahma decides to create a second god. By means of *tapas* sweat (*sveda*) is produced upon the Brahma's brow; this it punningly and mystically[2] regards as good knowledge (*suveda*), alluding perhaps in this way to the Brahmaveda (1). Through continued *tapas* more sweat breaks in streams (*dhārā*) from the Brahma's hair-sockets on account of which the Brahma proposes to sustain (*dhārayiṣyāmi*), create (*janayiṣyāmi*), and obtain (*āpsyāmi*) this all. Through a chain of more or less irrelevant additional puns the creation of the waters (*āpaḥ*, punning with *āpsyāmi*) takes place. The waters are the element of the Atharvan throughout, just as its divinity is the moon[3] (2). In these waters he beholds his own reflection; his seed falls into the water. The Brahma belabors the waters until they are divided into two, the saline undrinkable ocean, and the sweet waters. The latter being heated, the seed in it is dried up (*abhṛjyata*), and, lo, we have the Atharvanic sage Bhṛgu (3). The Brahma vanishes; Bhṛgu starts after it in various directions futilely, until the voice of the wind (Vāta) tells him to look for it below (*athārvāṅ*) in these waters. Therefore that became Atharvan and was exactly like Brahma (4). Brahma elaborates Atharvan into 10 Atharvan Ṛṣis, respectively *ekarca*, *dvyṛca*, etc., and 10 Ātharvaṇa Ārṣeyas, respectively *ekādaśa*, *dvādaśa*, etc. (symbolizing the 20 books of the AV.)[4]. From these the AV. is elaborated; from the latter the syllable *om* which (in the manner of the Upaniṣads) can be made to assume the function and virtue of the entire AV. (5). After the creation of the Veda of Atharvan comes the regulation cosmogonic act whose final outcome is the *trayī vidyā* with its divinities, elements, and *vyāhṛtis*, e. g., Rig-Veda, earth, Agni, and *bhūḥ*[5] (6). Just as the seed in the sweet waters produced Bhṛgu and in the sequel Atharvan, thus, next, the saline waters by successive cosmogonic acts (with puns) are made to yield the ocean (*samudra*), Varuṇa, Mṛtyu (Mucya), and by extracting from the limbs (*aṅga*) of Mṛtyu their sap (*rasa*) the final result, Aṅgiras, is reached[6]. The origin of Aṅgiras from the bitter waters of the ocean, next from Varuṇa who is taken here without doubt in his occasional sinister demoniac sense (as if Vṛtra)[7], and finally from Mṛtyu, is intended to turn forth the terrible side of the Āṅgirasa-Veda in contrast with the auspicious Atharvan and Ātharvaṇa-Veda, derived above through Bhṛgu. The latter is more particularly the substitute of Atharvan: *bhṛgvaṅgirasaḥ* = *atharvāṅgirasaḥ* (7). From the sage Aṅgiras the Brahma elaborates 20 Aṅgiras Ṛṣis[8] and from them 10 Āṅgirasa Ārṣeyas, the latter correlated respectively with 16, 18, 12, 1, 3, 4, 5, 6, 2, and 7 *ṛcaḥ*. This again alludes to the diaskeuasis of the Veda, but why these numbers, and why this order? From the Āṅgirasa-Veda comes the word *janat* which is the *vyāhṛti* of that Veda[9] (8). This is followed by an especial panegyric of the Aṅgirasaḥ, illustrated by a mantra of independent character[10]. (9). Brahma next elaborates from the six directions five other Vedas and from these the *vyāhṛtis*: *sarpaveda* and *vṛdhat*; *piśācaveda* and *karat*; *asuraveda* and *guhat*; *itihāsaveda* and *mahat*; *purāṇaveda* and *tad*[11] (10). From the near and distant regions he extracts *śam*, 'the high syllable', *ūrdhvam akṣaram*, with allusion, doubtless, to the *śānta-veda* (11). Brahma continues to create the moon, stars, plants and trees, and from 'his minor breaths the many other gods', winding up with the 'threefold, seven-stringed sacrifice consisting of 21 forms'. The text illustrates the latter by citing a pāda from the Paippalāda-hymn given in full Vait. 10. 17, and by referring to the śloka-chapter, GB. 1. 5. 25 (12). Brahma then institutes a sacrifice choosing certain divinities as special Śrauta-priests[12]. Candramās the divinity of the AV. figures as Brahman-priest, the Atharvāṅgirasaḥ as a special variety of Brahmans, called *goptāraḥ*. Prajāpati recommends that abundant fees be given to such priests lest there be injury to the *ṛtvij*, the sacrificer, and his offspring (13). Finally the functions of the Brahman-priest (and the *goptāraḥ*) as curers (*saṃdhāna*) of the flaws of the sacrifice (*viriṣṭa*) are defined[13] (14, 15). The entire cosmogony is original in that it establishes the Atharvan as the pivot about which the creative acts revolve, and in leading up dexterously to the presumably main object of a Brāhmaṇa of the AV.: the exaltation of the functions of the Brahman-priest who is, of course, understood to be an Atharvavedin.

[1] Cp. Bṛh. Ār. Up. 5. 4. — [2] *parokṣa*: GB. 1. 1. 7 (bis), 39; 2. 21 (bis); 3. 19; 4. 23, and similarly AB. 3. 33. 6; 7. 30. 4; TB. 1. 5. 9. 2, etc. — [3] GB. 1. 1. 20, 29, 39; 2. 16. 23; 3. 14; 5. 15, 19. The conception reaches back to the Saṃhitā itself, AV. 2. 22 and 23: see § 45. — [4] Cp. AV. 19. 22 and 23, and see § 35. — [5] The same subject is treated in an expanded form in the second cosmogony, 1. 1. 17—19. — [6] This etymology occurs also JBU. 2. 11. 9. — [7] Cp. BERGAIGNE, III. 144; GELDNER, Ved. Stud. II. 292. — [8] Cp. IS. XIII. 433. — [9] *janat* as the *vyāhṛti* of the Āṅgirasa-Veda is contrasted with *om* of the Ātharvaṇa-Veda also in GB. 1. 1. 20; 2. 24; 3. 3; 2. 2. 14. Neither Kauśika nor Vaitāna bring out any such distinction, *janat* being the general Atharvanic *vyāhṛti*: see the indexes to the editions, p. 381 (Kauś.), and p. 95 (Vait.). For the origin of *janat* cp. RV. 2. 21. 4; 4. 40. 2 (cp. also 3. 61. 4). — [10] Quoted with variants by Sāyaṇa in the introduction to the AV., p. 5. — [11] Cp. Kauś. 91. 10 ff. — [12] Emend in the text, *camasā, adhvaryavo* to *camasādhvaryavo*. — [13] Cp. Kauś. 9. 5 ff. The passage in GB. 1. 1. 14, *tad yathā lavaṇena* etc., is borrowed from Chānd. Up. 4. 17. 7; it is alluded to a second time in GB. 1. 3. 3.

§ 68. First Prapāṭhaka: 1. 1. 16—30. The Praṇava-Upaniṣad, being a cosmogonic account deriving creation from the om. — In the Persian translation of fifty Upaniṣads, the so-called Oupnekhat, which was made in 1656 for the Sultan Mohammed Dārā Shukoh in the city of Delhi, and which was afterwards (1801—2) translated by ANQUETIL DUPERRON into Latin, the Pranou figures as the 48th Upaniṣad of the collection[1]. WEBER, after erroneously identifying the Pranou with the Prāṇa and Prāṇāgnihotra Upaniṣads (IS. I. 249, 286), soon recognized its proper title to be Praṇava (IS. II. 394, 396; III. 326), and presented an account of it, condensed from ANQUETIL's Latin translation (IS. IX. 49 ff.). Manuscripts of an independent Praṇava-Upaniṣad are reported in the catalogues[2], but have not up to date come into the hands of students of the Upaniṣads. Thus DEUSSEN in his recent translation of the Upaniṣads (Sechzig Upanishad's, p. 858 ff.) felt compelled to present the Pranou in a German translation from ANQUETIL's Perso-Latin version, without, as he thought, having access to the Sanskrit original. Yet the Sanskrit text of the Praṇava has unconsciously been in the hands of

Indologists for more than 25 years: it is the part of the GB. here before us. A comparison of GB. 1. 1. 16—30 with DEUSSEN's translation shows that the differences between the two versions are unimportant: they are likely to be due to the blending of text and commentary in the Persian version, as well as to the peculiar tertiary character of DEUSSEN's final result. In its form as an independent Upaniṣad the Praṇava is divided into three Brāhmaṇas, embracing respectively sections 16—22; section 23; and sections 24—30 of GB. A quick survey of its contents and a comparison with GB. may be gotten with the help of DEUSSEN's translation.

This part of GB. represents obviously an independent account of creation by a different writer. It is probably of later date than the first cosmogony, and conceived under different impulses: The Brahma (neuter) creates Brahmā (masc.) upon a lotus-leaf. The latter by means of penance perceives the syllable *om* of two letters, four morae. With the first letter he perceives the waters and moisture[3], with the second brilliancy and the luminaries[4] (16). From the three vocalic morae (i. e., presumably, *o* plutied) a chain of cosmic, liturgic, and psycho-physical triads (cp. 1. 1. 6) are next derived: earth, atmosphere, heaven; fire (with plants and trees), wind, sun; RV., YV., SV.; *bhūr, bhuvaḥ, svaḥ*; *gāyatrī, triṣṭubh, jagatī*; etc. (17—19). From its first consonantal mora *v*[5] are derived water, moon (cp. 1. 1. 13), AV., *om* itself (! *om iti svam ātmānam*), *janat* (the *vyāhṛti* of the Aṅgiras; cp. 1. 2. 24), *anuṣṭubh*, etc. (20). From its second consonantal mora *m* the *itihāsa-purāṇa* and other literary varieties, which differ wholly from the corresponding account in the first cosmogony, 1. 1. 10; *vṛdhat* and the other Atharvanic *vyāhṛtis* (1. 1. 10); musical instruments, singing, and dancing; the metre *bṛhatī*; etc. (21). The second cosmogony leads up to the same climax as the first, the glorification of the duties of the Atharvanic Brahman-priest who heals with the *om* before and after the sacrifice all its defects (illustrated by AV. 10. 8. 9, and 9. 10. 18). The rather dignified chapter winds up with a hocus-pocus according to which *om* recited 1000 times grants all wishes (22). At this point ends the first Brāhmaṇa of the Praṇava. The remaining chapters of the *om*-cosmogony seem again secondary. In Brāhmaṇa-manner a conflict of the gods and Asuras about the city (*aindranagaram*) of the Vasordhāras (ANQUETIL's defective Sudhā) is narrated; the Asuras are victorious until the gods turn victors under the leadership of *om*, the oldest son of Brahma. The reward of the *om* is that no holy text shall be chanted without *om*. Hence the *om* figures as follows: *ṛcy ṛg bhavati, yajuṣi yajuḥ, sāmni sāma, śloke ślokaḥ, praṇave praṇavaḥ*, thus sayeth a Brahmaṇa-text. The AV. is omitted, pointing seemingly to the origin of the passage from a non-Atharvan source[6] (23). At this point ends the second Brāhmaṇa of the Praṇava. The next chapters contain a grammatico-philosophic disquisition on the *om* which betrays its very late and independent origin by statements not in accord with the preceding. Thus in section 25, as frequently in the later AV. Upaniṣads, four morae are ascribed to the *om* in a manner different from section 17. The etymology, pronunciation, and use of *om* are described with great detail, introducing a large number of technical grammatical terms[7]. In section 24 thirty-six questions about the *om* are posited. In section 25 Prajāpati explains the *om* to Indra: it is said to have different pronunciations in the four Vedas (*svaritodātta* in the RV., etc.). Its four morae are said to be respectively *brahmadevatyā, viṣṇudevatyā, īśānadevatyā, śarvadevatyā* (text *sarva*°); each has an individual color. In section 26 the questions asked in 24 are answered in detail. In defining the term *avyaya* the kārikā, Mahābhāṣya I, p. 96 (KIELHORN's edition) is introduced. In section 28 an evil divinity Doṣapati figures as a Rishi at the beginning of the *dvāpara*-age (see § 66, note 1). The chapter again leads up to the importance of the *bhṛgvaṅgirovidaḥ* (24—28). This in turn furnishes the occasion for an account of the four Vedas and renewed exaltation of the AV. The Vedas, their divinities (the moon, as usual, the divinity of the AV.), metres, and especially their initial mantras are stated: as opening mantra of the AV. the pratīka of 1.6.1 (*śaṃ no devīr abhiṣṭaye*) is given[8]. A renewed mystic exaltation of the *om* serves as the finale of the *om*-cosmogony (29, 30).

1 Cp. MAX MÜLLER, SBE. vol. J, p. LVII ff. — 2 See p. 21, note 52. — 3 Read, *apaḥ snehaṃ ca*, for *apasnehaś ca*, with BÖHTLINGK, BKSGW., February, 1896, p. 16 of the reprint. — 4 Cp., e. g., Chānd. Up. VI. 2 ff. — 5 Though *om* is said in 1. 1. 16, 25 to consist of four morae, its treatment here presupposes five. The *v* seems to be a transitional consonant derived from *o* = *av*, i. e., *au 3 v m*; cp. BÖHTLINGK, l. c. — 6 Cp. however SBE. XLII, p. XXXII ff. — 7 See BÖHTLINGK, l. c., p. 17. — 8 See Kauśika, Introduction, p. XXXVII ff., and above, p. 14.

§ 69. First Prapāṭhaka: 1, 1. 31—38. The Gāyatrī-Upaniṣad.— This text describes itself as an Upaniṣad, and deals with a theme suggestive of the Shavank Upaniṣad, though it is not at all like it (cp. DEUSSEN, l. c. p. 867). It has been translated by RĀJENDRALĀLA MITRA in the introduction to his edition of GB., p. 19 ff. It begins with the legend of a scholastic duel between Maudgalya and a strange sage Glāva Maitreya, apparently an adherent of the Sāma-Veda, judging by the fact that the name Glāva is mentioned in PB. 25. 15. 3; ṢB. 1. 4. 6; Chānd. Up. 1. 12, and, as far as is known, nowhere else. Glāva is defeated because he cannot explain 'the *sāvitrī*, the *gāyatrī*, of 24 syllables and 12 (cosmic) pairs, whose eye are the *bhṛgvaṅgirasaḥ*, on which all this is founded'. Maudgalya then explains (33) Savitar and the *sāvitrī* as consisting of 12 cosmic pairs (*mithunam*): mind and speech; Agni and earth, etc., winding up with the sacrifice and its fee (*yajña* and *dakṣiṇā*). Then follows a mystic correlation of the three pādas of the *gāyatrī* with three cosmic sets of twelve each, *pṛthivī*, *ṛc*, *agni*, etc., *antarikṣa*, *yajus*, *vāyu*, etc., each of which has the final outcome of *vrata*, religious devotion (cp. *vareṇya* in the text of the *gāyatrī*). With characteristic inconsistency the AV. itself is ignored in this apportionment of the *gāyatrī*, though it has been assumed that the *bhṛgvaṅgirasaḥ* are its eye. The subject ends with the statement, *śriyam aśnute ya ... evam etāṃ vedānāṃ mātaraṃ sāvitrīsaṃpadam upaniṣadam upāsta iti brāhmaṇam.*

§ 70. First Prapāṭhaka: 1. 1. 39. The ācamana-rite. — The first prapāṭhaka ends with a chapter on the *ācamana*, being the Brāhmaṇa-comment to Vait. 1. 19; Kauś. 3. 4; 90. 22. The opening pratīka, *āpo garbhaṃ janayantīḥ*, seems to refer to an independent (Paippalāda?) version of AV. 4. 2. 8 (*āpo vatsaṃ janayantīḥ*); other mantras (AV. 19. 69 and 70), formulas, and ślokas are also cited. The main prescript is, that the *ācamana*, the act of rinsing the mouth, shall take place three times; the Atharvan school-character of the chapter appears in the identification of the three *ācamanas* with the *purastāddhoma*, *ājyabhāgau*, and *saṃsthitahomāḥ* (Kauś. 3. 19; Vait. 1. 4, etc.). Finally the Bhṛgvaṅgirasaḥ are correlated with the waters by means of a śloka similar to the prose-statement in 1. 1. 29. The chapter is an independent, though late, Atharvanic lucubration: it may possibly have been suggested by the expression, *āpo jyotiṣi pratiṣṭhitāḥ*, in the preceding section.

§ 71. Second Prapāṭhaka: 1. 2. 1—9. The duties of the Brahmacārin. — The theme may have been suggested by the preceding treatise on the *sāvitrī*, whose acquisition is an important part of the training of the

Brahman disciple. The treatment is based upon AV. 11. 5, a hymn glorifying the sun as a Brahman disciple[1]; it is carried out with considerable originality, differing markedly from the presentations in ŚB. 11. 5. 4; TA. 2, and the Gṛhyasūtras. The Brahmacārin is urged to overcome the seven passions: caste-pride (*brahmavarcasam*), fame, sleep, anger, bragging, personal beauty, and fragrance, which are correlated respectively with the antelope, the teacher, the boa, the boar, water[2], maidens, trees and plants. If he clothes himself in the skin of the antelope he obtains *brahmavarcasam*; if he works for his teacher he obtains the latter's fame; if, though sleepy, he abstains from sleep he obtains the sleep that is in the boa; if, humble in spirit, he does not injure any one through anger he obtains the anger that is in the boar; if he does not perform braggart tricks in the water he obtains the braggadocio that is in the water; if he does not look at a naked maiden he obtains the beauty that is in the maiden; if he does not smell at plants and trees, after having cut them, he becomes himself fragrant (1, 2). The next four sections continue the duties and rewards of the Brahmacārin with allegories and illustrative legends (3—6). The next chapter contains mantras in expiation of certain sins to which he is liable: two of them occur Vait. 12. 7—9 (ĀpŚ. 9. 13. 11), but a third (*yadīdam ṛtukāmya* etc.) seems original with the GB. The Brahmacārin is next described as *devānāṃ pariṣūtam*, 'that which has been set in motion by the gods' (the sun), referring to AV. 11. 5. 23 in its Paippalāda-version[3] (7). In chapter 8[4] the Brahmacārin is urged to betake himself to a hermitage, after the pattern of the great sages of yore. The son of the great Rishi Vasiṣṭha recited the hemistich AV. 11. 5. 25^{ab} (11. 5. 24^{cd} in the vulgata) into the mouth of a shell, in order that a cold and a hot spring should issue therefrom. Then in the middle of the river Vipāś there arose the first hermitage Vasiṣṭhaśilā by name. This was followed by others: the names of the hermitages are for the most part original. After an account of an extraordinary feat of asceticism it is said that Śiva performed *tapas* during 48000 *brāhmya* years upon the back of the ocean (*salilasya pṛṣṭhe*). The chapter is Pauranic rather than Brāhmaṇa. Lastly, in chapter 9, as at the end of each of the preceding broader themes the text again finds its way to a statement of the preeminence of the AV. and the Brahman-priest (*bhṛgvaṅgiras*). After explaining the *brahmodya*-stanza AV. 13. 2. 27, the functions of the four Vedas and their priests are discussed and illustrated by mantras from the AV. and elsewhere, one stanza (*antarikṣe pathibhir* etc.) being RV. 10. 168. 3 with original variants.

§ 72. Second Prapāṭhaka concluded. Various subjects: 1. 2. 10—14. Disquisition on the sacrifice and the sacrificial place (*devayajana*). — A hungry priest, Vicārin the son of Kabandha Ātharvaṇa (cp. 1. 2. 18), too proud to seek subsistence, is sent out by his equally hungry mother. Having gone to a soma-sacrifice at the court of the emperor Mandhātar Yauvanāśva he proceeds at once to give instruction in marked Upaniṣad-style on the sacrifice and the choice of a sacrificial place: 'As all rivers having proper names lose their identity in the ocean, thus do all the Vedas and subsidiary literary categories lose their individual character in the sacrifice.' After a description of the ritualistic properties of the *devayajana* the relative position and functions of the four priests loom up once more: the Brahman-priest is, of course, the mind of the sacrifice (cp. 1. 3. 2, 14). The subject is disposed of with a final definition of the *devayajana* under four heads, *ātmā*, *śraddhā*, *ṛtvijaḥ*, and *bhaumam*, exhibiting points of contact with ŚB. 3. 1. 1.

1. 2. 15—17. The brahmaudana at the agnyādheya. — Here the GB. begins to address itself more directly to the task of acting as a Brāhmaṇa to the Vait. (5. 4; cp. 6. 6). Not, as might be expected, is this subject treated here in relation to the conspicuous *brahmaudana*-hymns, AV. 11. 1 and 12. 3, but with the superficial purpose of correlating the *cātuḥprāśya odana* (porridge sufficient for four priests) with the Atharvanic Vedic tetrad, the string upon which the Brāhmaṇa harps in and out of season. After reciting the familiar legend of Aditi who begot the Ādityas by eating the leavings of the *brahmaudana*[5], the *cātuḥprāśya* is correlated with the stereotyped cosmic and liturgic tetrads: the AV. comes in for the tetrad, *āpaḥ, candramāḥ, brahmaveda*, and *brahmatva* (function of the Brahman-priest). This is supported by liturgic explanations of the mantra *catvāri śṛṅgās* etc. (RV. 4. 58. 3, et al.)[6], and AV. 10. 10. 2. This is followed by the recommendation, rather striking in an extreme partisan text, that the first fee at the sacrifice be given to an Ātreya priest, descended from the Atri-stock, for the well-known reason that Atri freed the sun from darkness. The passage rubricates AV. 13. 2. 4^{cd}, 12, and seems to illustrate Vait. 21. 25 (cp. ŚB. 4. 3. 4. 21).

1. 2. 18—21. The iron-shod horse at the agnyādheya. — This horse, one of the main requirements of the *agnyādheya* (Vait. 5. 11; ŚB. 2. 1. 4. 16), is produced by Vāc from frightful, gruesome waters. The three Vedas fail to pacify the horse; then Śaṃyu Ātharvaṇa, the *śānti*-principle of the AV.[7], engages Vicārin, the son of Kabandha Ātharvaṇa (cp. 1. 2. 10), who prepares the 'holy water' (*śāntyudaka*) by means of 'holy' (*ātharvaṇa*) and 'witchcraft' (*āṅgirasa*) plants, and by the recitation of the appropriate lists of mantras[8] (18). The account of the horse is interrupted by an Atharvanic legend concerned with the origin and nature of the Brahman-priest and his assistants (cp. Vait. 11. 3): the latter are stated to be Sadasya, Brāhmaṇācchaṁsin, Potar, and Agnīdhra[9] (19). The text returns to the 'fire-footed' horse, explaining why it is called Agni Vaiśvānara in the mantra, *agniṃ tvāhur vaiśvānaram* (Vait. 6. 7; GB. 1. 2. 21), and to differentiate it from Agni Jātavedas, the fire at the *agnyādhāna* itself. The Brāhmaṇa (i. e. the Brahmanic religion)[10] carried Agni Vaiśvānara; the latter created these worlds. Then Agni Jātavedas in rivalry determines to exhibit his brilliancy and force, so that the Brāhmaṇa should carry him also. Jātavedas exhibits his virtues in four different ways; the last time 'he saw Virāj, the wife of the Brāhmaṇa', and gave her to him. Then the Brāhmaṇa built Agni Jātavedas; Agni Vaiśvānara, on the other hand, became the horse which frightened the gods, and Brahman (the Brahman-priest) calmed it with the above-mentioned stanza, and with the five stanzas, Vait. 6. 1. Next, anent Vait. 6. 8, the chariot (*ratha*) is mounted. It originated from the sap (*rasa*) of the Brahman, went to the gods, frightened them, but sundry stanzas appeased it also. Finally reasons are given why cows and gold are presented to the Brahmans at the *cātuḥprāśya* (Vait. 6. 6).

1. 2. 22—23. The sāṃtapana-fire. — From the time of RV. 7. 59. 9 the term *sāṃtapana* is associated with the Maruts, being ritualistically tinted from the start. As in Vait. 9. 2 the term appears everywhere in connection with the Maruts at the *sākamedha*-ceremonies (one of the seasonal sacrifices, *cāturmāsyāni*)[11]. Here, however, it appears as the name of a fire connected with *brahma*, the *brāhmaṇa*, and the *brāhmyaṃ havis*. Especially in the Gṛhya-ceremonies (*saṃskāras*) the Brāhmaṇa without the *sāṃtapana* suggests to the writer a clod in a pot that does not shine. It would seem as though the single fire of the house-practices, in which a single Brāhmaṇa is engaged,

were here called *sāṃtapana*. The subject-matter itself, and the reason for its presence here are far from clear.

1. 2. 24—1. 3. 5. Preeminence of the Atharvanic Brahman-priest.— The text returns to its pet theme, the Atharvanic Brahman (cp. Vait. 11. 2). An inane legend introduces the cosmic and liturgic tetrads (cp. 1. 2. 16), designed to shelter the fourth Veda, which figures in the series with *atharvāṅgiraḥ, brahmatva, āpaḥ, candramāḥ . . . om ity atharvaṇāṃ śukram, janad ity aṅgirasām* (cp. 1. 1. 20, and above, p. 8).

[1] SBE. XLII, p. 214, 626 ff. — [2] Read, *krodho 'paḥ ślāgham*, for, *krodhopaślāgham*, in the text, p. 23, last line. — [3] See ROTH, AV. in Kaschmir, p. 23. — [4] Marked 7 in the edition: the false numbering continues to 14; after that correctly 15, etc. — [5] Cp. TS. 6. 5. 6. 1; MS. 2. 1. 12; TB. 1. 1. 9. 1. — [6] This liturgic explanation of the mantra is parallel to, yet different from that presented by the scholiasts at VS. 17. 91; TA. 10. 10. 2; Nir. 13. 7. ROTH, AV. in Kaschmir, p. 23, points out that the writing *catvāri śṛṅgās* (GB., p. 34, l. 3) is that of the AVP. Three lines below, however, and at the end of GB. 2. 2. 6, we have the pratīka in the form, *catvāri śṛṅgeti*. — [7] See p. 8, and SBE. XLII, p. XXI. — [8] Kauś. 9; Vait. 5. 10 ff.; see JAOS. XI. 387 ff.; SBE. XLII, p. XVIII. — [9] Later, in passages that betray their origin from ritual-texts of the RV., the Brāhmaṇācchaṃsin, with Maitrāvaruṇa and Achāvāka, figures as one of the assistants of the Hotar: e. g. 2. 4. 14. — [10] Cp. ŚB. 1. 4. 1. 10 ff. — [11] WEBER, IS. X. 340; HILLEBRANDT, Ritual-Litteratur, p. 117.

§ 73. Third Prapāṭhaka. Various subjects: 1. 3. 1—5. Preeminence of the Atharvanic Brahman-priest (continued). — In 1. 3. 1 they that know the *bhṛgvaṅgirasaḥ* are called *devā brāhmaṇāḥ*; without them the sacrifice limps like a quadruped deprived of its allowance of four feet. Section 1. 3. 2 continues with an Atharvanic redaction of AB. 5. 32. 3 ff., with this conspicuous difference that the AB. says, *atha kena brahmatvaṃ kriyata iti: trayyā vidyayā*; but the GB. ascribes the *brahmatvam* to the Atharvan. This is followed in 1. 3. 3 by expiatory rules when priests break their silence at certain sacrifices. This is again an Atharvanic mouthing over of AB. 5. 32. 5—33. 4, with the difference that the GB. places *om* in front and *janat* after the expiatory formulas *bhūr*, etc.: obviously *om* represents the *atharvāṇaḥ*, *janat* the *aṅgirasaḥ* (cp. 1. 1. 20; 2. 24); the other formulas are, as it were, sandwiched in between these. In 1. 3. 4 the chief services for which the priests receive their fees are recounted after the pattern of AB. 5. 34. 1 ff.; those of the Brahman-priest (*devayajanaṃ me 'cīkḷpad* etc.) are of interest. This is followed (1. 3. 5) by an inconsequential legend showing how in a sacrifice undertaken with only three priests the fees were reduced by one half.

1. 3. 6—10. Mystic explanation of the new-moon and full-moon sacrifice. — This is an expanded treatment of ŚB. 11. 4. 1, giving the impression of direct dependence upon that text. Uddālaka Āruṇi, the son of Gotama, from the country of the Kurupañcālas, is chosen by his people to go to the Northerners (*udīcyān*), where he engages in a *brahmodya*-contest with Svaidāyana Śaunaka, the prize being a necklace. The separate acts of the *darśapūrṇamāsa* are correlated with facts and events in the development of the human body: Hair grows first on the head, later comes the beard and hair on the body; it turns grey first on the head, finally all over the body. Creatures are born toothless, the teeth coming later; they fall out in the seventh or eighth year, grow again, doomed all to fall out in the end. The lower teeth appear first, the upper later on; the lower are narrower and weaker, the upper broader and stronger; etc. The physiological review ends, *kasmād idaṃ śiśnam uccaśa eti nīcīpadyate kasmāt sakṛd* (? *śakṛd*) *apānam* (7). A specimen of the correlation of these facts with the practices at the *darśapūrṇamāsa* is as follows: Because the sacrificial straw (*barhis*) is first spread

in front of the altar (*vedi*), therefore these (human) creatures are born first with hair on their heads, etc. (9). Cp. Vait. 2 and 3.

1. 3. 11—16. Mystic explanations of acts at the agnihotra.—In continuance of the preceding legend another Brahman, Prācīnayogya by name, questions Uddālaka Āruṇi as to the mystic meaning of the acts of the *agnihotra*. The passage corresponds to ŚB. 11. 5. 3. 1—7[1], but the theme is handled independently and in close relation to the description Vait. 7, sharing with it some words elsewhere unknown[2]. This is followed (13, 14) by *prāyaścittas* for accidents that may befall the three Śrauta-fires, a theme foreign to the published text of Vait., but possibly dealt within its unpublished *prāyaścitta*-chapters[3]. ŚB. 11. 5. 3. 8 ff. has a closely parallel, yet independent treatment: the expiatory formulas differ in the two texts. The advantage of these expiations is illustrated in a chain of causation, introducing the familiar cosmic series of the four Vedas (*manas, candramās, āpas* for AV.; cp. 1. 2. 12, 16, etc.). Returning to the *agnihotra*, a legend is told concerning the family of Priyamedha Bharadvāja who thought themselves Veda-wise, 'knew it all', and did not consult any one skilled in the Vedas: they offered the *agnihotra* either once, twice, or thrice a day. They that offered it twice prospered most[4] (15). The next chapter contains a fanciful account of the nature and origin of *svāhā*; it is said to belong to the family of the Lāmagāyanas, a name familiar in the Sāman-schools: possibly the subject is derived from a text of that Veda.

1. 3. 17—23. Notes on the agniṣṭoma, especially on the consecration of the sacrificer (dīkṣā).—Abruptly the texts translates itself to the *agniṣṭoma*, in a legend about the priestly family of the Kārus who, because they were poor, performed that sacrifice with one cow (the so-called *ekagu*). The passage is a note on Vait. 24. 20. The *kāravo 'lpasvāḥ*, 'the poor clerics', typify the Brahmans in general who are thus excused from too great personal sacrifices (17). This is followed by an account of the *savanīya*-animal at the *agniṣṭoma*, suggested by Vait. 22. 21, but evidently derived from the closely similar account, AB. 7. 1. 1 = ĀŚ. 12. 9. Atharvanic traits are entirely wanting (18). Next the *dīkṣā* is treated in close correspondence with Vait. 11. 17. It begins with an explanation of the word *dīkṣita* (*dhiyaṃ kṣiyati*[5]), states the reasons why a *dīkṣita* may not rise and greet any one (Vait. 11. 18); explains the terms *vicakṣaṇavatī vāc* and *canasitavatī vāc*[6]; states why the food of the *dīkṣita* must not be eaten, nor his name pronounced; and how conflicting *dīkṣā*-ceremonies on the part of others are to be avoided[7] (19). This is followed by a legend in which points connected with the *dīkṣā* are discussed (20). Next come the rules of conduct for the *dīkṣita*, coinciding towards the end almost literally with Vait. 11. 21—26 (21). Then comes a *prāyaścitta* for transgressions of the rules of *dīkṣā* (Vait. 12. 1): the mantras are stated in full here as well as in Vait.[8] (22). Lastly come the practices of the *dīkṣita* when his wife is pregnant (Vait. 12. 14). The description of the *dīkṣā* makes the impression of being a secondary amplification of the statements of the Vait., rather than the product of independent school-tradition, parallel to that embodied in the Sūtra.

1 Cp. also AB. 5. 26. 6; TB. 2. 1. 7. 1; JB. 1. 21. — 2 *gavīḍā* 'cow that yields the milk for the *agnihotra*' (Vait. 7. 2); *samudvānta* 'boiling over' (Vait. 7. 3); *adbhiḥ pratyānī* 'to add water' (Vait. 7. 3). The word *pitryupavīta* is also Atharvanic (Kauś. 87. 26; Vait. 7. 15). — 3 See SBE. XLII, p. LXXI, note 1, and above, p. 16. — 4 See ŚB. 2. 3. 1. 18 ff.; KB. 2. 9 (end). — 5 Cp. the explanation of *dīkṣita* as *dhīkṣita* in ŚB. 3. 2. 2. 30. — 6 Cp. also GB. 2. 2. 23; AB. 1. 6. 8 ff.; KŚ. 7. 5. 7; ĀpŚ. 10. 12. 7. — 7 GB. 2. 2. 11, 15, 24. Cp. *saṃsava*, AB. 1. 3. 21; *vi spṛdh*, Vait. 16. 6; 17. 7: see GARBE's note on Vait.

16. 6. — [8] The majority of the mss. at Vait. present them in an abbreviated (*galita*) form.

§ 74. Fourth Prapāṭhaka. Mystic-theosophic exposition of the sattra of the year. — The dependence of this long and elaborate theme of GB. upon book 12 of ŚB. has been stated above, § 66. It extends through the fourth and fifth prapāṭhakas, with the exception of the last three sections (23—25) of the fifth. The first 6 sections = ŚB. 12. 1. 1, deal with the *dīkṣā* of the 16 Śrauta-priests — the 17th, the *sadasya*, is not mentioned (cp. Vait. 31. 1 and 11. 3). This is followed (7, 8) by a mythical derivation of the various *iṣṭis* and other acts of the *agniṣṭoma* from the divinities supposed to correspond to them, and an account of the rewards attending these ceremonies; the *agniṣṭoma* figures here as one of the main features of the *viṣuvat*-day of the *sattra* of the year[1], as well as many other days: see ŚB. 12. 1. 2. 1 and 12. 1. 3. 1—7, and cp. Vait. 11—17. The next two sections (9, 10) derive the separate parts and ceremonies of the normal *sattra*, the *gavāmayana*, from gods and divine personifications, with attendant rewards: see ŚB. 12. 1. 2. 2, 3 and 12. 1. 3. 8—22, and cp. Vait. 31. 7 ff. Next, two sections (11, 12) correlate the *sattra* and certain of its parts with the year: see ŚB. 12. 2. 3. 1. Then five sections (13—17) discuss the parts of the *sattra* from the point of view of the *mahāvrata*-days[2]: see ŚB. 12. 1. 3. 23 and 12. 2. 3. 2—4, 8. The discussion winds up with an expanded statement of ŚB. 12. 2. 3. 4: the position of the *abhiplava* in the *sattra* between two *pṛṣṭhya* is correlated with certain facts of ordinary life. Two sections (18, 19), essentially the same as ŚB. 12. 3. 3. 6, 7, compare the *sattra*-year with the wings of a great eagle, the *viṣuvat*-day in the middle being, as it were, the body of the eagle. Next (20 = ŚB. 12. 2. 2. 1) the character of the *jyotiḥ* (*jyotiṣṭoma*) as part of the *abhiplava* is discussed. Then follow two sections (21, 22 = ŚB. 12. 2. 3. 10, 11) with an account of the ascending and descending scale of the festival-divisions of the *sattra*-year, the *viṣuvat*-day in the middle[3]; the second part of this account is then (23) supported by a legend of the contest between the Ādityas and Aṅgiras[4] which is worked up rather differently in ŚB. 12. 2. 2. 9—12. This is dangerous ground for the GB. to venture upon, since the legends of the struggles between the Ādityas and Aṅgiras regularly exhibit the latter in the position of vanquished victims, similar to the Asuras in their struggles with the Devas; that, of course, is contrary to the spirit of the GB. where the Aṅgiras are especially revered. The mere appearance of such a legend in this text betrays its secondary origin; but for the fact that it does not in this instance present the Aṅgiras in too pronounced a position of disadvantage, it would be intolerable here. The prapāṭhaka is concluded (24 = ŚB. 12. 2. 2. 13—23) with a theological discourse (*brahmodya*) between Predi (ŚB. Proti) Kauśāmbeya Kausuravindu and his teacher Uddālaka Āruṇi in which the sacrifice, the year, as the single one (*ekam*), is said to consist of respectively ten, nine, eight, etc. days (*ahāni*). Very neat is the turn given by the GB. to the relation of the year with the number four. Whereas the ŚB. establishes this relation through the four-footed cattle, the GB. does not neglect to clinch its oft-repeated assertion that the Veda is fourfold: *catvāro vai vedā vedair yajñas tāyate*. It is not possible to doubt that GB. presents the secondary version of the two.

[1] Vait. 31. 10; KŚ. 13. 2. 7. — [2] See HILLEBRANDT, Ritual-Litteratur, p. 157. — [3] WEBER, Nakṣatra, II. 282, note; HILLEBRANDT, l. c.; cp. Vait. 31. 14. — [4] Cp. WEBER, IS. I. 291 ff.; Episches im vedischen Ritual, p. 46.

§ 75. Fifth Prapāṭhaka: 1. 5. 1—22. Exposition of the sattra of the year concluded. — The first section = ŚB. 12. 2. 2. 12, deals with the *abhiplava*, normally of six days, in mystic variations which enable it to embrace from five days to one. Next (2 = ŚB. 12. 2. 1. 1—9) comes a phase of the *sattra* called *gādhapratiṣṭhā*; and then three sections in which the *sattra* and its parts are correlated with the cosmic man (*puruṣa*) and his members (3 = ŚB. 12. 1. 4. 1 ff.; 4 = ŚB. 12. 2. 4. 1 ff.; 5 = ŚB. 12. 3. 2. 1 ff.). In these sections the GB. exhibits a good deal of independence; especially the two ślokas in section 5 differ considerably from those in ŚB. 12. 3. 2. 6, 7: they occur nowhere else in the published literature. Then (6 = ŚB. 12. 3. 5. 12—13) comes a statement of the identical grouping and numerical relation of the main events of the two *sattra* half-years on either side of the *viṣuvat*-day, which differs from those made in Vait. 31. 15; GB. 1. 5. 23.

At this point (7) the text introduces a *yajñakrama* stating the so-called *haviryajña* or *iṣṭi*, and the soma-sacrifices (*somasaṃsthāḥ*). It coincides with the order followed in the Vait. only up to the first of the soma-festivals, the *agniṣṭoma*[1]. Nor does this *yajñakrama*, or that exhibited practically in Vait., coincide with that stated farther on, GB. 1. 5. 23. The latter coincides almost perfectly with the classical *yajñakrama*, as reported on the authority of Gautama's Dharmasūtra 8. 19, 20[2]; the present account is more or less independent of all other known statements. This *yajñakrama* is merely a stepping-stone to the glorification of the *sahasradakṣiṇa*-sacrifice (8). Prajāpati performs all ceremonies in the order of the *yajñakrama*, obtaining only perishable results (*antam*), but when he follows up a *sattra* with the *sahasradakṣiṇa* he obtains imperishable results. The two sections bear every mark of secondary construction in behalf of Vait. 34. 21.

In renewed touch with ŚB., section 9 of GB. = ŚB. 12. 3. 5. 3—11 advises those that are devoting themselves to the *sattra* (*saṃvatsarasaṃsadaḥ*) to keep intact the other sacrifices, *agnihotra*, etc., which ordinarily would claim their attention. Next (10 = ŚB. 12. 3. 3. 1 ff.) there is a legend, in illustration of Vait. 42. 18, about the impossible *sattra* of a 1000 years[3], for which the *viśvajit* is substituted: the GB. characteristically substitutes five Vedas (*ṛci*, *yajuṣi*, *sāmni*, *śānte* = *atharvaṇi*, and *ghore* = *aṅgirasi*) for the three Vedas, ŚB. 12. 3. 3. 2[4]. Sections 11—20 expand considerably the subject of the three daily *savanas*, as treated in ŚB. 12. 3. 4. 1 ff. The GB. manages to import a good many Atharvan traits: in 11, à propos of *vidvāṃsaḥ*, the fourth (Brahman) priest is described in almost the same words as Kauś. 94. 3, 4. The four formulas, *mayi bhargaḥ* ... *mayi sarvam*, are correlated in ŚB. 12. 3. 4. 6—9 with three cosmic-liturgic forms, including the *trayī vidyā* and an indefinite fourth corresponding to *sarvam*, namely, *ye anye lokās* (*devās*, *vedās*, *prāṇās*) *tat sarvam*; the GB. changes this into a definite tetrad, so as to provide amply for an Atharvanic cosmos (*āpaḥ*, *candramāḥ*, etc.) in relation to the formula *mayi sarvam* (*sarvavidyā* = *brahmaveda*): see sections 15 and 19. Very noteworthy is the original version of the three formulas at the three *savanas* (12—14)[5]: the passage GB. 11—20 offers perhaps the most conspicuous instance of the manner in which this text, though removed by an almost immeasurable distance from the original springs of Śrauta-tradition, yet manages to adapt existing materials to its all-absorbing purpose, the glorification of the Atharvan. At this point (21) a legend introducing Dadhyañc Āṅgirasa, not found in ŚB., correlates the formulas, *oṃ śrāvaya*, etc., containing 17 syllables, with the year, or Prajāpati, or the sacrifice[6], and then leads up to the *pravara*, the invitation of the manes, Vait. 2. 15; the very words of that text as also the citation (AV. 6. 123. 3—5) are repeated in GB. The subject is concluded (22 = ŚB. 12. 3. 5. 11) with the *sāvitrapaśu* (cp. Vait. 22. 10).

§ 76. **Fifth Prapāṭhaka: 1. 5. 23—25. Metrical treatise on the sacrifice.** — The last three sections of the Pūrva-Brāhmaṇa lack a certain unity of structure, which makes it possible to imagine that they are not from the same hand. First (23) there is the ordinary *yajñakrama*; its account of the *haviryajña* and *somasaṃsthāḥ* (*sutyāḥ*) coincides with Gaut. Dh. 8. 19, 20: the *pākayajña* accord with the wording and order of Satyavrata Sāmāśrami in the Hindu Journal Ushā[7]. The apparent derivation here of the *yajñakrama* from schools of the SV. may lend significance to the presence in this section of ślokas that are paralleled by the Jaiminīya-Brāhmaṇa, also a Sāman-text. The rest of the section consists of questions and answers (*brahmodya*) devoted to the time-divisions of the sacrificial year. One of the stanzas is identical with Vait. 31. 15. Another (p. 85, l. 17) occurs in a variant form in Jaim. Br. 2. 73[8]; yet another stanza, Jaim. Br. 2. 71[9], exhibits a certain relationship with that beginning GB., p. 85, l. 13. The next section (24) contains a cosmogonic Atharvanic account of the origin of the sacrifice. Vaiśvānara heated with *tapas*, desiring offspring, pours semen into Śraddhā. From this union the world-conquering soma-toothed Aṅgiras is born. Then the resulting four Vedas[10] are described: 'The holy Atharvan and Aṅgiras praise with *prāyaścittas* and *bheṣajas*'. Next follows a list of the 17 Śrauta-priests, divided into four Vedic groups[11], to which are added four other functionaries, the wife at the sacrifice (*dīkṣitā patnī*), the butcher (*śamitar*), the householder (*gṛhapati*), and lastly Aṅgiras himself. The last section (24) is the final apotheosis of the Atharvan. After stating that all the 21 orthodox sacrifices, both of the present and of yore, resolve themselves in the Aṅgiras, the text enters once more upon an elaborate cosmic tetrad in behalf of the AV., similar to, yet somewhat different from the preceding ones[12]. The final outcome of the cosmogony is the sacrifice protected (*gupta*[13]) by the Atharvan. In addition to the regular sacrifice the formulas and offerings of the village[14] and forest also resolve themselves in the Aṅgiras; and, finally, the Atharvan secures the heaven of Brahma, whereas the *trayī vidyā* can only procure the *triviṣṭapaṃ tridivaṃ nākam uttamam*.

[1] See Garbe, Vaitāna-Sūtra, Translation, p. iv. — [2] Weber, IS. X. 326; Max Müller, ZDMG., IX, p. lxxiii; SBE. XXX. 357 ff.; Hillebrandt, ibid. p. 41. — [3] Weber, IS. XIII. 335; Hillebrandt, ibid. p. 158. — [4] See above, p. 8. — [5] See above, § 66, end. — [6] Cp. GB. 1. 3. 10; 5. 10; ŚB. 12. 3. 3. 3. — [7] Max Müller, SBE. XXX. 358; cp. above p. 116. The *somasaṃsthāḥ* coincide also with AŚ. 6. 11. 1; KŚ. 10. 9. 28. — [8] To wit: *ayutam ekaṃ prayutāni ṣaṣṭir, niyute dve nava cākṣārāṇi, sapta sahasrāṇi daśato daśa, etāvān ātmā paramaḥ prajāpateḥ.* — [9] *aṣṭāv etā navatayo bhavanty, ahorātrāṇāṃ parivatsarasya, aśītir asmin savanāni trīṇi ca, sahasraṃ ca pavamānāś ca sarve.* — [10] The SV. is alluded to with the probably late expression *sāmaghoṣa* 'noise of the Sāman', as in the Gṛhya and Dharma-texts. — [11] The *sadasya* is included this time among the Ātharvaṇas; cp. GB. 1. 4. 1—6; Vait. 11. 3. — [12] E. g. in 1. 5. 15 and 19. — [13] Cp. the *goptāraḥ*, GB. 1. 1. 13. — [14] Cp. the *grāmayājaka*, etc., SBE. XLII, p. xl, note.

C. CONTENTS OF THE UTTARA-BRĀHMAṆA (THE YAJÑAKRAMA[1]).

§ 77. **First Prapāṭhaka: 2. 1. 1—12. The new and full-moon offerings.** — The first section deals with three points: the purification of the Brahman's seat; the fetching of the *praṇītā*-water; and the placing of the *paridhi*-sticks around the fire. The first two themes are borrowed literally from KB. 6. 13, except for two characteristic touches. The formula, *idam aham arvāvasoḥ* etc., appears in its Atharvanic form, *idam aham arvāgvasoḥ* etc. (Kauś. 3. 7; 137. 39); and for, *bṛhaspatir ha vai devānāṃ brahmā*, in KB., the GB. reads, *bṛhaspatir vā āṅgiraso*, unto the greater glory of the

Āṅgirasa-Veda. The statement about the *praṇītā*-water, Vait. 2. 2, coincides with both GB. and KB., whereas that which concerns the *paridhis* (Vait. 2. 8, 13) does not appear in KB., but seems to be original with GB. The next three sections (2—4) deal with the *prāśitra*-food, Vait. 3. 7 ff. [2], beginning with the *prāśitra*-legend: Rudra being refused a share of the sacrifice cut off a portion of it, the *prāśitra*. This is given successively to Bhaga whom it makes blind; to Savitar whom it makes handless (and subsequently golden-handed); to Pūṣan whom it makes a toothless eater of gruel; to Idhma Āṅgirasa who loses by it his head; to Varhi (Barhi) Āṅgirasa whose body is disjointed by it; finally to Bṛhaspati Āṅgirasa (the typical Brahman-priest) who recites mantras over it that render it harmless [3]. Idhma Āṅgirasa echoes the well-known legend of Dadhyañc Ātharvaṇa or Āṅgirasa [4]. Neither Idhma nor Barhi are mentioned elsewhere, being clap-trap personifications; the three Āṅgirasas who figure here indicate the working over of the legend into an Atharvanic mould. The last half of section 3 corresponds closely to KB. 6. 14; section 4 to TS. 2. 6. 9. Next, individual points of the *darśapūrṇamāsa* are treated: the prohibition of the *dakṣiṇā*, because the *anvāhārya*-porridge is the ordained fee at these sacrifices [5] (5); the next section (6), à propos of the *anvāhārya*, is borrowed almost literally from MS. 1. 4. 6 (p. 54, l. 3 ff.); then (7) the *anvāhārya* is described as Prajāpati's share, the point being illustrated by the legend of the gods' sacrifice to Prajāpati, whereas the Asuras sacrificed into one another's mouths [6]. The need of performing the *darśapūrṇamāsa* before entering upon the soma-sacrifice is urged in section 8; an expiatory act on the rise of the moon when the priest is about to cook for the evening-offering is the theme of section 9 [7]; the mystic description of the *pūrvā* and *uttarā paurṇamāsī* and *amāvāsyā* is copied literally from Kauś. 1. 29, 30, and defined further in section 10. The rule that only one of the two full-moon and new-moon days shall be chosen (11) is copied almost verbatim, with shocking blunders on the part of the edited text, from TS. 2. 5. 5. 2 ff. Finally (12) certain oblations to Agni-Viṣṇu, and to Sarasvatī and Sarasvant, preparatory to the *darśapūrṇamāsa*, are described in accordance with Vait. 8. 1, 2 [8].

2. 1. 13—16. Kāmyeṣṭayaḥ. — The next three sections (13—15) deal with sacrifices for the fulfilment of special wishes. The Vait. has nothing to correspond; they are, indeed, an almost verbatim copy of MS. 2. 1. 10 [9]. Section 16 is the Brāhmaṇa of Vait. 11. 1 (beginning of the *agniṣṭoma*), in verbal agreement with GB.: he that wishes to perform a soma-sacrifice shall offer a freed steer (*usram anusṛṣṭam*) to Indra-Agni, in case his father and grandfather had not made a soma-sacrifice in their life-time. Since the theme is treated out of order it was perhaps conceived as a *kāmyeṣṭi*.

2. 1. 17—26. Āgrāyaṇa; agnicayana; and cāturmāsyāni. — The offering of the first fruits of the season (17) begins with the usual legend explaining the libations to Agni-Indra, the Viśve Devāḥ, and Soma [10]; otherwise the treatment corresponds closely to Vait. 8. 3—7. Judging from the mention, at the end, of the Atharvanic *purastāddhoma* and *saṃsthitahoma* (Kauś. 3. 19; Vait. 1. 4, etc.) this seems to be a somewhat original Brāhmaṇa. In section 18 the text, apparently without reason, undertakes a salto mortale into the *agnicayana*-ceremony, describing the use of the *apratiratha*-hymn in its Atharvan version (AV. 19. 13) at that ceremony. The Brāhmaṇa illustrates Vait. 29. 16, and is almost identical with MS. 3. 3. 7 (p. 40, l. 2 ff.); cp. also ŚB. 9. 2. 3. 1—5. The irregularity is the more marked because the next sections deal with the *cāturmāsyāni* which in Vait. 8 follow immediately upon the *āgrāyaṇa*. The remaining sections of this prapāṭhaka (19—26) deal with the

seasonal offerings; they are, as has been shown above (p. 102), taken from KB., and call for no further comment.

[1] See above p. 116. — [2] Cp. KB. 6. 13, 14; ŚB. 1. 7. 4. 5 ff.; TS. 2. 6. 8; RĀJENDRALĀLA MITRA, Introd. p. 29 ff. — [3] Cp. especially, TS. 2. 6. 8. 5 ff. — [4] WEBER, IS. I. 290, 384. — [5] Vait. 3. 19; cp. TS. 1. 7. 3. 3; ŚB. 1. 2. 3. 5. — [6] Vait. 3. 20; cp. TS. 1. 7. 3. 4. — [7] Very similar to TS. 2. 5. 5. 1 ff.; cp. KB. 4. 2. — [8] Cp. AB. 1. 1; ŚB. 3. 1. 3. 1. — [9] Cp. TS. 2. 2. 2. 1; KB. 4. 3. — [10] Cp. ŚB. 2. 4. 3.

§ 78. Second Prapāṭhaka: 2. 2. 1—4. The tanūnaptra-ceremony of the agniṣṭoma.—The first section opens in a rather perplexing manner with certain *kāmyeṣṭis* in which quadrupeds and birds are sacrificed by him that has built the holy fire (*āhitāgni*) in order to gain some special wish[1]. It interrupts the *yajñakrama* of Vait., which in chapter 10 deals with the *paśubandha,* unless the GB. regards this as a note on that very ceremony. Then (2—4) the text turns to the *tanūnaptra*, beginning with the legend in TS. 6. 2. 2. 1 almost verbatim[2]. Then comes the ceremony proper, again in close touch with TS., but with an Atharvanic improvement or two; e. g., the GB. substitutes *manas* (representing the Brahman-priest) for *prāṇa* in TS. The numerous mantras, however, accord in the main with Vait. (13. 16 ff.) rather than TS.[3] Apparently the GB. embellishes the acts of the Sūtra with the Brāhmaṇa of TS., without drawing upon independent tradition.

2. 2. 5—6. The pravargya-ceremony.—Section 5 again interrupts the *yajñakrama* of Vait. by one of those disquisitions on defects in the sacrifice which lead up to the glorification of the *bhṛgvaṅgirovid;* it may have been thought suitable here because of the *yajña*-legend in section 6. The discussion is based upon the word *makha*, introduced in the statement, *makha ity etad yajñanāmadheyam*, which is the language of the Naighaṇṭukas[4]. This section is almost certainly later than Yāska: sundry Pariśiṣṭa-ślokas also point to a very late date. Then comes the *pravargya*[5] (6), beginning with the usual myth, copied almost verbatim from AB. 1. 18 (cp. also AB. 1. 4. 9). The performance and the mantras accord in the main with Vait. 13. 25 ff. with which GB. at times agrees almost verbally (e. g. 13. 26, 30). The Vait. (14. 1) quotes the *gharma*-hymn from AVP. in full; the GB. cites it by pratīka (*gharmaṃ tapāmi*). Certainly GB. presupposes the Sūtra.

2. 2. 7—12. The upasad-days, and continuation of the agniṣṭoma.—Sections 7 and 8 deal with the legend and general matters pertaining to the *upasads*[6]; the legend is treated with some degree of independence[7]. Section 9 joins Vait. 15. 3 in the same recital of the divine women (*devapatnyaḥ*); both texts differ from the similar statements, MS. 1. 9. 2; TA. 3. 9. 1 ff.[8]. Section 10 is the Brāhmaṇa of Vait. 16. 5, partly in verbal agreement: the source of the legendary explanation of the 33 'forms of the sacrifice' (*yajñatanūs*) is unknown[9]. Section 11, in verbal agreement with Vait. 16. 6, prescribes how the soma-sacrifice of a rival may be frustrated[10]. Section 12 is the Brāhmaṇa of Vait. 16. 15—17, dealing with expiations for the overflow of the soma: the two texts agree verbally. The mantras of Vait. 16. 17 are quoted fragmentarily in GB. with explanatory remarks, quite as though the Vait. were in this instance the Saṃhitā of GB.

2. 2. 13—15. The stomabhāga-mantras[11].—Section 13 begins with the legend of their origin, substantially the same as TS. 3. 5. 2. 1, except that GB. omits very significantly the statement, *tasmād vāsiṣṭho brahmā kāryaḥ,* which is, of course, contrary to the doctrine of the Atharvan ritualists. The mantras in the sequel differ from those in Vait. and TS., but section 14 shares with Vait. 17. 16 the list of Atharvan *vyāhṛtis* (cp. GB. 1. 3. 3), and

prescribes the use of *om* and *janat,* one on each side of the ordinary ones (e. g., *oṃ bhūr janat*), for the purpose of protection (*ṛgbhir evobhayato 'tharvāṅgirobhir guptābhir*)[12]. The expression *apa gā* 'cease to sing' occurs only here and at Vait. 17. 4. Section 15, illustrating Vait. 17. 7, dwells upon the value of the *stomabhāgas* in overcoming the simultaneous sacrifice of a rival: the two texts share the long mantra, *stuteṣe* etc. The Brāhmaṇa, though making some show of independence, is later than the Sūtra. In continued touch with Vait., section 16 deals with the distribution of the *agnīdhra*-fire at the close of the *bahiṣpavamāna*, with the same *praiṣas* in both texts (Vait. 17. 12—18. 1; cp. ŚB. 4. 2. 5. 11). Section 17, anent Vait. 18. 5 (cp. TS. 3. 1. 10. 1), deals with the *pravṛtāhutis*, oblations on choosing the priests; sections 18, 19 (Vait. 18. 11—15) with the practices about the *sadas*. The mantra, *dhiṣnyebhyo namo namaḥ*, Vait. 18. 11, is alluded to fragmentarily in GB., as though the Vait. occupied the place of a Saṃhitā. À propos of Vait. 19. 6, sections 20—22 describe the Hotar-priest's oblations with the *prasthita*-cups at the three *savanas*. Since the Hotar is a Rigvedin these sections are purloined bodily from the AB. 6. 10; 6. 11. 6ff.; and 6. 12. 6ff. The prapāṭhaka ends with two seemingly inconsequential sections (23, 24), the first of which is again taken up with the explanation of the terms *vicakṣaṇavatī vāc*, and *canasitavatī vāc* (see 1. 3. 19); the last surprisingly bounds back to the *darśapūrṇamāsa*, urging the engagement of the gods (*parigṛhṇīyāt*) on the first of the new-moon and full-moon days, because these sacrifices are *savṛta*, i. e., undertaken by many at the same time[13]. The section seems to be the Brāhmaṇa of Vait. 1. 14.

[1] Cp. Vait. 43. 32, 33; ŚB. 11. 7. 1. 2; ApŚ. 7. 28. 8; MS. 2. 5. 11. — [2] Cp. AB. 1. 24; ŚB. 3. 4. 2. 1 ff.; MS. 3. 7. 10. See WEBER, IS. X. 362; HILLEBRANDT, Ritual-Litteratur, p. 127. — [3] But, *anabhiśastenyam iti*, in GB. 3, accords with TS. 6. 2. 2. 4: the Vait. 13. 18 has *anabhiśastiḥ*. — [4] Yāska's Nigh. 3. 17; Kautsavaya 45: cp. PAOS., October 1890, p. XLVIII ff. — [5] HAUG, AB., Translation, p. 41, note 1; WEBER, IS. IX. 218—20; HILLEBRANDT, l. c. p. 127, 134 ff. — [6] WEBER, IS. X. 363 ff.; HILLEBRANDT, l. c. 127. — [7] Cp. ŚB. 3. 4. 4. 3 ff.; AB. 1. 23; KB. 8. 8; TS. 6. 2. 3; MS. 3. 8. 1. — [8] BLOOMFIELD, ZDMG. XLVIII. 549. — [9] Cp. GARBE, Vait., Translation, 16. 5, note. GB. is cited by the scholiast to Pāṇ. 3. 4. 16. — [10] See the remark on 1. 3. 19, above, § 73, note 7. — [11] Vait. 17. 4 ff.; TS. 3. 5. 2; MS. 2. 8. 8; ŚB. 8. 5. 3; PB. 1. 9. 1 ff. — [12] Cp. above under 1. 3. 3. — [13] See the note on 1. 3. 19.

§ 79. Third Prapāṭhaka: 2. 3. 1—11. Agniṣṭoma continued: the vaṣaṭkāra and anuvaṣaṭkāra; ṛtugrahas; etc.—By way of illustrating Vait. 19. 8—12 which deals with the *vaṣaṭkāra* and *anuvaṣaṭkāra* (acts of the Hotar) sections 1—6 of GB. present with slight modifications AB. 3. 5—3. 8. Yāska, Nirukta 8. 22, also presents the opening of AB. 3. 8. 1; GB. 2. 3. 4 in a form different from each, but it is not necessary in this instance to credit him with independent tradition any more than GB.; both have mouthed over the text of AB. The second part of section 6 (Vait. 19. 18, 19) explains the blessing on drinking the soma, reproducing with verbal changes AB. 7. 33. 5ff. Sections 7, 8 treat the *ṛtugrahaṣ* (Vait. 20. 2): section 7 is partly identical with and wholly similar to AB. 2. 29; section 8 in part corresponds to AB. 6. 14. 5[1]. Section 9 presents a legendary explanation of the sound *hiṃ* (Vait. 20. 15, 16), being written in good archaic Brāhmaṇa-language[2], and deriving some interesting illustrations from every-day life. A closely similar passage has not been found[3]: it may have been derived from a Sāman-source with Atharvanic adaptations (*hiṃkṛtyātharvāṇo brahmatvaṃ kurvanti*). Section 10, dealing with the *āhāva* and *pratigara*-formulas[4] (Vait. 20. 15ff.), is copied almost verbatim from AB. 3. 12 (cp. KB. 14. 3), excepting that the formulas themselves are quoted in the spelling of Vait. which differs from that of all the other texts [5]. Section 11, illustrating Vait. 21. 3, 4, is copied with slight alterations from KB. 11. 4 and 5, including the expression, *iti ha smāha kauṣītakiḥ*, which leaves no doubt as to its origin: cp. above, p. 102.

2. 3. 12—19. The prātaḥsavana of the ekāha.— Section 12 begins with a legend, similar to AB. 3. 14, in which Prajāpati while performing an (*agniṣṭoma*-)sacrifice encounters Death whom he drives step by step from one of the *śastras* and *stotras* of the *agniṣṭoma* to the other. Sections 13—15 account for the three *śastras* (following the *ājya* and *praüga*) of the three assistants of the Hotar, the Maitrāvaruṇa, Brāhmaṇācchaṁsin, and Achāvāka [6]; these sections bear upon Vait. 20. 14. Although they contain many mantras which ought to guide to parallel chapters in other Brāhmaṇa-texts this is not the case; they seem original with GB., patterned perhaps after some RV.-sūtra (cp. ŚS. 12. 1 ff.). Thus the mantra, *ayam u tvā vicarṣaṇe* (RV. 8. 17. 7 = AV. 20. 5. 1) is not quoted outside of Vait. 21. 2 and GB. 2. 3. 14; *indra piba pratikāmaṃ sutasya* (RV. 10. 112. 1) only in GB. 2. 3. 14. Section 16 motivates by a Brāhmaṇa, which again seems independent, the fourfold use of the *āhāva* (*śaṁsāvom*) of the *prātaḥsavana* in relation to Vait. 20. 15 (cp. GB. 2. 4. 4 and 18). Sections 17—19 deal with the *dakṣiṇā*, the order in which it should be given to the priests, and the materials of which it shall consist (cp. Vait. 21. 24—22. 2): they are an almost verbatim copy of MS. 4. 8. 3.

2. 3. 20—2. 4. 4. The mādhyaṃdinasavana of the ekāha.—The subject is treated in the main in the order of Vait., borrowing considerably from AB., but, as in the case of the *prātaḥsavana*, some chapters seem to be original with GB. Sections 20, 21, reproducing almost literally AB. 3. 23, present the legend of the union of Sā (the Ṛk) with Ama (the Sāman), resulting in the junction of three *ṛcas* to produce one *sāman*, etc. (cp. Vait. 22. 8). Section 22, reproducing AB. 3. 24, deals with the *stotriya*, *anurūpa*, *dhāyyā*, *pragātha*, and *nivids* of the *niṣkevalya-śastra*, and bears upon Vait. 22. 10—12 [7]. Section 23 presents a legendary account of Indra's exclusive right to the *niṣkevalya-śastra* at the midday-pressure of the soma: 'In the beginning there was but one soma-pressure, in the morning. Then Prajāpati created the midday-pressure for his eldest son Indra'. The legend is quite different from that told AB. 3. 24. 10 ff. (cp. KB. 15. 4); it is original, if we may trust the quotation of the mantra RV. 7. 98. 5 = AV. 20. 87. 3, as this is not mentioned in any other text, not even the Vaitāna.

1 Cp. also KB. 13. 9. — 2 Cp. the sigmatic aorist *adrāg*, p. 127, l. 3. — 3 Cp. TS. 6. 4. 11. 3—4. — 4 HILLEBRANDT, l. c. 101 ff. — 5 E. g. *adhvaryo śaṁsāvom*, Vait. 20. 18; GB. here and 2. 4. 4; *adhvaryo śoṁsāva* KŚ. 19. 6. 26; *adhvaryo śoṁsāvo* KB. 14. 3; ŚS. 7. 19. 6; *adhvaryo śoṁsāvom* AB. 3. 12. 3; AŚ. 5. 14. 3; ApŚ. 12. 27. 12. — 6 See WEBER, IS. X. 353. The strictly Atharvanic division of the 17 Śrauta-priests does not assign the Brāhmaṇācchaṁsin to the Hotrakas, but makes him an assistant of the Brahman: see Vait. 11. 3; GB. 1. 4. 6. — 7 The word *prativīta* 'veiled' does not occur outside of GB. and Vait. (22. 12).

§ 80. Fourth Prapāṭhaka: 2. 4. 1—4. The mādhyaṃdinasavana concluded.—The *mādhyaṃdina* is continued in sections 1—3 with an account of the *stotriya*, *anurūpa*, *pragātha*, etc., of the three Hotrakas (cp. 2. 3. 13—15). They are based upon AŚ. 7. 4. 1 ff.; ŚS. 7. 22—24, worked over slightly into Brāhmaṇa-form. Section 4 accounts for the five-fold use of the *āhāva* of the *mādhyaṃdina* (*adhvaryo śaṁsāvom*) [1]: the Brāhmaṇa seems original; cp. GB. 2. 3. 16 and 2. 4. 18.

2. 4. 5—18. The tṛtīya-savana of the ekāha. — Continuing in the order of Vait., section 5 illustrates the *pātnīvata-graha* (Vait. 22. 3), and the

consumption of the Agnīdhra's share in the lap of the Neṣṭar (Vait. 25. 5). The Brāhmaṇa is borrowed from AB. 6. 3. 8—11[2]. Section 6 illustrates the offerings of shavings (Vait. 23. 12); the scattering of barley-grains in the *āhavanīya*-fire (Vait. 23. 13); the pouring of the soma-cups west of the *cātvāla*-pits (Vait. 23. 14): the Brāhmaṇa is borrowed from KB. 18. 7 and 8. Section 7 deals with the purification of the sacrificer, and is similar to, yet different from Vait. 23. 22. The mantras, *abhūd devaḥ*, and the *drapsavatyaḥ* (sc. *ṛcaḥ*) occur in both Vait. and GB.; but instead of the Paippalāda-hymn, *yat te grāvā*, of the Vait., the GB. has *saumībhiḥ*[3] (sc. *ṛgbhiḥ*): the Brāhmaṇa seems to be derived from an unkown Śrauta-source. Section 8, illustrating Vait. 24. 15, 16, describes the burning up of the *vedi* and the offering of grits (*saktuhoma*): TS. 3. 3. 8. 2 ff. presents a fairly close parallel. That the TS. is in fact its source seems likely, because the next section (9) interrupts the order of the Vait., yet is also derived from the same chapter of TS. Section 9 begins with a rite on the *ekāṣṭakā*-day bearing, out of order, on Vait. 31. 4, 5, and being a continuation of the Brāhmaṇa in TS. 3. 3. 8. 4—6, which is copied almost literally. But at the end the section returns to the order of Vait. (24. 14), describing the *agnisamāropaṇa* (cp. TS. 3. 4. 10. 4). Section 10 deals with the relation of the three *savanas* to the day and their symbolic connection with the three main positions of the sun: it is borrowed from AB. 3. 44.

At this point the GB. turns to the *śastras* of the *tṛtīyasavana*, in a treatment analogous to that of the first two *savanas* (2. 3. 12—19, and 2. 3. 30—2. 4. 4). Sections 11—14 introduce a legend, elsewhere unknown in this form. The gods Indra, Agni, Varuṇa, Bṛhaspati, and Viṣṇu prevented the Asuras from entering the evening twilight, and thus ruining the *śastras* of the evening. Agni changes into a horse (*aśva*) and enters the conflict first; hence the *sākamaśva-sāman* heads the *śastras* at the *tṛtīya-savana*[4]. The five gods, engaged in the conflict, are identified respectively with *vāc*, *prāṇa*, *manas*, *cakṣus*, *śrotra*, and through these '*prāṇas*' with Prajāpati; reasons are assigned why they are praised at the *tṛtīyasavana*. Finally, these gods, barring Agni who has been provided for in the *sākamaśva*, are distributed among the *śastras* of the three Hotrakas: Indrā-Varuṇa with the Maitrā-varuṇa; Indrā-Bṛhaspati with the Brāhmaṇācchaṁsin; and Indrā-Viṣṇu with the Achāvāka[5]. The next three sections (15—17) state the mantras for the *uktha, stotriya, anurūpa*, etc., of the Hotrakas, being based upon Rig-Vedic sources (cp. AŚ. 6. 1. 2; ŚŚ. 9. 2—4). Section 18 concludes the *agniṣṭoma* with an account of the fourfold *āhāva* of the *tṛtīyasavana* (*adhvaryo śaṁ-śaṁsāvom*) which seems original, like the parallel sections 2. 3. 16, and 2. 4. 4.

2.4.19. The ṣoḍaśin-sacrifice.— Section 19 concludes the prapāṭhaka with a brief explanation of this sacrifice, thus returning to the order of Vait. (25. 12). The Brāhmaṇa is borrowed from AB. 4. 1. 5—8.

1 Cp. AB. 3. 12. 3; KB. 14. 3. — 2 WEBER, IS. X. 390; HILLEBRANDT, l. c. 133. — 3 Cp. ApŚ. 13. 20. 8. — 4 Cp. AB. 3. 49; PB. 8. 8. 1—5. — 5 Cp. AB. 3. 50; PB. 8. 8. 6, 7.

§ 81. Fifth Prapāṭhaka: 2. 5. 1—5. The atirātra-performances.— These continue the order of Vait., chapter 26: the GB. is patched together out of passages of AB. and KB. (cp. above, p. 102). Section 1, almost identical with AB. 4. 5, explains the origin of the *atirātra* as typifying the expulsion of the Asuras out of the night by Indra and the metres, his allies; the three periods (*paryayas*) represent the successive acts of expulsion from the first part of the night, midnight, and the last part of the night. Section 2, borrowed from AB. 4. 6. 4—7, explains the advantages of the *śastras* at the three *paryayas* (Vait. 26. 3). Section 3, borrowed from AB. 4. 6. 8—14, explains how the *pavamāna-stotras*, which properly belong to the day alone, are also provided for the night; it also explains other features of the *atirātra* that are patterned after the soma-performances of the day[1]. Section 4, borrowed from KB. 17. 7, identifies the fixtures of the sacrifice with the members of the cosmic man (*puruṣa*), and the officiating priests with the breaths and other functions of the body. The first part of section 5 deals once more with the expulsion of the Asuras: this time the statement is borrowed from KB., in mechanical continuation of 17. 7, whereas the first discussion of the same theme was derived from the AB. The compiler has not taken the trouble to assimilate his excerpts. The second part of section 5, borrowed from KB. 17. 9, explains the distribution of the metres at the *śastras*.

2. 5. 6—10. The sautrāmaṇī, vājapeya, and aptoryāma rites.— The next two sections disturb the order of the Vait., which treats the *sautrāmaṇī* in chapter 30, after the *vājapeya* and *aptoryāma*. Section 6 presents one of the legends that have attached themselves to the *sautrāmaṇī*, being ŚB. 12. 8. 3. 1—2; section 7, illustrating Vait. 30. 16, 18, deals with the sāman-chants at the *sautrāmaṇī*: it almost copies ŚB. 12. 8. 3. 23—28[2]. In section 8 the text returns to the order of Vait. (27. 1—17), illustrating the *vājapeya*-ceremony by a Brāhmaṇa obviously copied from PB. 18. 7[3]. Sections 9, 10 deal with the *aptoryāma*[4]; the presentation is not in very close touch with Vait. (27. 18 ff.), nor has it been possible to find its source in the published Brāhmaṇas. Cp. in a general way PB. 20. 3. 2 ff.

2. 5. 11—2. 6. 16 (end). The ahīna-(sattra-)sacrifices.—To these performances[5] are devoted the remaining sections of GB., in general correspondence with the order and treatment of Vait. 31 ff. The Brāhmaṇas are borrowed en bloc from the sixth book of AB. with the usual slight alterations; the mantras are assimilated to some extent to those of Vait. Section 11 is composed of AB. 6. 17. 1, 2 and 6. 5; section 12 = AB. 6. 6; section 13 = AB. 6. 7; section 14 is very similar to AB. 6. 8; section 15 is almost identical with AB. 6. 18. 4 ff., introduced by a sentence from AB. 6. 17. 2, and ending in a passage from AB. 6. 17. 3, 4; cp. Vait. 31. 19, 20.

1 GB. shares with Vait. 20. 15 the expression, *uttamāt pratīharāt*. — 2 Both GB. and Vait. read *saṃśyāna* for *saṃśāna*, in ŚB. and elsewhere; cp. Garbe's note on Vait. 30. 16. — 3 Weber, Ueber den Vājapeya, SPAW., 1892, p. 765 ff. — 4 Eggeling, SBE. XLI, p. xx; Hillebrandt, l. c. p. 138. — 5 The GB. designates them as *anaikāhika* = *ahīna* (cp. also *ahargaṇa*): the word is wanting in the lexicons.

§ 82. Sixth Prapāṭhaka: The ahīna-sacrifices continued.— Section 1 is composed of AB. 6. 18. 1—3; 6. 19. 1—10 (cp. Vait. 31. 25). Section 2 continues from the middle of AB. 6. 19. 10 through to 6. 20, with some omissions on the part of GB. (cp. Vait. 32. 10). Sections 3—5 are almost identical with AB. 6. 21—23 (cp. Vait. 35. 12, and 35. 2, 4). Section 6 explains why the Hotar recites two *ukthas* and one *sūkta*, whereas his assistants, the Hotrakas, recite one *uktha* and two *sūktas*; the first part of section 7 specifies the *śastras* of the Hotrakas to their respective pairs of divinities. Neither of these passages seems to be derived from any known Brāhmaṇa; cp., however, AB. 6. 13 and 14 (especially AB. 6. 13. 7 with GB. p. 167, l. 3 ff.). The end of section 7, dealing with the so-called *śilpāni*, is nearly identical with AB. 6. 27. 1—5. Section 8 is almost identical with AB. 6. 27. 6—30. 4; section 9 with AB. 6. 30. 5—6. 31; section 10 with

AB. 5. 9 and 10 (cp. Vait. 31. 27); section 11 with AB. 5. 11—5. 12. 3, finishing with 6. 32. 1, 2. Section 12 is composed of a selection of passages some of which are identical with paragraphs of the AB.; others exhibit a certain degree of independence, yet seem to have been suggested by the same text: AB. 5. 19. 12 (cp. Vait. 32. 12); 6. 29. 1 (cp. Vait. 32. 13); 6. 29. 2 (the *vṛṣākapi*-hymn; cp. Vait. 32. 14); and 6. 32 (cp. Vait. 32. 19). Section 13 is compiled similarly from AB. 6. 33. 1—5 (cp. Vait. 32. 20; KB. 30. 5); 33. 16, 17 (cp. Vait. 32. 27; KB. 30. 7); 6. 33. 19 (cp. Vait. 32. 22); 6. 33. 18 (cp. Vait. 32. 23); 6. 33. 20 (cp. Vait. 32. 26). Section 14 is compiled from AB. 6. 34—36. 3 (cp. Vait. 32. 28—30); section 15 works over AB. 6. 36. 4—7 with a considerable degree of independence (cp. Vait. 32. 31); and, finally, section 16 is based upon AB. 6. 36. 8—17 (cp. Vait. 32. 33, 35).

LIST OF ABBREVIATIONS.

AA. = Aitareya-Āraṇyaka.
AB. = Aitareya-Brāhmaṇa.
Abhandlung = Abhandlung über den Atharva-Veda.
AG. = Āśvalāyana-Gṛhyasūtra.
AJPh. = American Journal of Philology.
APAW. = Abhandlungen der Kgl. Preussischen Akademie der Wissenschaften.
ApDh. = Āpastamba-Dharmasūtra.
ApG. = Āpastamba-Gṛhyasūtra.
ApMB. = Āpastamba-Mantrabrāhmaṇa, or Mantrapāṭha.
ApŚ. = Āpastamba-Śrautasūtra.
ArS. = Āraṇyaka-Saṃhitā.
AŚ. = Āśvalāyana-Śrautasūtra.
Ath. Paddh. = Atharva-(or Ātharvaṇīya-)Paddhati to Kauśika-Sūtra.
Ath. Pariś. = Atharva-Pariśiṣṭa.
Ath. Prāt. = Atharva-Prātiśākhya.
AV. = Atharva-Veda in the Śaunakīya school.
AVP. = Atharva-Veda in the Paippalāda school.
AWAW. = Abhandlungen der Kais. Akademie der Wissenschaften zu Wien.
Baudh. Dh. = Baudhāyana-Dharmasūtra.
BB. = Bezzenberger's Beiträge zur Kunde der Indogermanischen Sprachen.
BDh. = Baudhāyana-Dharmasūtra.
BKSGW. = Berichte der Kgl. Sächsischen Gesellschaft der Wissenschaften.
BṛhU. and Bṛh. Ār. Up. = Bṛhad-Āraṇyaka-Upaniṣad.
BRW. = Böhtlingk und Roth, Sanskrit Wörterbuch.
ChU. and Chānd. Up. = Chāndogya-Upaniṣad.
Contributions. = Bloomfield, Contributions to the Interpretation of the Veda.
DLZ. = Deutsche Litteraturzeitung.
Gaut. Dh. = Gautama-Dharmasūtra.
GB. = Gopatha-Brāhmaṇa.
GDh. = Gautama-Dharmasūtra.
GG. = Gobhila-Gṛhyasūtra.
GGA. = Göttingische gelehrte Anzeigen.
HASL. = History of Ancient Sanskrit Literature.
HG. = Hiraṇyakeśi-Gṛhyasūtra.
Introd. = Introduction.
IS. = Indische Studien.
IStr. = Indische Streifen.
JA. = Journal Asiatique.
Jaim. Br. = Jaiminīya-Brāhmaṇa.
JAOS. = Journal of the American Oriental Society.
JB. = Jaiminīya-Brāhmaṇa.
JBAS. = Journal of the Asiatic Society of Bengal.
JBU. = Jaiminīya-Brāhmaṇa-Upaniṣad.
KapS. = Kapiṣṭhala-Saṃhitā.
Kauś. = Kauśika-Sūtra.
KB. = Kauṣītaki-Brāhmaṇa.
Keś. = Keśava's Paddhati to Kauśika-Sūtra.
KS. = Kāṭhaka-Saṃhitā.
KŚ. = Kātyāyana-Śrautasūtra.
KZ. = Kuhn's Zeitschrift für vergleichende Sprachforschung.
LŚ. = Lāṭyāyana-Śrautasūtra.
Mahābh. = Mahābhārata.

MG. = Mānava-Gṛhyasūtra.
MHASL. = MAX MÜLLER, History of Ancient Sanskrit Literature.
MS. = Maitrāyaṇi-Saṃhitā.
MU. = Maitri-Upaniṣad.
Nakṣ. = Nakṣatrakalpa.
Nigh. = Nighaṇṭuka.
Nir. = Nirukta.
OLS. = Oriental and Linguistic Studies.
OST. = Original Sanskrit Texts.
Pān. = Pāṇini.
PAOS. = Proceedings of the American Oriental Society.
PB. = Pañcaviṁśa-Brāhmaṇa, or Tāṇḍya-Brāhmaṇa.
PBAS. = Proceedings of the Asiatic Society of Bengal.
Pet. Lex. = Petersburg Lexicon.
PG. = Pāraskara-Gṛhyasūtra.
RV. = Rig-Veda.
Rvidh. = Rig-vidhāna.
RVKh. = Rig-Veda Khila.
Sāy. = Sāyaṇa.
. B. = Śatapatha-Brāhmaṇa.
ṢB. = Ṣaḍviṁśa-Brāhmaṇa.
SBE. = Sacred Books of the East.
Seven Hymns = BLOOMFIELD, Seven Hymns of the Atharva-Veda.
ŚG. = Śāṅkhāyana-Gṛhyasūtra.
SMB. = Sāmaveda-Mantrabrāhmaṇa.
SPAW. = Sitzungsberichte der Kgl. Preussischen Akademie der Wissenschaften.
ŚŚ. = Śāṅkhāyana-Śrautasūtra.
st. and sts. = stanza, and stanzas.
SV. = Sāma-Veda.
Svidh. = Sāmavidhāna-Brāhmaṇa.
TA. = Taittirīya-Āraṇyaka.
TB. = Taittirīya-Brāhmaṇa.
TS. = Taittirīya-Saṃhitā.
Up. = Upaniṣad.
VāDh. and Vās. Dh. = Vāsiṣṭha-Dharmaśāstra.
Vait. = Vaitāna-Sūtra.
Ved. Stud. = PISCHEL und GELDNER, Vedische Studien.
Vend. = Vendidad.
Verz. = Verzeichniss der Sanskṛit- und Prâkṛit-Handschriften in der Kgl. Bibliothek zu Berlin.
ViDh. and Viṣ. Dh. = Viṣṇu-Smṛti.
VS. = Vājasaneyi-Saṃhitā in the Mādhyaṃdina school.
VSK. = Vājasaneyi-Saṃhitā in the Kāṇva school.
WL. = WEBER, Indische Literaturgeschichte.
WZKM. = Wiener Zeitschrift für die Kunde des Morgenlandes.
Yājñ. and Yājñav. = Yājñavalkya-Dharmaśāstra.
YV. = Yajur-Veda.
Yvidh. = Yajur-vidhāna.
ZDMG. = Zeitschrift der Deutschen Morgenländischen Gesellschaft.
ZIMMER = ZIMMER, Altindisches Leben.

TABLE OF CONTENTS.

I. SANSKRIT INDEX.

The references in both Indexes are to pages.

II. GENERAL INDEX.